GOLD

OF TH⊘ SO-AUZ-809

According to tradition, when Romulus, founder of Rome, asked for a divine sign, twelve eagles swooped down from the heavens. In ancient occult lore this portended twelve hundred years existence for Rome. The founding occurred in 753 B.C.; the last Roman emperor vanished from his throne in A.D. 476 . . . a glorious span of 1229 years.

In this colorful and straightforward history Donald R. Dudley covers the whole story of Roman rule: from the birth of the Republic to the collapse of the Empire, treating the rise and growth of Christianity as an integral part of the culture of the classical world.

He tells of military campaigns and conquests, and of a peculiarly Roman system of politics—the *clientelae*—where the noble Roman advised the foreign client on Roman affairs and presented his case to the Senate, while the client returned these favors with services to the patron in his own country, thereby strengthening the bond between Rome and non-Rome and extending her imperial power.

He studies the men who shaped Rome's destiny: Scipio, Tiberius, Caius Gracchus, Pompey, Crassus, Caesar, Sulla, Lucullus, Augustus, Nero, Trajan. He describes Roman architecture and art; studies domestic and social life; analyzes legal and political institutions.

He sets before the reader the vivid history of the power, the greatness, the glory . . . that was Rome.

THE

CIVILIZATION

OF ROME

by Donald R. Dudley

A MERIDIAN CLASSIC

NEW AMERICAN LIBRARY

A DIVISION OF PENGUIN BOOKS USA INC., NEW YORK
PUBLISHED IN CANADA BY
PENGUIN BOOKS CANADA LIMITED, MARKHAM, ONTARIO

To the memory of three great historians of Rome:
Martin Percival Charlesworth, Terrot Reavely Glover,
Michael Rostovtzeff

Copyright © 1960, 1962, by Donald R. Dudley

All rights reserved.

Library of Congress Catalog Card No. 84-62655

The Civilization of Rome previously appeared in a Mentor edition.

 MERIDIAN CLASSIC TRADEMARK REG. U.S. PAT. OFF. AND FOREIGN COUNTRIES
REGISTERED TRADEMARK—MARCA REGISTRADA
HECHO EN WINNIPEG, CANADA

SIGNET, SIGNET CLASSIC, MENTOR, ONYX, PLUME, MERIDIAN AND NAL
BOOKS are published *in the United States by*
New American Library, a division of Penguin Books USA Inc.,
1633 Broadway, New York, New York 10019,
and *in Canada* by Penguin Books Canada Limited,
2801 John Street, Markham, Ontario L3R 1B4

First Meridian Classic Printing, January, 1985

2 3 4 5 6 7 8 9 10

PRINTED IN CANADA

CONTENTS

PLATES

(The plates will be found as a complete section between pages 128 and 129)

1. The Tiber Island and the Pons Cestius.
2. The Capitol.
3. The Forum Romanum.
4. The Temple of Castor and Pollux.
5. Statue of a Vestal Virgin.
6. The Arch of Titus.
7. The Mausoleum of Hadrian.
8. Aerial view of "campaigning country" on the border of Wales.
9. Aerial view of part of Wroxeter.
10. Aerial view of a fort.
11. Aerial view of part of the Fosse Way.
12. Statue of Christ.
13. Roman coins.
14. Roman coins.
15. Roman coins.
16. Catacomb inscription.
17. Christian sarcophagus.
18. Foundation of a colony.
19. Imperial Eagle.
20. Cippus from the Roman Forum.
21. Celtic warrior.
22. Aeneas' escape from Troy.
23. Section of the Arch of Beneventum.

MAPS

ACKNOWLEDGMENTS

I am grateful to the following for permission to reproduce illustrations: Mr. Ernest Adams; Mr. Arnold Baker; Alinari; Museo della Civiltà Romana; British Museum; Foto Anderson; Institute of Christian Archaeology, Rome.

The map of Rome in Late Imperial Times Superimposed on Modern Rome is reproduced by permission of Methuen & Co., Ltd., and the map of Roman Communications by permission of Chapman & Hall. Mr. R. A. G. Carson and Mr. H. Mattingly of the British Museum have been good enough to advise me on the choice of coins. I am indebted to The Johns Hopkins Press, Baltimore, for permission to quote statistics from *An Economic History of Rome* by Tenney Frank. My colleagues, Dr. T. A. Dorey and Mr. Graham Webster, have been most helpful in offering suggestions and advice.

CHAPTER I

INTRODUCTION

About sixteen miles inland from the mouth of the Tiber a group of low hills—seven, by tradition—offers a favorable site for early settlement. On the hill whose broad and level summit would be the most attractive to herdsmen from the eastern mountains, archaeology shows the traces of a settlement dating from the ninth to the seventh century B.C. The cemetery of this community has been found in the valley below, and the graves have been excavated. The most notable objects they contain are models of round huts with a conical roof, like those *capanne* of wattle and daub still made by shepherds in the Roman Campagna. Such finds have been made at many places in Latium, but to this one a particular interest is attached. For the hill is the Palatine, and the valley the Roman Forum. Now according to tradition, Romulus, the founder of Rome, had his settlement on the Palatine, where a round hut, the "House of Romulus," was piously preserved as a national monument into imperial times. Several dates were given in antiquity for the foundation of Rome, but the one officially adopted was 753 B.C. Even the day was known. The Latin calendar found at Anzio has opposite the twenty-first of April the entry *"Parilia—Roma Condita"* ("The Festival of Pales—Foundation of Rome"). Pales was the divinity of flocks and herds, and the twenty-first of April is still observed as the birthday of Rome. Archaeology and tradition, then, agree that the origins of Rome go back to a settlement on the Palatine about 800 B.C. by herdsmen from the Latin hinterland. The shepherds, the round huts, and the festival of Pales afford a striking example of that continuity which is one of the keynotes of Roman history.

It is the task of the Roman historian to trace through rather more than twelve centuries the astonishing sequel to

9

these humble beginnings. By 600 B.C. Rome had become, by
the standards of the day, a wealthy and flourishing city,
under a monarchy probably not of native origin. In about 500
B.C. this monarchy was overthrown and succeeded by a republic. By 272 B.C. the Roman Republic controlled a great
confederacy of the whole Italian peninsula south of Genoa.
The wars of the next 150 years left Rome as the only great
power in the Mediterranean world, the successor to the universal empire of Alexander. Through the last century before
and the first after Christ expansion continued, reaching a
maximum in the reign of the Emperor Trajan (98–117
A.D.). At that time the "boundless majesty of the Roman
peace" (*immensa Romanae pacis maiestas*) stretched from
Scotland to the Sudan, from the Atlantic coast of Portugal to the Caucasus—an area two-thirds the size of the
continental United States of today, with, perhaps, a little
less than half its population. Into this world-wide empire the
entire cultural heritage of the ancient world—Greek, Oriental,
Semitic, West European—was absorbed and diffused. But the
stresses—economic, political, and social—of this expansion
shattered beyond repair the political fabric of the Roman
Republic. From the time of Augustus (31 B.C.–14 A.D.) the
Roman world was ruled by a strong centralized monarchy,
which controlled all the resources of the state. The three
centuries after Marcus Aurelius (161–180 A.D.) are those of
decline and fall, of barbarian invasion and economic decline.
By 476 A.D.—the finishing point of this book—the western
part of the empire had gone down in collapse, and in its ruins
were barbarian kingdoms out of which have evolved the
nations of modern Europe. Yet it must be noted that the
Eastern Empire, ruled from Constantinople, did not fall;
through most of the Middle Ages it was the most powerful
and civilized state in the world; it finally succumbed to the
Turks in 1453, on the eve of the discovery of the New World.
The intrinsic interest of these twelve centuries of Roman
history is in itself a claim to the attention of all intelligent
men. But there is something more. The legacy of Rome in
political institutions, in law, in language, in religion, in
literature and the arts, and in much else besides has been
an enduring and perhaps indestructible part of the fabric of
Western civilization. We must understand Rome if we are
to understand ourselves.

Unfortunately, the early chapters of this story, down to
at least the fourth century B.C., are notoriously obscure.
We have what purport to be continuous historical narratives,
notably those of Livy and of Dionysius of Halicarnassus, but

they are late, and are deliberately distorted. The great work of Livy (*From the Foundation of the City*, in 142 books) gives a patriotic, half-epic picture of Roman history, in which the heroic virtues of early Rome are strongly contrasted with the degeneracy of a later age. In the first ten books, Livy takes the story of Rome down to 293 B.C.; in a famous prologue he is frank about the legendary nature of at least the earliest part. Much less important, the *Roman Antiquities* of Dionysius went as far as the Punic War; the books we have go to about 271 B.C. As a Greek, the author is particularly interested in parallels—often imaginary—between Greek and Roman history, and portrays the Romans as of Greek descent. Both historians lived in the time of Augustus, and are thus five centuries later than the Rome of the kings. What were their sources? We know of a number of historians—Fabius Pictor, Cincius Alimentus, and the rest—working in Rome in the third and second centuries B.C. For the earliest period, they seem to have drawn heavily on a Greek historical tradition formulated in Sicily and southern Italy from about 400 B.C. onward. But this does not help much. The Greeks were only marginally interested in Rome; the Roman historians themselves were constantly led astray by a desire to dignify and embellish the origins of the city and to interpret the history of early Rome in the light of the political issues of their own times. There were of course official records, of a kind. From the early days of the Republic, the priestly colleges had maintained lists of magistrates, and to these were added notices of triumphs, treaties, prodigies, and the like, so that by the end of the fourth century B.C. there had been evolved an annalistic record comparable to the Anglo-Saxon Chronicle. But it is uncertain how much of this survived the Gallic invasion of 390 B.C., and even more doubtful whether any Roman historian could make systematic and critical use of such source material if it did reach him. Nor can archaeology make good—except occasionally—the defects of the historical narrative. Within the city, the immense buildings of the Empire have obliterated all but a few traces of early Rome. If we are to discard legends—and perhaps Livy was wise to retail them—we can only give a generalized picture of Roman history and institutions down to the fourth century B.C., set against the background of the geography and peoples of Italy.

On the map, the natural features of Italy look simple. The great arc of the Alps shuts it off on the north from central Europe. At the western end of this arc the Maritime Alps link up with the Apennines. Between Alps and Apennines

lies the plain of the Po valley, draining to the head of the
Adriatic. From the Gulf of Genoa peninsular Italy proper
extends southeast for more than 500 miles, nowhere more
than 150 miles wide. At its southwestern tip the peninsula is
separated by a narrow strait from Sicily. The Apennines
form a mountain backbone throughout, rising at several
points to more than 8,000 feet, and continued across the
Strait of Messina by the still higher mountains of Sicily.
But this seeming unity conceals a wide variety of climate
and soil; regional diversity has always marked the life of
Italy. Geographically, the Po valley belongs to continental
Europe. The Apennines are a mountain complex rather than
a single chain, and their remote valleys, deep glens, and
high plateaus foster the growth of isolated pastoral
communities. On the west, between the mountains and the sea,
three areas of plain and hill offer exceptionally favorable
conditions for agriculture—Etruria, between the Arno and
the Tiber; Latium, the area around Rome; and Campania, that
around Naples. The volcanic soils of the last two are especially
fertile, and the high yields when they were first cultivated
probably account for the legend of a primitive Golden Age
in Italy, when nature and the earth gladly answered all man's
needs. On the east, the mountains are closer to the coast, and
the only extensive plain is that of Apulia, famous for its
cattle and sheep. The rivers of the peninsula are short and
seldom navigable; travel must be by road or sea. The best
harbors are on the west. Today, Genoa, Leghorn, and Naples
are ports for ocean liners, and there are other good harbors
for smaller vessels. On the Adriatic coast, the ports of the
Gulf of Taranto give easy access to Greece and the Aegean.
Venice is a post-Roman creation. Her communications with
the outside world explain much of Italy's history. On the
northeast, easy passes across the Julian Alps lead to the Danube and Sava valleys, and then on to the great plains of
Hungary and the Black Sea. On the north and northwest the
passes to France and Switzerland are higher but still possible; even the high passes of the Pennine Alps have been
crossed by folk migrations and by invading armies. On the
south, Italy leads on to Sicily, and Sicily is only ninety miles
from Cape Bon in Africa. As we learned in the Second World
War, a strong naval power in Italy can sit astride the
Mediterranean; equally, Italy can be invaded from Africa.

Much remains uncertain about the archaeology and ethnol-
ogy of early Italy. Especially in the south, large tracts are,
archaeologically, still to be explored. What matters here is
to form some idea of the historic peoples whom Rome en-

countered as allies or enemies in her conquest of Italy, and of their development between 700 and 500 B.C. It is generally agreed that the oldest stocks—of Mediterranean origin like the Iberians in Spain—had by the beginning of the period been absorbed or pushed into the least favorable part of the peninsula by later invaders. The Ligurians have left traces of their occupation in the land that bears their name, but they play a very minor part in Roman history. Of the invaders, the earliest seem to have come across the Adriatic from the Balkans about 1000 B.C. One group, the Veneti, occupied the lands around the head of the Adriatic; another settled in the great plain of Apulia and much of Calabria. These people were stock raisers, famous for their breeds of horses and their horse-gods. The study of the native pottery is at present the chief source for knowledge of Apulian life: by the end of our period Canosa was producing extraordinary rococo vases, now to be seen in the Naples Museum, in which Hellenic and native styles were blended. Their languages were Indo-European, and can be studied from numerous place-names and about two hundred inscriptions. There is a small list of loan words in Latin. The Venetian dialect word "gondola" goes back to the Venetic *gandeia* (a small boat).

More important were those invaders from central Europe who by 700 B.C. were in possession of practically all the hill lands of the Apennines, and of whom the Latin peoples form one element. They seem to have settled as pastoralists in Latium not earlier than the Iron Age, the ninth and eighth centuries B.C. The area of first settlement was the Alban hills, a region of high, cone-shaped mountains and dark crater lakes which is one of the most beautiful in Italy. The common worship of Jupiter Latiaris on the Monte Cavo, the highest hill of the group, the cult of Diana in the sacred grove by Lake Nemi, and the stories of the early supremacy of Alba Longa, all support the view that here is the first home of the Latin peoples in Latium. The village settlement on the Palatine—easily visible across the plain—was an offshoot. But the Latins did not remain pastoralists only. They were the first to bring the plain of Latium into cultivation, thanks to the construction of an elaborate system of drainage. By the sixth century, some of their cities had developed a rich life, as archaeology has shown at such sites as Praeneste and Fidenae.

To the northeast were the Sabines, a sturdy stock of herdsmen and peasants. Like the Latins, they looked beyond their hills to the plain, and had established a settlement on the Quirinal hill of Rome at the same time as the Latin village on the Palatine. Later, traditionally in the fifth century B.C., there was a large-scale Sabine migration to Rome. Northward again, in the land that still bears their name, were the peoples collectively known as the Umbrians. Contact with the more civilized peoples of Etruria raised their cultural standards and led to the growth of cities. A kindred people, the Piceni, held the Adriatic coast between Ancona and the mouth of the Sangro. Their material culture may be studied in the museum at Ancona; it includes some fine products of Greek art, which probably came via Tarentum, and indicate a lively commerce in the Adriatic in the sixth and fifth centuries B.C. In the wilder lands known now as the Abruzzi, primitive shepherd societies remained throughout Roman times.

The wide belt of hill country east of Campania was the home of the Samnites, later Rome's most formidable enemies in the fight for Italian supremacy. At the beginning of the period their culture was primitive. Their clan system shows traces of totemism: pressure of population on food and grazing land caused them to send out bands of young warriors to conquer new lands, after the periodic celebration of a "sacred spring." But contact with the Greek cities of Campania provided a cultural stimulus. By the fourth century a powerful Samnite confederacy had developed, and there were rich cities, notably Capua, of a mixed Greek-Samnite culture.

All these peoples spoke closely related dialects, out of which three dominant languages emerged—Umbrian, Latin, and Oscan, the last the official language of central and southern Italy until the first century B.C. Their relation to Latin can be studied through inscriptions and through two documents of some length. The *Tabulae Iguvinae*, found in the fifteenth century at Gubbio (Iguvium) in Umbria, record the acts of a priestly college like that of the Arval Brethren in Rome. The *Tabula Bantina*, found at Bantia in 1793, is a list of municipal regulations. A comparison of these with archaic Latin shows (roughly!) that Oscan and Umbrian are "brother" languages, with Latin as a "cousin."

Last of all the invaders of Italy were those Celtic peoples, whether from Gaul or from the Danube, who crossed the Alps into the Po valley in the sixth century B.C. They pushed the Etruscans out and the Veneti into a corner, and became so dominant in this region that it was called Gallia Cisalpina—"Gaul this side of the Alps." Many of the famous cities of northern Italy—Milan, Verona, Brescia—can be traced back to Celtic *oppida* of this period.

The highest civilizations in Italy were those of the Greeks

in southern, and of the Etruscans in central, Italy. The latter at one time seemed likely to win hegemony over the whole peninsula. The material remains of Etruscan civilization are among the most remarkable in Italy, especially at such sites as Caere, Tarquinii and Vulci, with their great cemeteries and richly decorated tombs. New techniques of investigation are likely to lead to even more spectacular discoveries from the many Etruscan sites still to be explored. Etruscan art is strikingly displayed in the museums of Florence and Rome. In modern times, Etruscan studies have become highly specialized, with Italian scholars in the lead. Even so, many problems remain unsolved. The Etruscan alphabet, closely akin to Greek and Latin, can be read; the phonetic values of its twenty-six letters are known. But, although short inscriptions can be read, the language is known very imperfectly; it does not seem to belong with the other Indo-European languages of Italy. Above all, there is the problem of the origin of the Etruscans. Did they come from Asia Minor, as Herodotus said in the fifth century B.C.? And, in that case, were they offshoots of the civilization which flourished in Anatolia at the end of the first millennium? Or were they of native Italian origin, as Dionysius of Halicarnassus supposed? The debate continues.

But our interest lies in contacts between Rome and Etruria, and in the nature of Etruscan influences on Rome. Here the picture is fairly clear. When Rome first knew the Etruscans, the heart of their power lay in those lands between the Arno and the Tiber that still bear their name— Etruria or Tuscany. Their civilization, like that of classical Greece or Renaissance Italy, was one of city-states: twelve cities (a sacred number), made up the Etruscan League. Politically these cities seem at first to have been ruled by kings; in some of them, the dynasty was replaced by an oligarchy. Their wealth was based on metalworking and on trade. They exploited the iron of Elba and the copper of Etruria, and were skilled workers in gold, silver, and ivory. They had close trading connections with Greece proper, with Egypt, with the Levant, and above all with Carthage. Trade rivals of the Greeks of Massilia and Sicily in the western Mediterranean, it was natural that they should become allies of Carthage. As their wealth grew, their power expanded beyond Etruria. Many Latin cities fell under their control, including Rome. For a time they were dominant in the Po valley and in Campania, though from both they were later expelled.

No literature survives, and their history is known from hostile sources. Only through their art can we come into

direct contact with the Etruscans. Derivative in technique
and style, this art had certain characteristics which could
produce masterpieces. It excelled in portraying the grotesque
and the supernatural—fantastic animals such as the Chimera
of Arezzo and the Wolf of the Capitol, divine figures of
superhuman vitality such as the Apollo of Veii. The same
gifts caused it to excel in portraiture of a highly realistic
kind. Etruscan art depicts vividly a life of luxury and pleasure on earth, of gloom and punishment beyond the grave.

Roman tradition agrees that the Etruscans were obsessed
by the supernatural. They excelled all other people in the art
of divination—of interpreting the will of the gods through
the observation of lightning, the entrails of sacrificial victims, and other omens. This was the famous "Etruscan discipline" which the Romans incorporated in their own religious ritual.

Such, in bald outline, was the Etruscan civilization, a
powerful but recessive influence on the early history of Rome.

The Greek settlements in Sicily and southern Italy were
part of a great colonizing movement of the eighth to the sixth
century B.C. By this, the Mediterranean coasts from Spain
to Russia were planted with that most fruitful of all Greek
inventions, the *polis*, the Greek city-state. Cumae was the
oldest in Italy, being founded in 750 B.C., about the same
time as Rome itself. The sites for these new cities around the
Gulf of Taranto, on the coasts of Campania and eastern
Sicily, were chosen with the utmost care by experienced
prospectors, and the fact that many of them are important
towns and cities today shows how well that work was done.
Such are Naples (Neapolis), Taranto (Tarentum), Syracuse,
Reggio (Rhegion). The word "colony" in the modern world
has certain associations which in no way apply to these
cities of the western Greeks. Independent from the first of
the mother city, they frequently surpassed it in wealth and
civilization. The luxury of Sybaris has become proverbial.
By the fourth century B.C. Syracuse was the greatest city of
the Hellenic world. So vigorously did Greek civilization
flourish on Italian soil that southern Italy became known as
Magna Graecia, Greater Greece. The names of Pythagoras
(fl. 530 B.C.), Empedocles (fl. 450 B.C.), and Archimedes
(287–212 B.C.) are evidence for the great contribution made
by the western Greeks to philosophy and science. They fostered the Sophistic movement of the fifth century B.C., a
stimulus to education and enlightenment. Literature and the
arts were highly developed; as for architecture, Paestum and
Segesta may stand with Delphi and Olympia as examples of

the Greek achievement. The western Greeks, then, were full partners in Hellenic civilization, the most brilliant and advanced of the age. As such, they are of the first importance as a cultural influence in Italy from the seventh to at least the second century B.C. But there was never any prospect that they would dominate Italy politically. Indeed, they never formed a unity among themselves, sharing as they did to the full the weakness as well as the strength of Greek civilization —the fatal rivalry between city and city, and endemic class struggle within the city itself. Even the rulers of Syracuse at their most powerful never controlled the whole of Sicily. The Greek cities of Italy were to prove no match for the growing power of the Italian communities, first of the Samnites, and finally of Rome.

The peoples of Italy before the expansion of Roman power were of diverse racial origins, speaking different languages, and ranging in cultural development from brilliant urban civilizations to semi-nomadic tribal societies. Political unity was to be imposed by slow degrees; only with the admission of Gallia Cisalpina to Italy in the time of Julius Caesar did it finally extend from the Alps to the Strait of Messina. After the collapse of the Western Roman Empire, such unity was never attained again until 1870, with the creation of the modern Italian state. Cultural unity was slower still. In the second century B.C. the poet Ennius said that he had three hearts, because he spoke Greek, Latin, and Oscan. Not until the time of Augustus could men speak of Rome and Italy as a unity, sharing a common destiny. *Sit Romana potens Itala virtute propago,* ("Such shall be the power of Roman stock, allied to the valor of Italy"); this, in Virgil's view, is the explanation of Roman rule over the world. To create Italy was the first great historical achievement of Rome; to make a political and cultural unity of the whole Mediterranean world was to repeat this task on a larger scale.

CHAPTER II

EARLY ROME TO 500 B.C.

A Latin settlement on the Palatine, a Sabine settlement on the Quirinal—these do not, as yet, make *Urbs Roma*, the City of Rome. The tradition that Rome was founded by Romulus on April 21, 753 B.C., contains this truth: that in early Italy the foundation of a city was a deliberate politico-religious act, carried out by a single leader in exact accordance with a solemn ritual. Yoking together a bull and a cow, the hero-founder must trace with a bronze plow the sacred furrow, the *pomoerium*, that is to delimit the area of the city. Within it, on the highest hill, dwellings are assigned to the gods who will henceforth be its protectors. Then the lines of the two chief streets will be laid out: north-south, the *cardo*, east-west, the *decumanus*. Thus marked out, the sacred area (*templum*) of the city corresponds in miniature to the *templum* of the heavens, with the four cardinal points and the four quarters of the sky. Such were the foundation rites. But what was the extent of the first city, and who was the hero-founder? Neither question can be answered for certain, although some archaeologists claim to have traced the lines of *cardo* and *decumanus* beneath the foundations of later buildings, and to have found their crossing-place (appropriately) by the ancient Temple of Vesta in the Roman Forum. These rites, and the religious ideas behind them, are known to have been Etruscan; and on the Capitol, the acropolis of Rome, was enshrined the great Etruscan trinity of Jupiter, Juno, and Minerva. Certainly it was under Etruscan influence, perhaps with an Etruscan king as founder, that the ritual inauguration of the city of Rome took place. From that moment its individual life, its *fatum*, ran its predestined course, known to the gods and revealed to men through the science of augury. It was a union of Latin,

Sabine, and Etruscan elements, provided in the Capitol with a fortress and a center for a common worship. Between the three hills lay a marshy valley which could be drained to provide a common center for economic and political life. The Cloaca Maxima, the great culvert which drains the Roman Forum, can still be seen entering the river by the Tiber Island, through a monumental archway of Augustan date.

Once established, the new city flourished because of other advantages of its site. The Tiber Island, lying in the river just below the Capitol, offered a fine position for a crossing. Close by was the sacred Pons Sublicius, built and maintained by a priestly college which derived its name from that function —the *pontifices* or bridge builders. Early Rome and the crossing at Tiber Island can be compared to early Paris and the Ile de la Cité. The route that crossed the Tiber here was an important one, connecting Etruria and Campania, the two most flourishing regions of Italy. Northeast, another important route led up the Tiber Valley, and thence by easy passes across the Apennines to the valley of the Po. At Ostia, near the mouth of the river, were important workings of salt, one of the prime commodities of the time. So Rome flourished as a center of commerce and trade by the end of the sixth century, though she was to have a long struggle to win control of the Tiber Valley from her rival, the Etruscan city of Veii.

This urban life could only be supported on a basis of agriculture. The extent of the first farmlands of the Roman people can be judged by the Ambarvalia, a sacred procession conducted by the priestly college of the Arval Brethren to bless the crops of each year. Four of the stopping places of the procession are known, set five or six miles from the city on the roads radiating south and east. A territory, then, on the east bank of the river, some twelve miles long and about six in depth, with a bridgehead west of the river including the Janiculum and Vatican hills, this was the first countryside (*rus*) which fed the city of Rome. Later it was extended to cover most of the plain of Latium.

It was not an easy land to farm. Only after the construction of an elaborate drainage system could the soil be made dry for crops and healthy for man and animals. At the end of the nineteenth century, archaeologists explored the amazing system of channels (*cuniculi*) cut in the tufa which extend over practically the whole of the Roman Campagna. They are about five feet deep and two or three feet wide, and represent a major piece of engineering carried out under central direction and maintained by successive generations.

As the Dutch won their land from the sea by patience and toil, so did the Roman people win theirs from the marsh.

Cereal crops were the basis of this early agriculture. Vegetables were grown for the vegetable market (*forum holitorium*) of the city. Of fruits the fig came early, the vine and the olive only later, perhaps from contact with Greek agriculture. Cattle and sheep grazed the pastures, and pigs were fed in the still extensive woodlands. The landowners and peasants who worked these lands through the centuries were the strength of the Roman nation, which by 500 B.C. may have numbered a few hundred thousand people in all, with perhaps twenty to twenty-five thousand inhabitants of the city itself.

The domestic unit was the family (*familia*), husband, wife, their unmarried children, and the household slaves, living together in the home (*domus*). In a sense, the dead lived there as well, for the ancestors were honored by an annual festival, and their waxen effigies were kept in the house, and, carried by mourners, followed the dead to the grave. The source of authority in this small community was the father (*paterfamilias*), reinforced by a legal view of his powers (*patriapotestas*) that gave him not only rights over all property belonging to the family, but even power of life and death over his dependents. Roman tradition ranked among its heroes some of the heavier fathers, who did not hesitate to put their own sons to death for disloyalty to the state. In practice, it seems that this absolute authority was tempered by family councils, to whom the gravest issues were referred.

Related families made up the *gens,* the Roman clan, another great social institution. The aristocratic *gentes* were proud of their lineage, going back to some honored founder, human or divine. The *gens Julia,* to which Julius Caesar belonged, went back through Aeneas and Anchises to the goddess Venus. Some Welsh genealogies, it may be said, go back to Priam, but they boggle at the final step. Although the *gentes* played no formal part in Roman politics, in practice they counted for much. Intermarriage among the aristocratic *gentes,* and their control of the state in the third and second centuries B.C., meant that a few great families at that time dominated Rome as thoroughly as did the great aristocratic families in eighteenth-century England.

The position of the Roman woman is a paradox. According to what seems to be the older form of Roman marriage, the bride and all her possessions passed absolutely into her husband's power (*in manum*). Legally, her relation to him was that of a daughter, and she renounced links with her family to become a member of his. Actually, as a Roman matron (*matrona*) she was treated as a partner in the marriage. She managed the home and brought up the children. She was never shut up in the women's part of the house like the women of fifth-century Athens, but went about the city, attended public ceremonies, and sat as hostess at the dinner table. Moreover, another form of marriage ceremony became increasingly common, whereby the *in manum* concept did not apply. Some have seen in this a survival of a matriarchal society, or ascribed it to Etruscan influence. It is most likely that it derived from a working out of the implications of the Roman view of marriage (*matrimonium*). This was that marriage is the lifelong union of one man and one woman, entered into voluntarily for the sake of the procreation of children, and maintained on the basis of constant mutual affection (*affectio maritalis*). On this a single illustration is better than pages of exposition. Here, in archaic Latin that cannot be later than the second century b.c., is the epitaph of a Roman wife and mother:

> Hospes, quod deico paullum est, asta ac pellege.
> Heic est sepulcrum hau pulcrum pulcrai feminae:
> nomen parentes nominarunt Claudiam.
> Suom mareitom corde deilexit suo:
> gnatos duos creavit: horunc alterum
> in terra linquit, alium sub terra locat.
> Sermone lepido, tum autem incessu commodo.
> Domum servavit. Lanam fecit. Dixi. Abei.

Stranger, what I say is short, stay and read. Here is the unbeautiful grave of a beautiful woman. Her parents named her Claudia. She loved her husband with her whole heart. She bore two sons: one of whom she left alive on earth, the other she buried in the earth. Her speech was gay, but her bearing seemly. She kept the home. She made the wool. I have spoken. Go away.

Despite the license of later times, there is ample evidence to show that the view of marriage of Claudia and her husband was maintained to the end of the Empire. Thence, fortified by Christianity, it has continued in unbroken succession to modern times.

Throughout their history, Roman religion mirrors the historical experience of the Roman people. In this early stage, it is remarkable for two features—the primitive nature of its concepts, and the legalistic organization of its ritual. Before reason and logic, primitive man saw the world around him as governed by unseen powers, whose operations are made manifest in the phenomena of nature—night and day, the seasons, the winds, the weather, growth and decay of vegetation and animals, the events of human life from birth to death. These powers the Roman called *numina* (spirits in action), and he confronted them in a personal relationship. The whole view has been aptly described, in a recent study by scholars of the University of Chicago, as the "I-Thou relationship to the universe." Such *numina* were infinite in number, but a man would be concerned only with those whose operations affected him, some regularly like the spirits governing crops and herds, some occasionally or even uniquely, like the divinity Aius Locutius (Up and Spoke) whose sole manifestation was to utter a warning of the approach of the Gauls. Relations between man and these *numina* were regularized, and a code of accepted practice was established. There is as yet no question of temples, cult statues, mythology. The object of a religious act is to induce the *numen* to perform its function in a way favorable to yourself—to strike a bargain with it, in fact, *do ut des,* I give you something, you give me something. Every man, therefore, was his own priest for dealing with the *numina* affecting his own house and farm—the Penates, who looked after the store-cupboard, Janus, in charge of the door, Terminus, of the boundaries of the farm, Seia, who watched corn in the ground, Segetia, presiding over standing grain, Flora, goddess of flowering corn, Runcina, who supervised its removal from the ground, Tutilina, who guarded it in the barn. What was given to the *numen* was a sacrifice—an animal, or part of it, an offering of milk, honey, cheese, or a sacred cake. The value of this depended on the size of the favor expected. Often the sacrifice was not completed until the service had been rendered; it was expressed in promissory form as a "vow" (*votum*): on completion of the terms, this had to be discharged. Hence the formula, frequent on inscriptions: V.S.L.M. (*Votum solvit libens merito*), "He gladly discharged the vow to a god who had earned it." On top of this archaic animism there developed—probably under Etruscan influence—the worship of a number of anthropomorphic divinities, and especially those worshiped by the state. Jupiter, Juno, and Minerva were established in their great temple on the Capitol. As Rome grew to universal empire, so did Jupiter become the Lord of Heaven. Saturnus, originally an agricultural god, had a temple in the Roman Forum from very early times. Vulcanus, god of earthquakes and volcanoes, had a sacred place near by: it is a district where he has often shown his powers. Mars was worshiped as the god of sowing and of war, both seasonal operations beginning in his month of March. More important, and probably older, was the cult of Vesta, who never took on human form, and whose archaic round temple stands in the center of the Forum. In it burned the sacred flame that must never be allowed to go out, and it housed the mysterious objects which Aeneas had brought from Troy, in whose keeping was bound up the safety of Rome. The maintenance of this all-important cult was the duty of the Vestal virgins, the remains of whose house and garden with its honorary statues of superiors of the order (*virgines maximae*) is one of the most interesting things in Rome. For the upkeep of these state cults called for permanent organization; hence the College of the Pontifices, originally three, then nine, later fifteen in number, and presided over by the Pontifex Maximus. They preserved the sacred formulae, saw to all public religious observances, and drew up the calendar of festivals, attributed to Numa, which is the earliest of Roman calendars. Another sacred college, that of the augurs, interpreted the will of the gods from lightning, from birds, from the feeding of sacred chickens, from four-footed animals, and from omens. Their advice was handed to the magistrates before every great act of state; it was for the magistrate to accept or reject it. Such was Roman religion as we first know it—completely devoid of any spiritual satisfaction for the worshiper, and offering no code of morals. Hence the ready adoption by the Romans, at a later stage, of foreign cults which could satisfy these basic human needs.

From what has been said, it will be clear that modern historical criticism will not admit anything that could be called a political or narrative history of early Rome, except in the most general terms. There was a formal foundation of the city, and it may well have been about the traditional date, in the middle of the eighth century B.C. There was undoubtedly a monarchy. The traditional names of the six kings may represent historical figures, in the same way that Arthur of Britain was an historical figure. That some of the kings were Latin, others Sabine, and others Etruscan would accord with what is known of the ethnic make-up of the Roman people. That the last Etruscan kings were expelled by an oligarchic revolution at the end of the sixth century is perfectly credible. It is further clear that this was a reaction of the native landed aristocracy against the mercantile interests of the city, a conflict which was to play a part in the later class struggles of the early Republic. Beyond this outline political history, and a generalized picture of Roman society and its institutions, it is scarcely possible to go. We are left with the Cloaca Maxima instead of the Rape of Lucrece, and the drainage channels of the Roman Campagna instead of Horatius at the Bridge. It may seem a barren triumph.

But, in another way, the modern historian must take cognizance of the stories in the first ten books of Livy and in Macaulay's *Lays of Ancient Rome,* "the touching story of Coriolanus, the still more touching story of Virginia, the wild legend about the draining of the Alban Lake, the combat between Valerius Corvus and the gigantic Gaul," and all the rest of them. Worked up by Roman historians into a traditional patriotic narrative, they formed the mental picture the Romans had of their own past and their own character. They became a dynamic social myth and, as such, had a profound effect on political action in later times—for example, Cato and the "old Roman" party of the second century B.C. In just the same way, what is known or believed about the Founding Fathers or the War of Independence has often influenced politics in the United States. Nor have these Roman legends lost all their dynamism today. In France, at the height of the Stavisky scandals, a performance of *Coriolanus* caused riots in the streets of Paris.

Early Rome displays political institutions which can be widely paralleled in Italy and Greece, and which were also widespread among the Celtic and Germanic peoples. First, there was the king (*rex*). Even if historical traditions were not unanimously in favor of his existence, it could be deduced from many fossil survivals in religion and politics. The title *rex* was borne by certain priests who had taken over his religious functions; the Pontifex Maximus lived in the palace (*regia*) that had been the traditional home of King Numa. The oldest inscription in Rome, that on the archaic *cippus* under the Lapis Niger in the Forum, declares that "the sacrifical animals are sacred to the King." Under the Republic, if one of the consuls died or resigned, an official called *interrex* was chosen, and his period of office was known as an *interregnum.* But if the existence of the king is certain, the nature and scope of his powers is a matter of dispute. The monarchy seems to have been elective rather than hereditary, the election being made by the heads of the great aristocratic families (*patres*), and probably confirmed by the people. The taking of auspices played a cardinal role in this election; the king must be assured of the favor of the gods. Once elected, his powers seem to have been far-reaching, if not absolute. He made war and peace, and was the su-

preme commander in the field. He was the source of law
and the head of the state religion. Over the citizens he held
power of life and death, symbolized by the rods and axes
(*fasces*) of the lictors. It has been well said that the powers
of the king in the state are the counterpart of those of the
paterfamilias in the family. The purple robe, the triumphal
procession, the lictors with their axes, were all taken over
from the monarchy by the consuls as officers of the Republic.

The aristocracy were the wealthy landowners, claiming descent from the heads of the chief families (*patres*) who had
taken part in the foundation of the state. The germ of the
Roman Senate is the council of (traditionally) one hundred
aristocrats which advised the king. The first Roman class
struggle—and no doubt a long one—was the contest between
the monarchy and the aristocracy which ended in the establishment of the Republic. The word *populus* seems to have
meant, originally, the whole Roman people, irrespective of
class, organized for military or political purposes. The origin of the later popular assemblies lay in the meetings in
which the *populus* was called to signify its assent to such
great proposals as the election of a king or the declaration
of war. The *plebs* was that part of the community debarred
by poverty or humble birth from the ranks of the aristocracy.
There seems no reason to think of them as the urban poor,
as distinct from the peasantry, nor to postulate a separate
racial origin, as is sometimes done. The roots of the great
class struggles of 500–300 B.C. clearly lie in this period, but
cutting across them was the curious social institution of
clientship (*clientela*). In this, a number of poorer citizens
would place themselves as clients under the protection of a
wealthier man who became their patron (*patronus*), and gave
them legal and financial support. But the advantages were
not all on one side. The clients could render important political services to their patron, and here again political features of the Republic are foreshadowed. The whole structure,
entered upon for mutual advantages, but resting on a moral
basis of loyalty (*fides*) and obligation (*pietas*), is something
peculiarly Roman. In Virgil's picture of the Underworld, the
harshest punishments are exacted from those sinners who
have cheated a client in life.

We are still two centuries from the beginnings of Latin
literature, for nobody now believes in the tribal lays which
Niebuhr once postulated as the vehicle for the legends of
early Roman history. But there is much to show that Rome,
under Etruscan influence, was in the sixth century B.C. one
of the chief centers of artistic development north of Magna

Graecia. The cult statues and the terra-cotta decorations of
the temple of Jupiter on the Capitol were the work of the
Etruscan artist Vulca. They were swept away in the reconstruction of the temple in the time of Sulla, but a century
later Pliny speaks admiringly of similar ancient statues of
the gods which survived in some numbers in Rome and the country towns, and which clearly had for his generation the appeal that Romanesque architecture or Italian primitives have
for our own. The discovery in modern times of the superb
statues of Veii and Conca enable us to understand what he
means. Again, in the fourth century B.C., Rome seems to have
been the center of the manufacture of bronze objects of very
high quality, such as the Ficorini casket now in the Villa
Giulia, and it is likely that the origins of this art go back a
century or so earlier. One masterpiece of the lost art of early
Rome does survive—the great bronze wolf which in all prob-
ability is the original Wolf of the Capitol, dating from the
sixth century B.C.

Preliterary Latin is known only from a few inscriptions,
from hymns such as the *Carmen Saliare* and the *Hymn of
the Arval Brothers,* and from a few pieces of archaic Latin
quoted by later authors. Scanty as they are, these fragments
confirm what is said by Polybius, that this early Latin was so
different from the language of his time (the second century
B.C.) as to be scarcely intelligible. But the study of semantics
shows how early Latin, the language of a simple agricultural
community, was transformed, as was Roman religion, by the
historical experience of the Roman people. For example,
laetus originally meant "fat" or "rich," of land or crops, *lae-
tare* "to manure," and *laetamen* "dung." In the language of
augury a *laetum auspicium* foretold prosperity; hence the
meaning *laetus* "joyful" or "prosperous." *Egregius* and *exi-
mius,* both meaning "excellent," were originally used for a
prize animal selected out of the flock. *Cohors* was originally
part of a farmyard or pen: then part of a military camp:
finally the unit stationed there. *Agmen* meant first any flock
of driven animals, later a column on the march. *Impedire*
and *expedire* meant hobbling and unhobbling animals; later
they acquired specialized military meanings as well as the
general sense of "obstruct" and "set free." *Probus* was used
of crops which grow properly, *luxuria* of vegetation run to
seed, *pauper* of land or animals giving a poor yield. Only
later do they acquire a general and moral significance. The
vast majority of Latin proverbs, like those of England and the
United States until very recent times, reflect the experience
of generations of country dwellers.

CHAPTER III

ROME AND ITALY TO 280 B.C.

Two great themes dominate the first two centuries of the
Roman Republic: internally, the class struggle between the
aristocracy and the plebeians, and externally, the expansion
of Roman power over the whole of Italy from the Gulf of
Genoa to the Strait of Messina. It is by no means an easy
period to interpret. A half-legendary coloring pervades the
historical sources down to the Gallic invasion and beyond.
Coriolanus belongs to myth rather than history. Cincinnatus
and Camillus are undoubtedly historical figures, but the story
of their deeds has been embellished to suit their roles as
heroes of a patriotic, epic history. Toward the end of the
fourth century the mists clear; Appius Claudius Caecus (consul in 307 and 296) has been called "the first clear-cut personality in Roman history." At the beginning of the period,
the Romans win the battle of Lake Regillus by the direct
intervention of the heroes Castor and Pollux; at the end
they are engaged in a war with Pyrrhus, one of that progeny
of great commanders littered on the world by the conquests
of Alexander. It is as though English history passed in two
centuries from Alfred the Great to the wars of Marlborough.
With the political struggle between the orders the case is
rather different. In the historical narrative, it unrolls in an
orderly succession of phases, each marked by the enactment
of legislation whose details reveal new concessions gained by
the *plebs*. Generations of schoolboys have been made to
memorize these laws as though they were as definite and ar-
ticulate as the bones of the human skeleton. But, in fact, this
very orderliness is suspicious. In the great class struggles of
the second and first centuries B.C., the early struggle of the
orders was used for political propaganda by all parties; it is
not easy to say how much has been retrojected in the his-

torical narrative from the later period to the earlier. More-over, it is often not easy to tell when a particular provision was asserted by the *plebs* as a right, and when it was con-ceded by the patricians as having the force of law. But it is at least possible to appreciate the objectives and strategy of the two sides, and to see the machinery of the Republic in action in a long struggle which has in many ways enriched Western political thought. Similarly, in the conquest of Italy, we shall be less concerned with the details of campaigns than with the broader issues of Roman treatment of her de-feated enemies, the extension of Roman citizenship, and the function of those great institutions, the Roman *colonia* and *municipium*.

Rome's relations with the Latins were of crucial impor-tance. During the regal period she had held the primacy in a Latin league whose original purpose was the common wor-ship of Jupiter Latiaris on the Alban Mount. It is likely that this came to imply some degree of political supremacy, and when the kings were expelled from Rome, the Latins saw their chance to shake it off, no doubt on the grounds that the treaty of alliance had been made with the king. Whether the young Republic tried to reassert its claim is uncertain; if so, it was unsuccessful, for in 493 B.C. Rome and the Latins con-cluded a treaty on equal terms—the famous *Foedus Cassia-num,* which still survived, engraved on bronze tablets, in the Forum in Cicĕro's day. An abstract of the treaty is given by Dionysius (VI. XCV. 1-3):

> Let there be peace between the Romans and all the Latin cities so long as heaven and earth are still in the same place. Let them never make war on each other, nor call in foreign enemies, nor grant safe passage to any third party making war on either, but let them help each other with all their force when attacked, and let each have an equal share of all spoil and booty won in wars in common. Let all cases relating to pri-vate contracts be judged within ten days among the people where the contract was made. Let nothing be added to nor taken from this treaty except by the joint consent of the Romans and all the Latin cities.

This is a classic example of a *foedus aequum,* a treaty be-tween equals, though it is to be noted that Rome treats with all the Latin cities combined.

On the secure basis of a Latin alliance, Rome was able to consolidate her position against the Etruscan cities on the north, the Sabines on the northeast, and the Aequi and Volsci of the Apennines proper, these last more barbarous peoples and fierce opponents. The wars were long and progress was slow, for the campaigning season was confined to early summer, and it was practically impossible to take a walled city. Some parts of the historical narrative are hard to understand; for example, the story of the migration of the Sabine Attus Clausus and his five thousand dependents to Rome, where he was given land and received into the patrician order —the origin of the famous *gens Claudia*. Does this represent the expulsion by the Sabines of a pro-Roman party? Or does it mask a Sabine conquest of Rome? The legends of the ten-year siege and final capture of Veii (396 B.C.) by Camillus are stranger still, and only to be understood by entering into the world of magic, divination, and destiny of the *disciplina Etrusca*. Both cities, rivals for so many years, were approaching a crisis in their life cycle. For Veii, eight ages had gone of the nine or ten after which the Etruscan nation was fated to be destroyed. Rome was nearing the fatal number of 365 years from her foundation by Romulus. Both faced sudden death; one might win a new lease of life. That one was Rome, thanks to the superior occult generalship of Camillus. By the terrible ceremony of *evocatio* the gods were summoned out of Veii, and the city captured and destroyed. The whole strange story has recently been elucidated by a Belgian scholar; * it is as heavy with doom as the conquest of Mexico by Cortes. Reverting to sober history, it is clear that by the time of the conquest of Veii Rome was firmly in control of the lower Tiber valley, southern Etruria, the whole plain of Latium, and much of the hill country farther east.

But within a few years, a sudden disaster threatened to sweep all these gains away. This was the great Gallic invasion of 390 B.C. An earlier chapter showed how in the sixth century the Gauls had invaded the Po valley in search of new lands to settle. But this was no folk migration; it was simply a plundering raid on a large scale. The first attack was on the Etruscan city of Clusium, and when Rome tried to protect Clusium, the Gauls turned on her. On the banks of the Allia River, a few miles north of Rome, a Roman army faced for the first time the ferocious charge of Celtic warriors. There was panic, and a disgraceful defeat; ever afterward July 18, the "day of the Allia," was a black day in the calendar. The Gauls pressed on to plunder and burn the city, though the garrison on the Capitol probably held out. Brennus became the first barbarian conqueror of Rome, to be suc-

* J. Hubaux: *Rome et Veies,* 1958.

ceeded by no other for eight hundred years. After exacting
a humiliating tribute, the Celts withdrew northward across
the Apennines, leaving behind a name which did not wholly
lose its terrors until the conquest of Gaul by Julius Caesar.

The economic distress and internal struggles which followed the Gallic invasion postponed any further Roman
conquests in Italy to the second half of the fourth century
B.C. Then followed seventy years of almost continuous warfare, at the end of which Rome emerged victorious over all
her enemies, and ready to play a major role as a Mediterranean power. It was a period of achievement, in war and
diplomacy, hardly less remarkable than that following the
Second Punic War. Unfortunately, our historical sources give
only the Roman side of the story, and even so there is a
good deal that is obscure. If we were better informed, such
men as Lucius Papirius Cursor, Publius Decius Mus, Appius
Claudius Caecus might not seem inferior to the soldiers and
statesmen of the age of Cicero. And in the powerful confederacy of the Samnites Rome met her most resolute and
formidable enemy until the Second Punic War. For by 350
B.C. the Samnite power had spread from their mountain
homeland to the coastal plains east and west. Their contact
with Greek civilization had led to the growth of wealthy
cities in Campania, chief of which was Capua, the greatest
manufacturing center in Italy, noted for its production of
bronze and iron goods and of ceramics. Between the Hellenized Samnites of the coastal plains and their more primitive
kinsmen of the hills there was friction, while the Greek cities
such as Neapolis were looking around for a protector against
Samnite domination before it was too late. For both, the only
champion was Rome, and it was on the invitation of Neapolis that Rome intervened in Campania. Little is known of
the first Samnite War, but in gaining control of Campania—
whenever it was done—Rome gained a prize of immense importance. Apart from the wealth of Capua, it was the most
productive agricultural land in Italy, the fertile volcanic
soil yielding three main crops a year in the best localities.
Along the coast were a series of fine harbors—notably Puteoli and Naples—with an established overseas trade.

The cities of the Latin League, faithful allies for nearly a
century and a half, looked on this increase of Roman power
with jealous eyes. They had been getting a raw deal for some
time; forced to contribute to Roman wars, they had not had
a fair share of Roman victories. Now the conquest of Campania enabled Rome to outflank them, and gave her economic gains that, once consolidated, would tip the balance

against them beyond redress. But their first thoughts were not of war. They approached Rome for a revision of the *Foedus Cassianum*, the treaty on which the alliance was based; it is likely, though not certain, that the proposals they put forward were for a federal union, one consul and half the senate at Rome to be Latins. The Romans would have none of it, and the Latins, rebuffed, turned to war. They were joined by the Volsci, Aequi, Hernici, and some of the newly conquered cities of Campania, and Rome faced a formidable coalition of kindred peoples, whose armies were trained and equipped in the same way as her own. There followed three years of bitter fighting, in which it is possible, for the first time, to discern a well-planned and well-executed Roman military strategy. At the end of it the Latin League was beaten and forced to sue for peace. The settlement that followed (338 B.C.) affords the clearest evidence we possess for the political side of Roman supremacy in Italy. Rome refused to treat with the Latin League as such, and the league thus ceased to exist. She then negotiated with the Latin cities individually on the merits of each case. Some were admitted to full Roman citizenship, others to citizenship without the right to vote or hold office in Rome. Certain of the most persistently hostile had their fortifications destroyed and their leading politicians exiled. But the vast majority retained their own laws and their own magistrates; they had the duty of serving in Roman wars, but also the right to share in Roman conquests. Individually, their citizens had *ius commercii* and *ius connubii* with Rome; that is, they could enter into contracts with Roman citizens, enforceable under Roman law, and intermarry with Romans without either party losing rights. Moreover, they could in most cases acquire full Roman citizenship by migrating to Rome or joining a Roman colony. The spirit displayed in these settlements was generous by any standards, and by those of the ancient world, astonishingly so. The whole system of graded privileges and interlocking loyalties may some day repay study by the nations of the Atlantic Alliance. But Rome was at the center; all roads led to Rome.

The Samnites were not likely to accept the loss of Campania as final so long as their military power was unbroken. For thirty years Rome was engaged in a series of campaigns against them which have come down in the traditional account as the Second Samnite War (326–304 B.C.) and the Third Samnite war (298–290 B.C.). Modern scholars do not put much trust in Livy's account of these years. It is hard to avoid the impression that Livy is treating them as a kind of curtain-raiser to the still more terrible wars against Carthage, and that many of the episodes he describes are "doublets" of the events that really belong to the Punic Wars. Thus the disaster of the Caudine Forks and the Roman reaction to it are parallel to the disaster of Cannae and its sequel, and the unquenchable hostility of the Samnite leaders Gavius Pontius and Gellius Egnatius is like that of Hamilcar and Hannibal. But at least it is clear why the wars with the Samnites lasted so long. First, the Romans had to learn mountain warfare the hard way. The Roman legion was meant for warfare in the plains; the mobile units of the Samnites were much better adapted to the hills. Hence such disasters as the Caudine Forks (321 B.C.), where an entire Roman army was forced to surrender, and the battle of Lautulae a few years later. Secondly, the Samnites had to be conquered piecemeal, glen by glen; there was no single center where capture would end the war. The Roman strategy was to shut them up in their mountains, split their forces, and gain control of the main passes by planting fortresses. One of their most effective measures was to deprive the Samnites of their winter pastures by holding the plains. In the Third War the Samnites tried to break out of their corner, and did succeed in building up a great anti-Roman coalition in which the Gauls, the Umbrians, and the northern Etruscans were the other main allies. Gellius Egnatius, to whom this policy is ascribed, must have been an astute statesman as well as a general. It was an hour of grave danger for Rome, but in a desperately fought battle at Sentinum in Umbria (295 B.C.), she shattered the northern coalition. The last round was at hand, and Livy has a dramatic picture of the effort the Samnites made to raise an army, and the terrible oath by which their soldiers were bound to conquer or die. The Roman victory at Aquilonia over this last of Samnite armies (293 B.C.) brought the war to an end, and the defeated enemy were admitted to the second grade of Roman citizenship. In Roman tradition the struggle with the Samnites left a grim and terrible memory; it was "the inexpiable war." And many of the Samnites were unreconciled: they were to be the core of resistance to Rome in the Social War two centuries later.

Far otherwise does tradition represent the war against Tarentum and King Pyrrhus of Epirus (280–275 B.C.). The Roman victory over the Samnites had alarmed the Greek cities of the Gulf: Tarentum, the largest and wealthiest, called in Pyrrhus as her deliverer. The Greek world after Alexander, like Europe after Napoleon, was full of capable generals of high talents and higher ambition. Pyrrhus of Epirus was one of these. He had had dreams of winning Macedonia itself; now the Tarentine engagement offered hopes of a great western empire, rivaling the conquests of Agathocles or Dionysius of Syracuse. So Pyrrhus came to Italy with a mercenary army of 20,000 Greeks, the most highly fancied professionals of their day, twenty elephants, and his own knowledge of how to employ the invincible Macedonian phalanx. He came; he saw; he won two battles (by a precarious and diminishing margin), drew one, and lost one; and he went away. He was the first great Hellenistic general the Romans had encountered, and they beat him in the end—small wonder that in Roman tradition he acquired the status of favorite enemy. Henceforward supremacy in Italy is to be a cardinal doctrine of Roman policy, and to play a part like that of the Monroe Doctrine in the New World.

The struggle on the internal front was as arduous as the wars of conquest in Italy. The revolution that established the Republic had been the work of the landed aristocracy. The executive powers of the king, the administration of the law, his command of the army, his religious functions, were now discharged by a variety of magistrates, themselves aristocrats, and effectively controlled by the great organ of the aristocracy, the Roman Senate. Popular liberties had gained nothing by the change, and it is not surprising that the rest of the Roman citizens were in no mood to tolerate a state that condemned them to economic, social, legal, and political inferiority. So the struggle of the orders began early in the fifth century B.C., and was to last for more than two hundred years before the *plebs* gained all their objects. The Roman *plebs* in the fifth century B.C., and even more in the fourth, was made up of elements as diverse as those that combined to force through the Reform Bill of 1832 in England. There were at least four main groups among them: urban artisans not tied to the aristocracy by the client system, free peasants, wealthy traders, and poor immigrants. Their first need was for political weapons to carry on the struggle, and a highly simple and effective one was to hand— *secessio*, secession, leaving Rome in a body. This they did more than once, though how many times is uncertain. Traditionally, the first secession was in 494 B.C., and it is clear that the first round of the struggle was fought in that decade. From it the *plebs* emerged with their own magistrates, the tribunes, and their own political organ, the *Concilium Plebis*, (Assembly of the People) to match the magistrates and Senate of the other side. Fully evolved, the powers of the tribunes were far-reaching. They could veto the acts of any magistrate, or any laws or resolutions of the Senate, which were contrary to the interests of the *plebs* or of any individual plebeian. They had the right of doing business with the people in the Assembly, and getting them to pass resolutions (*plebiscita*). Their persons were sacrosanct, and the *plebs* jealously protected them against violence. But they worked under certain limitations. They were not magistrates of the Republic, they did not possess the power of command (*imperium*), they could not interfere with commanders in the field. Above all, one tribune could veto the acts of another. Even so, the *plebs* had now become organized as a state within the state.

Their next great victory came in the middle of the fifth century, when they secured a written code of law. This was the famous Twelve Tables, "the fount," says Livy, "of all Roman law, public and private." Previously, the interpretation of customary law, dependent on oral tradition, had been reserved to the aristocracy, and had been one of the main props of their privilege. They cannot have given it up lightly, though the details of the struggle are obscure. What is certain is that a board of ten commissioners was set up (*decemviri legibus scribundis*) and the constitution suspended while they were at work. They seem to have undertaken some comparative legal study, and are said to have visited Athens, where the laws of Solon had been in operation for more than a century. Certainly they would have visited the cities of Magna Graecia, famous for their jurists and codes of law. The result of their work was a codification of public, private, religious, and criminal law which was passed as a statute through the Assembly of the People and engraved on bronze tablets in the Forum. It was learned by schoolboys in Cicero's day, and some of the provisions remained in force until Byzantine times. About a third of it is known to us from various sources, mostly in a modernized Latin which suggests several revisions, and this forms the starting point for all historical treatment of Roman law.

It is rather puzzling to find, so soon after the Twelve Tables, a further plebeian offensive which resulted in 445 in a law allowing intermarriage (*connubium*) between patricians and plebeians. It looks as though the aristocracy had managed to keep this vital social concession out of the Twelve Tables and it was forced out of them as a kind of appendix. It would, of course, benefit only the wealthy plebeians.

Again, it was they who gained from another concession made at this time, that one of the consuls might be a plebeian. But here the patricians took back with one hand what they gave with the other. The office of consul, in the old form, was abandoned; its place was taken by military tribunes with consular powers, three in number, who might be either patricians or plebeians. A new office, that of censor (443), was brought in, reserved for patricians, and given very important powers, for the censor had charge of the register of citizens and their property, assigned for service with the cavalry, and kept up to date the list of the Senate. The control of public morals, by which such men as Cato the Elder made famous the office of the censorship, was a later development, but even at the end of the fourth century Appius Claudius Caecus based a political program on the tenure of the position.

It might be thought that the poorer plebeians had so far obtained very little. But probably the foundation of colonies and the redistribution of public land were sufficient, before 390, to relieve the worst of their economic grievances, and they were little interested in the opportunities for a career in politics. But the distress that followed the Gallic invasion caused the struggle to be renewed, and in its new phase it was chiefly concerned with the grievances of the poorer plebeians, chief of which were land hunger and the harshness of the Roman laws of debt. The two were closely connected. Agriculture was the basis of the Roman economy, and the clash of interest between the big landowners and the peasants the basic political issue. The big estates could be made to pay simply because their owners had the capital to pay for improvements and to tide them over bad years. The small holdings were uneconomic to farm, and the laws of debt made the position hopeless. For the peasant could not raise a mortgage on the security of his land; all he could put up was his person, which meant the economic value of his labor. This created a bond (*nexum*) between him and his creditor, which literally had to be worked off, thus reducing the debtor to the status of a serf. If he failed, he could be imprisoned, sold into slavery, or even put to death. Undischarged debts could be passed on to his sons, so that a child might inherit at birth a burden of labor which he could not discharge in his entire working life. The only source from which land hunger could be appeased was the *ager publicus*, land won in wars of conquest. Some of this had always been distributed as peasant holdings, but most of it had been sold to those who could afford to buy it, and it had thus fostered the growth of large estates. Now the amount to be held by any one person had to be limited, and this was the object of the famous *Lex Licinia Sextia* of 367 b.c. What

1. Italy

these limits were is less certain: tradition says 500 *iugera* of arable land, or the grazing of 500 sheep or cattle; but so much use was made of the supposed provisions of this law in the later agrarian crisis of the second century b.c. that it is hard to be sure of its original terms. None the less, it is beyond doubt that a major agricultural reform was carried out at this time, and that it was fiercely resisted; tradition tells of a ten-year struggle before the bill was carried. Agricultural reform was always political dynamite in the Greco-Roman world.

The new system of land grants, and the operations of a kind of state bank to provide advances and loans, seem to have relieved the worst economic evils. But the *nexum* system remained unreformed until 326 (or 313; accounts differ), when the *Lex Poetilia* gave what Livy calls a new charter of liberty to the *plebs* by abolishing bondage or imprisonment for debt, and permitting the mortgaging of land.

The agrarian reforms of 367 also brought political gains, for the consulship was revived, and it was agreed that one of the two consuls must be a plebeian. Again the patricians tried to recoup their losses by the creation of a new office, this time that of the praetors, who took over from the consuls most of their legal duties. But plebeians were admitted to the censorship in 339 and to the praetorship in 337; and the last stronghold of the patricians, the great priestly colleges, were opened to the *plebs* sometime after 292 b.c. The last stage of the struggle was reached in 287 b.c., when the passing of the *Lex Hortensia* gave the force of law to resolutions of the *Concilium Plebis*.

After two centuries of struggle the *plebs* had thus obtained all their objectives, and that with a minimum of violence and through due process of law. In both ancient and modern times this process has evoked admiration and has underlined the contrast of the bloody class struggles which characterized the Greek city-states. It is fair enough to see in it the high-water mark of the political achievement of the Roman Republic, and to remind ourselves from such words as "senate," "popular assembly," "plebiscite," "vote" (and indeed "dictatorship"), how much that political achievement has left by way of legacy. But its sequel was surprising. The aristocracy now had no legal basis for privilege left; their position in the state now rested on what they could command through *auctoritas* and *dignitas,* the unofficial status conferred on them by their wealth, their numerous clients, their family reputation, and the personal achievement of each man. But for the next century and a half, down to the

Gracchi, these were enough to make it the great age of aristocratic supremacy in Rome. The issue of the struggle of the orders had been, in a sense, a victory for democracy, but the Roman Republic was never a democracy, either then or later.

When, about a century later, the Roman constitution was studied by experienced Greek political observers like the historian Polybius, they saw in it a perfect embodiment of the virtues of the "mixed constitution." The popular assemblies were a democratic element, the Senate stood for the aristocratic principle, and the powers of the king were exercised by the magistrates—above all, by the consuls. This mixed constitution, they thought, conferred on Rome a political stability that was the real cause of its success. The Greek Polybius and the Roman Cato were agreed—as they would have been on little else—that this constitution had the great virtue of being the product of centuries of political experience. "Our Republic," said Cato, "was not made by the services of one man, but of many, not in a single lifetime, but through many centuries and generations." And Polybius emphasizes that the Romans did not sit down to think out their constitution, but evolved it in the hard school of political experience.

A modern observer will be struck by these features above all: first, that all three branches, magistrates, Senate, and popular assemblies, could initiate legislation; second, the small number of the magistrates holding executive powers. Two consuls, one or sometimes two praetors for legal administration, two quaestors for finance, four aediles for policing and supervising the city, two censors, though these only at intervals—barely a dozen in all, far fewer than the cabinet of a modern parliamentary state. The dangers of leaving power in so few hands were minimized by limiting their terms to a single year, and giving the magistrate in each grade one or more colleagues who could oppose him. The Roman people, through their several popular assemblies, did in a sense exercise ultimate authority, since they elected the magistrates, heard capital cases, and decided issues of peace and war. But they met only on the summons of a magistrate. The Senate was in regular session, was better fitted for debate, and contained nearly everyone of political experience. It was to the Senate, rather than to the people, that the magistrates deferred, for they were members of the Senate, and after their term of office their political future lay with it. It was therefore a natural tendency for the magistrates to become more and more the executive arm of the Senate, rather than to follow policies of their own. It was this, plus the prudence with which, on the whole, it exercised its powers, that accounts for the effective supremacy of the Senate in Roman politics from 300 b.c. to the time of the Gracchi.

Modern observers have also commented on the generosity of Rome's policy in Italy during this period. One of the reasons why Rome could afford such a policy was the success of the system of colonies. Compared with the Greek colony, the Roman colony belongs to another order of being. The former was a private venture, splitting off from the mother country to found a new community. The Roman colony was founded as an act of state, its site was chosen for strategic as well as economic reasons, and the number of colonists was determined in advance. As the name shows, the economic aspect was the earlier; *colere* means "to cultivate the land," and a *colonus* was, primarily, a tenant farmer. In some colonies all citizens were possessed of full Roman citizenship, which could thus be acquired by anyone settling there. Others were founded jointly with the Latins, and in them the citizens enjoyed "Latin rights." The dates of foundation, particularly the early ones, are not too reliable, but they seem to fall into two main periods, 450–390 and 350–263 b.c. Between these limits, we hear of twelve colonies of Roman citizens and thirty Latin colonies, which may in all have provided land for about sixty thousand citizens and their families. Of these, the best known archaeologically is Ostia, whose whole development has been explored from the colony of the late fourth century (or earlier?) to the great harbor city of imperial times. Air photography often shows in the neighborhood of Roman colonies the system of "centuriation," the division of public land into blocks of one hundred allotments which was the basic unit of the grants. They were sited on river crossings, harbors, or other positions suitable as a base for a field army. In peace, they were a focus of Romanization; in war, a bulwark for Rome. Their loyalty did not falter even in the terrible times of the Second Punic War. No wonder that the Roman author Aulus Gellius called them "the image and reflection, in little, of the Roman people." Thus early, and on the soil of Italy, there was a vigorous development of an institution which was to play a great part in the Romanization of the western provinces. Most of these forty-two colonies are today vigorous Italian cities; many of the historic cities of Europe, such as Cologne and Lincoln, began life as Roman colonies. A comparative study of Roman colonization and the opening up of the American West is greatly to be desired.

The *municipia* of Italy had a different origin, which begins with the extension of Roman power to Campania. A number of Campanian cities were given the status of *municipium*, signifying that they had entered into alliance with Rome and had exchanged social rights. But they retained their own magistrates, constitution, and religious rites, and their citizens could acquire Roman citizenship only by emigration to Rome. Like the *colonia,* the *municipium* was extended to the western provinces, where it developed along new lines.

Technology also played its part in the unification of Italy. In 312 B.C. the censor Appius Claudius Caecus began the building of the great highway from Rome to Capua (132 miles) that still bears his name—the Via Appia. It was the first of the great Roman roads that have meant so much for the civilization of Europe. Constructed in four layers, flags, rubble, cement, and top dressing, carefully graded, crossing rivers by bridges or paved fords, and the Pontine marshes by a viaduct, it provided an all-weather artery for the movement of men and goods between Rome and Campania. After the war with Pyrrhus it was extended to Brundisium (234 miles). At the same time a great northern highway, the Via Flaminia, was built from Rome to Ariminum (Rimini, 230 miles) on the Adriatic coast. In the next century an extension from here to Placentia (176 miles) was called the Via Aemilia, and played the same part in the opening up of Cisalpine Gaul that the Canadian Pacific Railway did in that of Canada. Other trunk roads connected Rome with the principal towns of Etruria on the northwest and Samnium to the southeast. The modern reader may perhaps think more readily in terms of motorways than of railways. It is a useful comparison; in particular, these roads may well be compared to the autobahn and autostrada of Germany and Italy in the 1930's. For, like theirs, the prime purpose of the great Roman roads in Italy was strategic—the safe and rapid movement of troops and supplies. Later, their economic importance became dominant, though for the movement of heavy freight they could never play the same part as a modern highway. In the ancient world, where only draft animals and pack mules were available for land haulage, heavy goods went, where possible, by sea.

This great system of trunk roads, inaugurated in Italy, was later extended to every part of the Empire. It was a purely Roman thing—the great Hellenistic kingdoms could show nothing like it—and it made land travel easier and faster than it was to be again until the railway age.

The army with which Rome won Italy was a citizen militia, called out when need arose. Every able-bodied citizen was liable to military service as part of his obligations to the state. He discharged it at his own expense, at first, serving without pay and providing his own weapons and equipment. A military system whereby the richest class of citizen provided the cavalry, the next wealthiest the heavy infantry, and the poorer classes the light-armed troops is traditionally attributed to the king Servius Tullius, in the sixth century b.c., but more probably belongs to the mid-fifth century. As campaigns grew longer and were fought farther from Rome, this system became inadequate, and in the final struggle against Veii a decisive step was taken by providing pay (*stipendium*) for military service. Later, the state began to provide standard weapons and equipment—the first stage toward a professional army, although that development still lay in the future.

The main unit was the *legio* or division, of 5,000 infantry and 300 cavalry, and perhaps in the fourth century, certainly in the third, each consul commanded an army of two legions. Tactics were based on Greek models, perhaps themselves learned from the Etruscans. We hear of three lines of battle, based on age groups; first the young men, who were spear throwers (*hastati*), next the main heavy infantry (*principes*), and in reserve, the veterans (*triarii*). Cavalry was used to protect the wings of the infantry formation, rather than in its own right. This produced an army well adapted to fighting in level country, but the long campaigns in the mountains of Samnium showed that something more flexible was needed, and the legion was accordingly broken down into maniples (*manipuli*), capable of acting as independent companies. Finally, the allies were obliged to furnish auxiliary troops to take part in the campaign; often these were of arms in which the Romans were not strong, such as cavalry.

By the standards of fourth-century Italy, this was a formidable army, and it was certainly a versatile one. It faced and beat the Celtic fervor of the Gauls, the specialized tactics of the Samnites, and the professional competence of Pyrrhus and his Greeks. But it had weaknesses, which were soon to be exposed. Weapons and equipment were insufficiently standardized. The troops, though brave, were inadequately trained, and their main concern was to get the war done and go back to their farms. Above all, there were grave inadequacies in the higher command. One of the consuls might be an able commander, but the odds were long against both being competent. Of course, a man with a good record in the field might be brought back in an emergency as consul or dictator, as was Camillus. But no one at Rome understood the higher strategy, because there was no one to think about it full time. By Greek standards, Rome had no generals as yet, and was to have none before the Second Punic War. Indeed, it was the lessons learned in that grim struggle that turned the Roman army into the force that was to dominate the world for the next five centuries. The difference between the Roman armies before and after Hannibal is that between the armies of Bull Run and those of Gettysburg.

The return of Pyrrhus to Greece in 275 B.C. left Rome supreme in Italy. There were a few mopping-up operations before that supremacy became absolute: Rhegium was captured in 270 B.C., Brundisium in 267; the Piceni revolted in 268 and were reduced the following year. But when, in 266 B.C., Apulia and Messapia had been received as allies the process was complete. It was a little more than 120 years—four generations of men—since the low point of the Gallic invasion of 390 B.C.

The settlements which Rome made between herself and the various Italian communities were, on the whole, like those which had been made with the Latins in 338 B.C. There was the same policy of divide and rule, balanced by the granting of privileges, carefully graded according to capacity, to ex-enemies and new allies alike. Full Roman citizenship, it is true, was more sparingly extended; only the Sabines received it at this time. The Samnites, Etruscans, and Umbrians received what may be called half-citizenship (*civitas sine suffragio*): they could not take part in Roman politics, and probably could not acquire full citizenship by residing in Rome. The historic Greek cities of the South became allied states (*civitates foederatae*). Collectively, all those new additions to the Roman confederacy were known as "Italian allies" (*socii Italici*) and formed a sort of outer ring less fully privileged than the Latins. But, like them, they retained their own constitutions, elected their own magistrates, made their own laws, and worshiped their own gods. They paid no tribute to Rome, though they were bound to supply contingents to the Roman armed forces. The *pax Romana* prevailed over the Italian peninsula from Pisa and Rimini to the Strait of Messina, as later it was to do over the whole Mediterranean world. Roman law and the Latin language began that extension which was to make them dominant by 150 B.C. It was, in fact, the starting point of the cultural, social, and economic unification of Italy which has never since been wholly lost, even in the Dark Ages.

The advantages to Italy of settled peace and increased prosperity were great. To Rome, they were greater still. Her lands—the *ager publicus populi Romani*—had been extended in the wars of conquest to about ten thousand square miles, a fifth of the whole peninsula. It was a rich and varied estate, ripe for development. Much of it was allotted for small holdings, the traditional type of Roman agriculture. But there was also a share of the *pascua,* the great pastureland of Samnium, Apulia, and Calabria. Here were the summer and winter grazing grounds for sheep and cattle, and the immemorial drove roads (*calles*) along which huge flocks of animals passed twice a year, as they did along the drovers' roads from Wales to England before the railways. This was a new type of farming for the Romans, and on it huge fortunes were to be built by a few men rich enough to buy or rent large pastures from the state. In contrast to the smallholders, the immense gangs of shepherds (*pastores*) that later worked these big ranches grew into a lawless element that readily turned to brigandage and rebellion. Then there were the forest resources of Italy, still largely untouched, especially such regions as the Sila in Bruttium, as important for ship-building as the English oakwoods for the wooden ships of the old navy.

Roman Italy about 260 b.c.—the start of the First Punic War—covered some 52,000 square miles, and its population, at an estimate very widely accepted, was perhaps 4 million. Both figures accord very closely with those of the state of North Carolina today. Rome itself may have had a population of 125,000. In the world of the third century b.c., Roman Italy had about the same population as the kingdom of Macedonia. The other two great Hellenistic kingdoms were much bigger, Egypt being about 10 million and Syria about 30 million. But the events of the next century were to show that in the solidity of her institutions and the morale of her citizens Rome had resources superior to those of any other state in the world.

CHAPTER IV

ROME AND THE MEDITERRANEAN: 280–133 B.C.

An indelible impression was left on the mind of Rome by the appalling series of wars with Carthage known as the Punic Wars. The First Punic War, after twenty-three years, ended in something like mutual exhaustion. The second brought Rome to the brink of destruction at the hands of her great enemy Hannibal. The third pushed Carthage over it, ending with the annihilation of Punic power and the physical obliteration of the city. That is what is meant by the grim phrase "a Carthaginian peace." Small wonder that looking back, Roman writers saw this struggle—and especially the Second Punic War—as the Great War, "the struggle for universal empire by land and sea," in the words of Lucretius. Virgil, with the imagination of a poet, saw the two cities as predestined enemies from their origins; Aeneas' betrayal of Dido marks their first clash; Hannibal is the avenger who arises to fulfill Dido's curse. But, in fact, Rome and Carthage were on friendly terms for more than two centuries. The first treaty Rome made with a power outside Italy was that with Carthage in 508 B.C., and it was renewed in 348 and 278; on each occasion the object was to restrict Roman trade in the western Mediterranean and to limit Carthaginian interests in Italy. It was only when her conquests brought her to the Strait of Messina that Rome became the heir of the old dispute between Greek and Carthaginian in Sicily.

The great adversary that now confronted Rome was the wealthiest city in the western Mediterranean. It had been founded about 800 B.C. by colonists from Tyre in Phoenicia —whence the Latin name "Puni" for the Carthaginians— whose first object seems to have been to exploit the murex beds, the shellfish that yielded the highly prized purple dye. But they had been quick to realize the natural advantages of the site, which in modern times have led to the rise of a great city at Tunis. The headland of Cape Bon is only eighty miles from the western corner of Sicily; a power that dominates this seaway can cut the Mediterranean in two. East of Cape Bon, there are good harbors in the Gulf of Tunis, and the fertile valley of the river Bagradas leads on to a hinterland very suitable for high farming. With these natural advantages, and under an oligarchic constitution admired by Greek political thinkers for its stability, Carthage had become a great power. She had a rich carrying trade with Egypt and the Levant, and was building up a monopoly in the western Mediterranean, where Corsica and Sardinia were firmly in her grasp. In the long struggle with the Greeks in Sicily neither side had been able to expel the other; the Greeks, led by Syracuse, were dominant in the eastern, the Carthaginians in the western part of the island. But the golden opportunities lay in the west, where Carthage was the heir of the old maritime empire of Tartessus in southern Spain. Apart from the rich and growing Spanish trade, she held a series of trading posts down the west coast of Africa. The great Carthaginian explorer Hanno (c. 500 b.c.) had reached at least Sierra Leone and perhaps the mouth of the Congo. Northward from the Strait of Gibraltar her ships sailed to the Bay of Biscay and perhaps beyond, although the link between Carthage and Cornish tin looks less likely than once it did.

A wealthy commercial oligarchy, like that of Venice, drew the profits from this huge overseas trade. Other magnates developed great agricultural estates in Africa, and some historians have seen a political weakness in the rivalry between these interests. The military resources of Carthage were formidable. Although mercenaries made up a large part of her army, she did not lack for good mercenary troops, infantrymen from Spain and the Berber lands, cavalry from Numidia. Her commanders were versed in the most up-to-date Hellenistic methods of warfare, and the greatest fleets of the world rode in her twin harbors, one for the navy, the other for the merchant fleet.

The First Punic War was sparked off by a Carthaginian attempt (backed for once by Syracuse), to gain control of Messana, from which they would have been able to dominate the strait between Italy and Sicily. For twenty years the city had been in the hands of a disreputable body of Italian mercenaries, the Mamertini. When these "sons of Mars" appealed to Rome for help, the Senate was hesitant; but the Popular Assembly insisted on war (264 b.c.), though it is unlikely that they realized where it would lead.

The clearance of Carthage from northeast Sicily, and the transference of Syracuse to the Roman side, were only the first phase. Carthage fought on, and Rome, no doubt at the instigation of Syracuse, undertook to drive her out of the island. This meant breaking Carthaginian command of the sea, and led to Rome's first great effort to become a naval power. It was remarkably successful. The inscription still survives in which Caius Duilius recorded his victory off Mylae in 260 B.C.: "He was the first to present the Roman people with the spoils of a sea battle, and the first to lead free-born Carthaginians in a triumph." There followed a series of the greatest naval battles ever fought in the ancient world. After a victory off western Sicily in 256 B.C., the Romans were able to by-pass the enemy forces still in the island and to land an army in Africa for a decisive blow at Carthage itself. This bold venture failed. Next year the army was defeated and the bulk of it, with its commander, Regulus, captured; a fleet sent to take off survivors was wrecked with immense loss of life. Indeed, throughout the war the Romans found it easier to defeat the Carthaginian navy than to master the sea. The last phase of the war was therefore a renewed campaign in western Sicily and around its coasts. The Carthaginians found a great general in Hamilcar, and maintained a desperate defense of their two surviving bases of Lilybaeum and Drepana (the modern Marsala and Trapani). Both were still in Punic hands when peace was made in 241 B.C., on the terms that Carthage should evacuate Sicily "and all the islands between Sicily and Italy" and pay a huge indemnity.

But the end was not yet. The great mercenary army which Hamilcar had led back from Sicily rebelled against the government, and Carthage was involved in the terrible struggle known as "the Truceless War." It was a chance for Rome to give another turn to the screw. She annexed Sardinia—an island between Sicily and Italy?—and virtually doubled the demand for indemnity if a new war was to be avoided. Beaten and humiliated, Carthage could only accept (238 B.C.). But she was left thirsting for revenge, and Hamilcar was there to plan it. In Spain, too, she had suffered in these years, though the details are obscure. But it was probably the power of Massilia that had pushed back the Carthaginians in Spain until they held little more than a bridgehead at Gades. In Spain lay the chance to revive the power of Carthage and to renew the struggle with Rome.

Rome also was faced with acute problems at the end of the First Punic War. None were more pressing than the need to find the right form of government for the territory which had resulted from Rome's first overseas campaigns. Roman expansion in Italy had brought about the formation of a great confederacy of Roman citizens and Italian allies covering the whole peninsula. In theory, this system might have been extended across the strait of Sicily. But there were good practical reasons why another course was taken. The immediate problem was to deal with the former colonial possessions of Carthage in the western part of the island, partly backward Sicel communities, partly Carthaginian settlements, but all alike once subjects of Carthage and paying tribute to her. Now what Rome asked of her allies in Italy was not tribute but military service; this these alien Sicilian communities could scarcely provide, nor would it have been fair to expect them to do so. Much easier to leave them to pay tribute, only now to Rome, not to Carthage. Rome would, of course, have to provide for the administration of the whole area and for the adjudication of suits between persons of different communities, as well as for the collection of tribute. But there were precedents to hand. Magistrates with the powers of praetors had been responsible for the judgment of cases between Italian allies, while quaestors had looked into financial questions. It was therefore natural to send out a praetor as governor, exercising his power (*imperium*) within the sphere (*provincia*) of western Sicily. He was assisted on the financial side by quaestors, and also had a small staff of aides. This was in 241 B.C., and western Sicily thus became the first Roman province, the kingdom of Syracuse remaining for the time outside. The same machinery was used in Corsica and Sardinia, which—after a good deal of fighting—were formed into a single province in 227 B.C.

When, in 211 B.C., the kingdom of Syracuse was incorporated with the province, it was in some respects a new situation, for here were historic Greek cities, above all, Syracuse herself, the greatest city of the Greek West. But one mark of high civilization is an efficient system of collecting taxes, and Syracuse had the most up-to-date system in the Hellenistic world, spoken of with admiration by Cicero nearly 150 years later. This had been drawn up by Hiero on the model of Ptolemaic Egypt, where the whole land was a royal estate and its inhabitants were all the subjects of the king. So to the king of Syracuse went the dues from the tithe on harvested crops, the rents from pasture lands, and the 50 per cent from harbor dues. The whole code was remarkable for its equity and flexibility: what more natural than that the Romans should take it over and incorporate the kingdom of Syracuse into the Province of Sicily? It was therefore of momentous consequence that the first overseas peoples Rome was called on to govern were, first, the alien or backward peoples of western Sicily, Sardinia, and Corsica, and second, the subjects of a highly centralized monarchy. The methods adopted produced a profound change in the nature of the Roman state, which now acquired subject peoples and subject lands tributary to Rome herself, not to the other members of the Roman confederacy. Thus piecemeal, almost casually, and with an eye to the past rather than the future, there developed a system of provincial government which was to have far-reaching effects on Rome and on the whole Mediterranean world.

Roman expansion in these years was not confined to lands won from Carthage. A series of campaigns in Liguria extended her hold beyond Pisa to the Maritime Alps. Then, in 225 B.C., Italy was again menaced by a great Gallic invasion, almost on the scale of that a century earlier. Rome had to raise a large army, which routed the Celts at the battle of Telamon. To avoid such dangers in future, she pushed northward into Cisalpine Gaul and began the long process which reduced that land to the shape of a province. Colonies were founded at Placentia, Cremona, and Modena, from which have grown famous cities of the Lombard plain. In the Adriatic, the activities of pirates from bases on the coast of Dalmatia forced her to take naval action, and to establish a base of her own in Epirus, the modern Albania, which brought her into diplomatic contact with Macedonia and with Greece proper.

All this had meant a consolidation of Roman power. But the expansion of Carthage in Spain was of a more spectacular kind, and its prime architect was Hamilcar Barca. It would be worth much to have the full story of his nine years as governor in Spain, for as a colonial administrator he seems to rank with such men as Lyautey. Even so bitter an enemy of Carthage as Cato the Elder, visiting Spain half a century later, refers with admiration to the work he did and the abiding memory he left. Hamilcar was accompanied on his mission by members of the oligarchic Council of Carthage, and the Carthaginian citizens serving in his army met from time to time as a popular assembly—clear evidence of the high importance attached to the project. Before this time, the interests of Carthage had been in Andalusia, with the old colony of Gades (Cadiz) as its capital, Malaca (Malaga) as an important port, and a string of trading posts and fishing harbors along the Atlantic coast west of Gibraltar. This was the land of the ancient native kingdom of Tartessus, whose wealth was founded on the rich mines of the Sierra Morena.

But under Hamilcar another and richer province was acquired in southeastern Spain, with Alicante as the chief base, extending along the coast as far as Cape Nao. New mines were opened, cinnabar as well as copper, agriculture was developed, cities were founded, and, above all, a great colonial army was recruited from the Spanish tribes. It was a formidable accession of power to Carthage, for the Spanish soldiers have always been good—and at times, the best in the world. No wonder that Rome and her ally the Greek city of Massilia, took alarm, and that a Roman embassy was sent to see what was happening (231 b.c.). They got the polite reply that all this was being done to ensure prompt payment of the indemnity owed by Carthage! Hamilcar's real feelings are better expressed in the story—true or false—that when he took his son Hannibal out to Spain, he made the nine-year-old boy swear eternal enmity to Rome. When Hamilcar was killed in 228, his son-in-law Hasdrubal was an energetic successor; he began the conquest of the great central plateau, and founded a new and splendid capital for the whole province at Nova Carthago, the modern Cartagena. In 226 a treaty with Rome defined the Ebro as the limit of Carthaginian power on the north. Five years later Hasdrubal was assassinated. Hannibal, now aged twenty-five, succeeded as the third and perhaps the greatest governor of his line. In two campaigns across the Spanish plateau he got as far as Salamanca and the Douro River; almost two-thirds of the Iberian peninsula was now at least nominally in the control of Carthage. Across the Pyrenees, there were diplomatic contacts with the tribes of Gaul, which menaced Massilia and even Italy. When Saguntum, one of the few independent Spanish cities south of the Ebro, appealed to Rome for help, both sides were glad of a pretext for war.

So the moment had come for Hannibal's grand design, and Carthage could really repay her debt to Rome. Hannibal's strategy in the Second Punic War, and the series of battles which form its set pieces, are among the classics of military history, and he has a secure place among the greatest commanders of the world. As with Robert E. Lee, it was a mark of his genius that he was able for so long to hold the initiative against an enemy who disposed of greater resources. Ever since Polybius, historians have admired the boldness of Hannibal's plan to carry the war to Italy, despite Rome's command of the sea, her hold on Sicily, and the huge forces she could muster in Italy, amounting to 700,000 infantry and 70,000 cavalry. But he was putting into operation a plan that had been well considered and long prepared. Across the

Alps, he would be among the Gallic tribes whom Rome had only recently subdued, and who would be anxious to shake off her yoke. All turned, of course, on his ability to beat Roman armies in the field, but of this he was rightly confident. And the allegiance of at least Samnium and Apulia would be shaken by a series of Roman defeats. Once in southern Italy he could be reinforced from Carthage, and Sicily either captured or neutralized. Success on this scale might bring Macedonia into the war; Rome could then be attacked from three sides and perhaps destroyed, or at least lose her command of Italy.

Such were the hopes with which, in April of the year 218 B.C., Hannibal left New Carthage with an army of perhaps forty thousand men. By mid-August he had reached the Rhone, to which the Romans had sent a consular army, under Publius Scipio, to stop him. But the Punic army moved up the river and vanished. Scipio saw what had happened—Hannibal was crossing the Alps. At once he sent his army on to Spain to sit astride the Punic lines of communication—a wise decision that was to stand Rome in good stead. He himself went by sea to confront Hannibal in northern Italy. Hannibal's route across the Alps has been a standing controversy from Polybius to the present day, and has afforded many a happy holiday to scholars intent on its solution. Perhaps the Mont Cenis and Mont-Genèvre passes are the most likely. Late in September he brought a tired and diminished army to the Po valley. Scipio, rightly, tried to engage him before he could recover. At the river Ticinus the Romans got the worst of a cavalry battle. A few weeks later they were heavily defeated at the battle of the Trebia, and got an ominous taste of Hannibal's powers as a tactician. Hannibal had now won what might be called the Battle of the Po Valley, for Roman forces were withdrawn across the Apennines to await the campaign of 217. Cremona and Placentia were left to stand siege; they held out for the whole of the war.

No fewer than eleven legions were put in the field for that year, two being sent to Spain, two to Sicily, and four, under the new consuls Servilius Geminus and Caius Flaminius, to block the road to Rome. Hannibal was forced to cross the Apennines by the pass now used by the railway from Bologna to Florence, and suffered from snow in the mountains, even in May, and floods in the valley of the Arno. So far, for the Romans, so good. But Flaminius was no match for Hannibal, who lured him to disaster on the shores of Lake Trasimene. On a misty morning, the Roman army entered the flat ground between the lake and the hills, which were held by Hannibal. When they were all in the trap was sprung; the Roman forces were surrounded, and lost two legions with their commander. It was a disaster that could not be disguised: "We have been defeated in a great battle" were the words used to break the news in Rome. Both sides had much to reflect on from the way the war had gone. For Rome it was clear that it was, at present, hopeless to face Hannibal in the field. The Carthaginian, on the other hand, found himself unable to capture a strongly defended city, and no Roman ally had yet come over to his side. Occupation of central Italy would yield no further dividends, and he used his victory to move south along the Flaminian Way to Apulia. For the rest of the war southern Italy was to be his main base.

No such freedom of maneuver was open to Rome. First, the state had to be put completely on a war footing; to this end, the old device of appointing a dictator was tried again. Quintus Fabius Maximus as dictator was the choice of the aristocratic party. But party feeling had not yet been sunk in the common emergency. Instead of letting Fabius choose his own Master of Horse, he was given Minucius, a nominee of the democrats. But at least Fabius began to apply a strategy based on the realities of the situation. Hannibal was not to be faced in the field, but he could be harassed, cut off from supplies by a scorched-earth policy, drained of strength in minor engagements. Time would work for Rome. It was the strategy of the Russians against Napoleon in 1812—and it won for Fabius the nickname Cunctator (the Delayer), while "Fabian tactics" is a phrase well known today. But it calls for stern discipline to use such tactics, though it was done for the rest of the year 217. Roman forces watched in helpless anger while Hannibal ravaged the rich lands of Campania. When Hannibal spared the estates of Fabius and his friends, it looked bad; when he got back across the mountains to Apulia by a ruse that not only deceived Fabius but made him look a fool as well, the game was up. Led by Minucius, the democrats won the consular elections for 216 with a policy of facing and defeating Hannibal in Apulia. So in the August of that year a great Roman army, under the consuls Caius Terentius Varro and Lucius Aemilius Paulus, confronted Hannibal on terrain of his choosing—as a killing ground. The battle of Cannae is the model for an overwhelming victory. It was Rome's greatest disaster. Twenty-five thousand men were killed and 15,000 taken prisoner; Varro with some 10,000 men managed to escape. The years after Cannae were the darkest of the war. Samnium and Apulia fell away, and Hannibal gained control of Capua, the second city of Italy. A military alliance was made between Hannibal and Philip of Macedon. Worse still, King Hiero of Syracuse died; Hannibal's agents won over his young successor, a Punic fleet appeared in the harbor of Syracuse, and the greatest Greek city in the West was lost to Rome, with the prospect of the loss of Sicily as well.

But the allies in central Italy were still loyal, and Rome faced her troubles with a dauntless spirit. When Varro came back after his disastrous defeat, he received an official vote of thanks—"because he had not despaired of the Republic," and he was even employed again and met with much success. Meanwhile, with grim determination, Rome set out to employ her two advantages, time and numbers. Twenty-five legions were raised, and Fabian tactics were used in earnest. A cordon of mobile armies penned Hannibal in southern Italy. Syracuse was besieged by a huge force under Marcellus. A double ring of Roman armies invested Capua and sat down to starve it out. Nothing could break the anaconda grip on these two cities. Syracuse had the most formidable fortifications in the world, and could call on the genius of the great mathematician and engineer Archimedes, but it was captured by Marcellus—after a siege of two and a half years. To raise the siege of Capua, Hannibal made a spectacular march from Capua to the very gates of Rome. But the Romans were not frightened. The ground his camp was standing on was sold at auction and fetched a very good price; not a man left Capua. In 211 both Capua and Syracuse fell. The balance had at last swung to Rome in the Italian theater of war.

But at the same time news of disaster came from Spain, where Roman armies under the brothers Scipio had fought a most valuable series of campaigns ever since 218 B.C. Not only had they stopped reinforcements to Hannibal, but they had crossed the Ebro and carried the war to the enemy. But Spain could be reinforced by Carthage more easily than by Rome; the Scipios had allowed their armies to become over-extended, and both were destroyed. A successor had to be found, and the young Publius Cornelius Scipio put himself forward. It was a choice that was to determine the issue of the war, for this young man was the first really great Roman commander. There is a curious parallelism between Scipio's career and that of his great rival Hannibal. Scipio, too, took up a great command at the age of twenty-five to win a revenge due to his family. He was confident of his knowledge of the art of war, in which his model was Hannibal, not Fabius Maximus Cunctator. When he reached Spain, he made a daring and successful attack on New Carthage, the main Punic base. Soon afterward, he won his first great battle at Baecula, against Hasdrubal, Hannibal's brother and a fine general in his own right. Only one hope of victory now remained to Carthage—to reinforce Hannibal in Italy. In May, 207 B.C., another Punic army under Hasdrubal descended from the Alpine passes to the Po valley. It raised grim memories of the invasion of 218 B.C., as the German offensive in the Ardennes in 1944 raised memories of the fearful break-through of 1940. But the war was in a new phase, and the Roman response was prompt and daring. Four legions blocked Hasdrubal's road to the south at the River Metaurus. They were reinforced by troops whom Claudius Nero had detached from the forces covering Hannibal and led on a forced march which covered 240 miles in six days. The combined Roman forces won a brilliant victory, the first major defeat of a Punic army in Italy. Hannibal learned of it ten days later when his brother's head was thrown into his camp, and withdrew to Bruttium, his last stronghold in Italy.

Between 208 and 206 B.C. Scipio, in a series of masterly campaigns, rolled up the Carthaginian armies in Spain and drove them into the sea. Then he returned to Rome, to be elected consul in 205, and to put forward the audacious plan of an African campaign which would knock out Carthage and end the war. In this he was opposed by Fabius, still fighting the earlier years of the war, or perhaps remembering the fate of Regulus. It was with a small army, largely equipped from volunteer sources, that Scipio sailed for his great campaign on African soil. In two years (204–203) of war and diplomacy he brought Carthage to an armistice and the brink of peace. But the war party in Carthage was still strong, and there was one throw left—the recall of Hannibal. After fifteen years in Italy the old general brought his Old Guard back to Africa for the last round of the struggle. At Zama, in the autumn of 202 B.C., the two greatest generals of their age met. The comparison with Waterloo cannot be evaded. After a terrible day-long battle—"a damned near-run thing!"—the old master was beaten by his younger rival in the defeat that cancels all victories. Nothing was now left for Carthage but to sue for peace.

The terms could not be light, for Rome could not risk the renewal of a danger which she had barely escaped with her life. So Carthage gave up her navy and her overseas possessions, was saddled with a huge war indemnity, and retained only her own lands in Africa. Masinissa, king of Numidia, was installed on her frontiers as an ally of Rome. Carthage was thus deprived of any future as a Mediterranean power, and Rome succeeded to her position in Spain and the West.

The effect of the Second Punic War sheared through the whole fabric of Roman life, economic, social, and political. There was, first, an immense loss of life and property. To borrow a modern phrase, the red-hot rake of war had been drawn through the fair land of Italy. But in the Second Punic War it had been drawn up and down, slowly and agonizingly, for fifteen years. Especially in southern Italy, the devastation was appalling; some think that its effects can still be seen today. We hear of four hundred villages being blotted out in Apulia in the fighting that followed Cannae. At the capture of Tarentum, thirty thousand of its citizens were sold into slavery. It was the small farmers of Italy who had manned the Roman armies, to die in their thousands at Trasimene and Cannae. Those who fought in the later, victorious campaigns came back to find that huge areas of land had gone out of cultivation, farm buildings were destroyed and farm animals killed—all their capital equipment was lost. Many would lack the means, or the inclination, to take up farming again, and would drift off to the towns, especially to Rome, to swell the ranks of the urban poor, dependent for their living on a wealthy patron or on the state. But, as always, there were men who had done very well out of the peace. Immense fortunes had been made out of war contracts, and for the first time Rome had a class of wealthy businessmen. In the postwar world, men with capital had tempting opportunities for investment, especially from buying or renting land owned by the state (*ager publicus*), which had been greatly increased by confiscations from rebellious communities in southern Italy. The land was going cheap, and there was plenty of cheap labor to work it in the slaves provided by the wars in Africa, Spain, Cisalpine Gaul, and Italy itself. Pasture was the thing now, not arable—cattle or sheep rearing on huge ranches worked by gangs of slaves. For smaller estates, money could be made out of vineyards, market gardens, or olive growing, where a bailiff and his wife could be left in charge of a labor force of twenty-five to fifty slaves, with periodic inspections by the owner to see that he was not being cheated. Such is the rural scene depicted in Cato's treatise *De Agricultura,* written about 160 B.C. So the small farmer disappeared from large parts of Italy, especially from Apulia, Latium, and Etruria. The social consequences were far-reaching, and in two generations led to the great upheaval of the time of the Gracchi.

In politics, the war greatly strengthened the position of the Senate, and left the democratic party in eclipse. Their political leaders had a bad war record, for they were associated with the rash and ill-fated policies which had led to disaster at Trasimene and Cannae. But from the Senate had come both the successful defensive policy of Fabius and the brilliant and successful offensives of Scipio. And indeed, the tenacity and courage of the Senate had provided the central direction essential to success. War does not wait on debates in the popular assembly, it can only strengthen the executive power; and in Rome that meant the Senate. So the half-century from 200 to 150 B.C. is, *par excellence*, the period of senatorial supremacy, with an inner ring of great families holding a virtual monopoly of high office. Of the consuls elected between 234 and 134 B.C., half came from ten families, four out of five from twenty-six families. Even eighteenth-century England was not an oligarchy on this scale.

But the biggest change of all was in Rome's position in the Mediterranean. A new colossus had arisen in the west. Within twenty years from Zama, Rome had shattered forever the balance of power that had been maintained in the Hellenistic world for more than a century. In another fifty years, the Roman provincial system extended from Spain to Asia, and Rome was a great imperial power, as she was to remain for the rest of her history. Yet the Empire was not acquired by any deliberate policy of imperialism, nor by a consciousness of manifest destiny. The Senate was long reluctant to support the acquisition of territory overseas, especially in the eastern Mediterranean. As late as 168 B.C. Roman armies were withdrawn after the defeat of Macedon, and the kingdom was broken up into four independent republics. But the end of the period saw another and darker aspect of Roman policy, signalized by the brutal destruction of Carthage and Corinth in 146 B.C., and there can be no doubt that the provinces of Macedonia (148), Africa (146), and Asia (129) were acquired for the advantages they would bring to Rome.

This period was one of the most decisive in Western history, and it is fortunate that we have the account of a man who had exceptional qualifications and unique opportunities for observation—the Greek historian Polybius. A citizen of Megalopolis, Polybius played a leading part in the politics of

the Achaean League from 183 to 168 B.C. Then he was de-
ported to Rome with a thousand of his countrymen for the
equivocal part the Achaean League had played in the Third
Macedonian War. Thanks to his friendship with Aemilius
Paulus, and later with Scipio Aemilianus, he saw Roman
politics from the inside, and was present at such great events
as the capture of Carthage and the destruction of Corinth.
The task which Polybius set himself—and for which no other
man of that age was so well fitted—was to explain the rise of
Rome for Greeks and Romans alike. His views on the function of history make it clear to whom his book was addressed.
It was not meant to gather dust on library shelves. History
must be practical, the instructor of men of affairs; Polybius
was writing for statesmen. The defeat of the Macedonians
at Pydna in 168 he regards as the decisive event: "By this time,
all had been forced to admit that for the future nothing remained but to accept the supremacy of the Romans, and to
obey their commands."

But in 200 B.C. such a consummation must have seemed
remote. The diplomatic pattern of the Hellenistic world had
seemed set for more than a century. There were the three
great powers of Macedon, Syria, and Egypt, successor states
to the Universal Empire of Alexander the Great, stretching
from the Adriatic to the Punjab. An able or ambitious monarch of any of them might regard himself as Alexander's
heir and try to recover his patrimony. Several tried, but none
succeeded. In so far as the Universal Empire was revived, it
was by Rome, but with the center of gravity shifted to Italy
and with gains in the west to offset the loss of the lands east
of the Euphrates.

There were great differences between the three Hellenistic
kingdoms. Macedon, perhaps, stood highest in prestige as
the home of Alexander and of the phalanx with which he had
conquered the world. The core of her strength lay in the old
Balkan kingdom, where the plain of Macedonia supported
a large population, and in which there were highly important mines of silver, gold, copper, and iron. From this heartland Macedonian power extended over the rich cornlands and
vineyards of Thrace and some of the islands of the northern
Aegean. To the south there was a fluctuating suzerainty over
much of Greece proper, exercised since the days of Philip.
After the eclipse of Carthage, Macedon was Rome's nearest
powerful neighbor, a possible source of danger across the
Adriatic, as had been shown in the alliance between Hannibal and Philip V.

In Egypt the Greek dynasty of the Ptolemies was the successor to the native Pharaohs, exploiting through a highly organized bureaucracy the great natural resources of the Nile Valley. The land was thickly populated, productive of grain, rich in gold, copper, and iron, and with a great range of building stones and marbles. The papyrus trade, of which Egypt possessed a monopoly, was an important source of revenue; it supplied the most widely used writing material of the time. The cosmopolitan city of Alexandria was the greatest city and port of the world. It was also the leading center of culture, famous for its library and for the museum, a research institute of scholars and scientists. But Egypt was not able to sustain the role of world power. In the reign of Ptolemy V Epiphanes (210–180 b.c.) she lost all her possessions outside Africa except Cyprus, and entered a period of decline marked by weak rulers and dynastic quarrels. This very weakness was the reason why Egypt was the last of the Hellenistic kingdoms to fall into the power of Rome.

Syria, ruled by the Seleucid monarchs from their capital of Antioch-on-the-Orontes, was the largest and most heterogeneous of the three kingdoms. Here, at the crossroads of traffic between Europe, Asia, and Africa, where the great caravan routes across the deserts brought the goods of India and the Far East to the Mediterranean, was a possible seat for world power. But the separatist tendencies in the old native states beyond the Euphrates were a standing weakness to Seleucid power. It is true that under Antiochus III (241–187 b.c.) Greek control was re-established over most of the huge kingdom on a firmer basis than at any time since Alexander, but this revival was not to last.

In the midst of these great kingdoms, a number of powers of the second rank managed to preserve their independence. The maritime republic of Rhodes had built up a great commerce in the eastern Mediterranean in the third century b.c., and protected it against piracy by the best navy of the day. Here something of the high culture and political freedom of the best days of Greece had survived and adapted themselves to a new age. In northeastern Asia Minor a wealthy kingdom had been built up by the Attalid rulers of Pergamum. They had a diversified agriculture and mineral resources; the parchment of Pergamum was becoming a rival to the papyrus of Egypt. Their capital was the finest example of town planning in the Hellenistic world, and a great center of art and culture. In Greece proper, hostility to Macedon had led to the organization of two federal systems, the Achaean and Aetolian Leagues, which were to be the last but by no means the least of Greek political experiments.

Finally, there were the historic city-states of Greece, Athens, Sparta, and the rest, rich in prestige, shrunken in power, still cherishing dreams of "liberty" on the old pattern.

Such was the world into which Rome was drawn at the end of the Second Punic War. Diplomatically, there was always a three-cornered struggle between the great powers, and since the interests of the minor states naturally favored the preservation of a balance of power between them, a system had grown up not unlike that which obtained in Europe between 1815 and 1914.

It was natural that Rome's first conflict should be with Macedon. In the war against Philip V (200–196 B.C.) she fought as the head of an alliance of Greek states, chief among them the Aetolian League. The Popular Assembly at first refused a declaration of war, but the Senate thought it unwise not to respond to a request for help from Rome's allies and was apprehensive of the long-term danger to Rome of an alliance that had recently been made between Syria and Macedon. The climax of the war was the battle of Cynoscephalae (197 B.C.), the first direct clash of the two greatest weapons of warfare of their day, the Roman legion and the Macedonian phalanx. The day went in favor of the legion, but as the Romans had enjoyed the advantages of terrain, the military argument remained open.

In the peace discussions that followed, the Romans favored much easier terms for Macedon than did the Greeks. The Aetolians, indeed, pressed for the death or deposition of Philip, and received a lecture from the Roman commander, Quinctius Flamininus, on the wisdom of generosity to a beaten enemy, with the treatment of Carthage after the Second Punic War as an example. In the settlement, Philip retained his throne, but was forced to withdraw his garrisons from Greece, cut down his armed forces drastically, pay an indemnity to Rome, and undertake not to wage war outside Macedon without her permission. Macedon had thus had her wings clipped. There followed the famous scene at the Isthmian Games of 196 B.C., where Flamininus announced through the heralds that all the Greek cities once subject to Philip should be "free, exempt from tribute, and subject to their own laws." Greek skepticism could find little to fasten on except the fact, pointed out by the disgruntled Aetolians, that the former Macedonian fortresses were now in Roman hands. Even this argument lost its force when Flamininus, at a council held in 194, announced the evacuation of the fortresses and a Roman withdrawal from Greece. Greek political wisdom was left to digest the implications of this policy of enlightened self-interest on the part of Rome. They were to read the signs badly, in the event, but not so badly as did the King of Syria.

If it is success that clouds judgment, Antiochus III ("the Great") could claim sufficient excuse. Between 212 and 206 he had reasserted Seleucid sway over huge areas of Asia. Now, the humbling of Philip and the weakness of Egypt opened the prospect of regaining old possessions of Syria in Thrace and Asia Minor. It was the Aetolian League that lured him on to the invasion of Greece, promising that the democratic parties everywhere would welcome him as a "liberator" against the pro-Roman oligarchies then in power. Conversely, Pergamum and Rhodes embroiled Rome with Antiochus by attributing to him grandiose plans of conquest in the west, all the more credible because he was using Hannibal as a military adviser. So the Romans first pushed Antiochus out of Greece, then followed him to Asia and defeated him at the great battle of Magnesia (189 b.c.). Thanks to the Rhodians, the Syrian navy was also knocked out as an effective force.

Once again, the settlement is instructive. Antiochus had to renounce all his lands north and west of the Taurus Mountains and undertake to stay out of Europe. He paid a large indemnity, surrendered most of his navy, and agreed to hand over Hannibal. Syria had thus been penned back into Asia. Rome now proceeded to deal out rewards and punishments to the lesser parties. Pergamum got most of the surrendered Syrian lands; Rhodes gained some territory and important commercial privileges; the Aetolian League was quickly brought to heel and reduced to a dependent ally of Rome. Within ten years, Rome had separately engaged the two greatest Hellenistic powers, invaded their territories, and struck them down. She had acquired no new territory for herself, but it was clear that any problem in the Hellenistic world in which Rome took an interest was likely to be decided as Rome wished.

Twenty years later, this was proved in a manner that could not be denied. In the last years of the reign of Philip V (d. 179 b.c.), and still more in that of his successor Perseus, there was a remarkable revival of the power of Macedonia. The mines were worked with energy, the army was brought up to strength, and the diplomatic position of Macedon was quietly improved, especially in Greece, where Rome was making the discovery that the strongest power cannot expect to be loved as well. For some years there was talk of another war between Macedon and Rome; in 172 b.c. Pergamum

once again sounded an alarm; war began in 171. It was a
hard struggle which at first did not go well for Rome. But a
good general was found in Aemilius Paulus, and at the battle of Pydna (168) the legion and the phalanx met at last on
equal terms. Long after, Paulus would tell of the panic he
felt as he saw the phalanx bear down on his position, but the
victory he won that day established the legion for four centuries as arbiter of the world's battlefields.

This time there could be no question of the Macedonian
monarchy surviving the peace. Perseus was taken to Rome,
appeared in the splendid triumph of Paulus in 167, and died
in captivity two years later. Macedonia was split up into
four independent republics, and the lucrative gold and silver
mines were closed down. Rome thus took care to cripple her
enemy but declined territorial or economic advantages herself, a striking commentary on the absence of "imperialism,"
in its modern sense, from her policy at this time. But, odd as
it might seem to the Romans, the Macedonians liked their ancient monarchy and had little liking for the new republics.
A pretender called Andriscus appeared and had some success; when he was put down there were others. By now it was
clear that there was only one solution—Rome must adminis-
ter the country herself. Accordingly, in 148 B.C. Macedonia,
together with Epirus and Illyricum, was declared a Roman
province. It was a momentous change of policy, and its full
effects were soon to be seen outside Macedonia.

Immediately, they were seen in Greece, where Roman patience had for some years been wearing thin. In 146 B.C. the
Achaean League became involved in a quarrel with Sparta,
who appealed to Rome for help. Rashly, they offered resistance to a Roman army under Lucius Mummius, with appalling results. Their military forces were at once defeated, and
Corinth, their leading city, was totally destroyed. Most of
the men were killed, the women and children were sold into
slavery, and the famous art treasures of the city were looted
or sold. It was an act of calculated brutality which shocked
the Greek world, and it came just fifty years after the "lib-
eration" proclaimed by Flamininus. The Achaean League
was then dissolved, and the Greek cities, except those who
had treated with Rome, were brought under the governor of
Macedonia.

Meanwhile, in Africa, the new brutalism was being demon-
strated on an even more impressive scale. It has always been
difficult to understand the motives of Cato and the conserva-
tives in Rome who engineered the Third Punic War and the
destruction of Carthage. Even the modern totalitarian states

have usually found it necessary to invoke some theory of racial superiority or Marxist determinism to cloak the naked desire to stamp out an enemy. So the attack on Carthage has been ascribed by some historians to economic rivalry, to the desire of the great Roman landowners to crush the Carthaginian export trade in wine and olives. Others have explained it as the result of a Machiavellian calculation that Rome would be wise to destroy Carthage before its superb site fell into the hands of the king of Numidia. Neither explanation seems sufficient. Perhaps the Second Punic War had left an obsessional fear of Carthage, for it seems clear that Cato and his friends were bent on her destruction and gave her no chance of escape. The Third Punic War began in 149 B.C., and Carthage withstood a three-year siege, longer than that of Syracuse. In the spring of 146 the fortifications were breached, and six days of hand-to-hand fighting put an end to her long agony. By the solemn ceremony of *evocatio*, practiced two centuries earlier at Veii, the great goddess of Carthage, Juno, was called out of the doomed city and induced to migrate to Rome. Polybius watched the final scenes at the side of the Roman commander, the "liberal" Scipio Aemilianus. The city was burned and razed to the ground, the plow was driven over it, salt was sown, and a curse pronounced on anyone who should try to restore it. Fifty thousand survivors were then sold into slavery. The African lands of Carthage with their large grain-growing estates were converted into a new Roman province, that of Africa. It was, after all, a solution of the Carthaginian problem.

The story of Rome's relations with the other Hellenistic states at this time is soon told. No ruler of comparable stature occupied the Syrian throne after the death of Antiochus the Great, and Roman policy aimed at keeping that kingdom from becoming powerful. The occasion when Antiochus IV Epiphanes meekly and instantly abandoned an invasion of Egypt at the bidding of a Roman envoy who drew a circle around the King with his stick (168 B.C.)—"Answer me yes or no before you step out of that circle"—was an impressive demonstration of Roman power. After 160 B.C. the decline of Seleucid power was rapid, and gave rise to new Asiatic kingdoms which were later to be a source of much trouble to Rome, notably those of Pontus, Armenia, and, above all, Parthia. Egypt remained weak, and retained her independence because she was useful to Rome as a counter to Syria. Rhodes experienced to the full the difficulties of being a Roman ally and retaining a measure of self-respect. After the battle of Pydna she was treated with hostility and suspicion;

her commerce was deliberately damaged by the foundation of
the free port of Delos, and with her navy unable to keep the
seas piracy in the Aegean reached formidable proportions.
Pergamum, farthest from Rome, was more successful
than any of the others in keeping on the right side of the
superstate. But the cost was high and the uncertainty great,
and the decision of Attalus III to bequeath his kingdom to
Rome on his death (133 B.C.) showed that, by now, the status
of subject was preferred to that of ally. After a last bid for
independence under the pretender Aristonicus had been
crushed, the kingdom was organized as the Roman province
of Asia (129 B.C.), and the Roman provincial system extended
to a third continent. It was a splendid new accession of
power to Rome, like that of the Louisiana Purchase to the
United States.

In Spain the going was harder throughout the century.
Rome had no mind to let go the lands she had won from
Carthage, and in 197 the two provinces of Hither and Further
Spain were set up. But it was the work of two centuries
to expand beyond these to the conquest of the whole Iberian
peninsula. The land itself is of great extent, highly differen-
tiated in geography and climate; its peoples were of various
racial origins and different levels of culture. In particular, the
resistance of the tribes of the central plateau involved the
armies of the Republic in some of their hardest-fought wars,
and earned for Spain the reputation of being *"horrida et bel-
licosa provincia"*—a savage and warlike province. Two episodes of this struggle are famous. The first was the fierce resistance in Lusitania (Portugal) under Viriathus, who held the
field for eight years (147–139 B.C.); of him the historian
Appian remarked that "considering he was a barbarian, he
showed the most outstanding qualities as a commander." The
second was the even more desperate resistance of the
Celtiberi of middle Spain, whose strength lay in the construction and defense of immense hill forts. The siege of one
of these forts, Numantia, was only ended after an eight-
month siege, when Scipio Aemilianus, the conqueror of Carthage, with a Roman army of sixty thousand men, starved out
the four thousand defenders. "Such was the passion for freedom of a single barbarian town."

But gradually the two provinces of Spain were consolidated
and developed. Roman colonies were planted at Italica and
Carteia. The mines were actively exploited; those of New
Carthage are said to have employed forty thousand men. A
big export trade was set up in corn. There was much money
to be made in Spain, and the province provided some of the

earliest and most flagrant examples of bad governors. Yet an occasional good governor such as Tiberius Sempronius Gracchus could win a response from the natives that foreshadowed the intensive Romanization of the peninsula under the empire. After the capture of Numantia, a great strategic road, a thousand miles long, was built from the Pyrenees to the Strait of Gibraltar.

But the full story of the growth of Roman power cannot be told in terms of her relations with independent states and the extension of the provincial system. Side by side with these, the official actions of the Roman state, there was at work the influence of an extraordinary system of private relationships —the *clientelae*, which linked powerful Roman nobles with non-Roman communities or potentates in Italy and beyond. This extended through the whole Mediterranean world the relationship of patron and client which we saw as a feature of Roman society in the earliest days of the Republic. A recent study by E. Badian has shown how far-reaching were its effects, and how hard to assess. Between the Roman noble as patron, and the foreign community, whether independent or provincial, as client, a relationship was set up that had a powerful moral basis but no strict basis in law. Moreover, it might last for several generations and influence Roman domestic politics as well as foreign policy. Such were the ties the Scipios had in Spain and Numidia, the Fabii in Spain, Flamininus in Greece, the Domitii in Gaul, the Claudii Marcelli in Sicily. The Roman patron would afford hospitality to his clients when in Rome, advise them on Roman policy, and present their case in the Senate if need arose. They would return hospitality, render him services in money and kind, and contribute by their relationship to his dignity and standing in Rome. Here was a powerful bond between Roman and non-Roman. Clearly, it could serve the extension of Roman power; equally, it could further at Rome the interests of her dependents.

Domestic politics at Rome in the first half of the second century B.C. were dominated by the aristocracy and its great organ, the Senate. Wealth and birth were the qualifications for entry to this exclusive order, and it was rare, at this time, for a new man to force his way in. But in so far as ex-magistrates were admitted, there was an element of popular election. Forbidden to engage in trade or to undertake public contracts, the senators were landowners, with the conservative outlook of that class. Their personal dignity was enhanced by their distinctive dress, by the long train of friends who waited on them in public, and by a place of

honor at state ceremonies. The Senate itself had three hundred
members, whose membership was permanent, unless they
were expelled by the censors. It met when summoned by a
magistrate, either in the Curia, the Senate House proper
(still surviving, though often rebuilt, in the Roman Forum),
or in a temple. One of the consuls presided, and a report presented by a magistrate introduced a debate, in which individual senators would be asked to express their opinion
(*sententiam dicere*) according to an order of precedence. Like
the English and the Irish House of Commons in the eighteenth century, the Senate was a great arena for oratory, the
highest in the land. The debate would be followed by a vote,
resulting in a decree of the Senate (*senatusconsultum*). The
debates were not reported at this time, but *senatusconsulta*
were registered in the public treasury. The business brought
before the house was varied, and included all the public issues
of the day. In practice, the Senate decided questions of war
and peace, though they needed the ratification of the Assembly. They received embassies from foreign powers, appointed
commissions of investigation, ratified treaties, fixed tribute,
assigned provinces to the consuls, let out public contracts, and voted supplies of money to magistrates. When it
is added that they also had supreme control of law and of
religions, it is clear that most of the powers of the state
were exercised by them. They could quickly bring a powerful
individual to heel, even Scipio Africanus, the conqueror of
Hannibal.

Within the Senate an inner ring of powerful families was
dominant. It was a tight circle, drawn tighter by intermarriage and adoption. Rome was ruled by a great cousinship.
For example, Scipio Africanus married Aemilia, sister of
Aemilius Paulus; one of their sons, being childless, adopted
the son of Aemilius Paulus, who took the name of Scipio
Aemilianus. A daughter, Cornelia, married T. Sempronius
Gracchus; this lady is the famous "mother of the Gracchi."
Scipio Aemilianus, in his turn, married her daughter Sempronia, his cousin; but this did not prevent a bitter political hostility between him and his wife's brother Tiberius Gracchus.
There were more or less permanent *factiones* (factions)
among the nobility, renewing their rivalry in the annual elections of magistrates. The German scholar Münzer has analyzed
these factions and their influence. Sometimes their differences
would appear as a clash of principles, as for example, the opposition between the conservative, puritanical, chauvinistic
group led by Cato and the liberal, progressive, philhellene
group of the Scipios. But no permanent political parties or

programs could really develop from this homogeneous background.

The great Roman noble could expect a lifetime of service to the state. He would fill in turn all the magistracies, govern a province, command an army in the field, serve on important commissions, and play his part in the Senate. The archaic Latin of the third century b.c. epitaph of Lucius Scipio shows how a public career counted above everything else:

> Honc oino ploirime cosentiont Romai
> duonoro optume fuise viro
> Lucium Scipione, filios Barbati
> consol, censor, aedilis hic fuet apud nos,
> hic cepit Corsica Aleriaque urbe
> dedet Tempestatebus aede meretod.

> Most Romans agree that this man, Lucius Scipio, was the best of good men. He was the son of Barbatus, and served among us as consul, censor, and aedile. He captured Corsica and the city of Aleria, and dedicated a temple to the Tempestates in discharge of a vow.

The same spirit pervades another epitaph, far removed in time and space.*

It remains to note a development closer to Italy. As soon as the Second Punic War ended, Roman power was reasserted in Cisalpine Gaul, which had had to be abandoned before Hannibal. A vigorous program of colonization and development was put in hand. The Ligurians and the Boii were pushed back into the mountains in a series of sharp campaigns. Forty thousand of the Apuani were removed from their homes and settled on war-devastated lands in southern Italy—an early example of the forced migration that so many peoples were to experience under the Empire. In reverse, large numbers of war veterans and land-hungry peasants came north to the cleared lands of the Po valley. Colonies were founded at Aquileia, Bononia (Bologna), and Luca (Lucca), all to grow into great cities. Roman settlers appeared near Mediolanum (Milan). Marshes were drained, rivers channeled, and a network of roads built. No colonization undertaken by Rome was to be more successful than this, which has made the Po valley forever part of Italy. In

---

* "Here was buried Thomas Jefferson, author of the Declaration of American Independence, of the statute of Virginia for religious freedom, and father of the University of Virginia."

all, we know of twenty-one colonies founded between 200
and 170 B.C. in Cisalpine Gaul, Picenum, Campania, and
southern Italy. Tenney Frank estimates that between forty
and fifty thousand citizens were settled by these means on at
least one million acres of good farming land. It is an impressive extension of small farming, but it is outweighed by
the growth of the huge ranches, worked by slave labor,
whose full effects were being felt by the mid-century.

The Roman achievement in literature of this period was
considerable, though often it is not given its due. In part,
this is because so much has perished. Of the ten chief come-
dians of the second century B.C. only Plautus and Terence
are represented by complete plays. No complete tragedy survives. The epic poets Naevius and Ennius survive only in
fragments, as does the great satirist Lucilius. Only one complete work of Cato—the *De Agricultura*—represents Roman
prose and his own extensive literary output. The historians
have all gone, and a few passionate fragments of Tiberius
Gracchus stand for Roman oratory. Of this period above all
others is it true that we see Roman literature as we see an
iceberg—a small visible portion above a vast submerged
mass. Again, Roman authors, then and later, were so punctil-
ious in acknowledging their debt to Greece that it is natural
to regard them as derivative and second-rate. None the less,
the origins of Roman literature are to be sought in Roman
conditions. The first dated piece of Latin prose is the speech
of Appius Claudius Caecus on the peace negotiations with
Pyrrhus, which was extant in the first century B.C.; Roman
historiography goes back to the annals which were compiled
by members of the Roman aristocracy. True, from 240 onward, the influence of Greek literature, whether by way of
Sicily or southern Italy or Greece proper, is paramount. But
it was adapted, not slavishly imitated, and always the genius
of Rome and Italy had a contribution to make.

The coming of drama on the Greek model to Rome can
be dated at 240 B.C., when at the *Ludi Romani* a Greek play
was performed in a Latin translation by Livius Andronicus.
He also translated the *Odyssey* for use in schools, and was
the first to see that there was a public for Greek literature in
Rome. Roman comedy was derived not from the old comedy
of Aristophanes, which depended on the free political life
of fifth-century Athens, but from the "new comedy" of the
next century, which took its themes from private and domestic
life, and in which the great name was that of Menander.
It was a smart, sophisticated world that Menander portrayed,
in many ways much to the taste of a Roman audience. The

topic of sexual laxity was handled with an amused tolerance in contrast to the stern moral code of Cato; social historians were quick to remark that the first divorce in Roman society followed within five years of the first play. But Greek new comedy lacked action, the tempo was languid, there was too much psychology and oversubtle characterization. The Roman audience wanted a strong infusion of gusto and slapstick, more buffoons and comic characters, and a livelier pace. Plautus, who supplied these needs, won and kept a faithful public. Terence, who remained faithful to the spirit of Menander, was never really popular. For comic gusto, uproarious fun, and invention the best of Plautus (251–184 B.C.) can be compared to Aristophanes and the comic scenes of Shakespeare: his plays are full of knockabout, drunken scenes, quarrels; there is a large element of song and dance, so that they can be described as gay musical comedies with a happy ending. His diction presents us with twenty thousand lines of racy Latin, the authentic voice of the generation that faced Hannibal. By contrast, the plays of Terence (195–159 B.C.) are refined drawing-room comedies, full of psychology and philosophy. His characters give the impression of having been to the best finishing schools, and they talk the pure and refined Latin of the circle of his patron, Scipio Aemilianus. Twenty-one comedies by Plautus survive, six by Terence; they have had a far-reaching influence on the comedy of manners in Italy, France, England, and Spain.

Of Roman tragedy we know much less, but it looks as though it kept closer to the Greek originals than did comedy —as though behind each Roman tragedy stood a Greek tragedy—with Euripides the Greek tragedian most in vogue. The Trojan War was extremely popular as a subject, and this suggests an interest in the legends linking early Rome with Troy, the great theme of the *Aeneid*. Even in the surviving fragments we can trace certain concessions to Roman tastes. The Roman feeling for melodrama and the horrific is evident, and the whole spirit of Roman tragedy was dominated by rhetoric; the characters rant at each other in long, formal speeches like rival politicians in a debate. These characteristics all reappear later in the plays of Seneca, and Shakespeare's *Titus Andronicus* is of the same lineage.

The Roman element was still stronger in the two great epic poems of the period, the *Bellum Punicum* of Naevius (c. 270–207 B.C.) and the *Annales* of Ennius (239–169 B.C.). If in form and treatment they looked to Homer as model, their subject matter was purely Roman, the great wars against Carthage in which both men had fought. Naevius, using the native Saturnian meter, wrote of the First Punic War and the origins of Rome and Carthage; it is probable that the story of Aeneas and Dido first appears with him. Ennius dealt with Roman history down to 171, but the Second Punic War is his greatest theme. In his use of the hexameter he begins the splendid line of Roman poets which includes Lucretius and Virgil; in his knowledge of Greek, Oscan, and Latin he united in himself the cultures of the Italy of his time.

Rome, the city and its life, provided the raw material for the satires of Lucilius (180–102 B.C.)—postwar Rome, with its increase of wealth and luxury, its corruption and debauchery. In the words of the later satirist, Juvenal, "Lucilius thrashed the town": here for the first time was a really rich crop of vice for a Roman satirist to thresh. The first great Roman patrons also appear at this time, chief among them the Scipios and their friends. Scipio Africanus was the patron of Ennius, and a great philhellene. Of all the spoils of the Macedonian War, Aemilius Paulus took for himself only the library of Perseus, the first notable private library in Rome. In the circle that surrounded Scipio Aemilianus we see Roman patronage at its best, with wide interests in literature, philosophy, and law, and comprising both Greeks and Romans. Scipio and his friend Laelius were the two leading statesmen of the day, Polybius the historian and Panaetius the philosopher the most eminent representatives of Greek culture, Lucilius and Terence the chief Latin authors. These men understood all that was best in Greek and Roman civilization, and tried to interpret it for their mutual benefit. Among these men, too, was worked out the important concept of *humanitas*—a common bond uniting all men, and transcending differences of race, nationality, color, or creed. It was to have a salutary influence on Roman political thought and on Roman law.

Art and architecture made less progress than literature. A number of wealthy Roman nobles became connoisseurs and collectors of Greek art, but this did not stimulate a native Roman style. There was, of course, a great deal of building in the city because of the increase in its population, which cannot have been less than half a million in 150 B.C. Some of the nobles built town houses that were thought luxurious at the time, though a century later it was their simplicity that evoked comment. Now too began the construction of great tenement houses (*insulae*) to house the Roman poor, and the growth of slums. On the credit side, there was a good deal of bridge building, street paving, and extension of

the sewers. Several temples were built, notably that of Magna
Mater on the Palatine, whose lofty *podium* is still to be seen,
and the marble temple of Apollo in the Campus Martius,
adorned by captured Greek sculpture. The first basilicas
were built in the Roman Forum, among them the Basilica
Aemilia, the finest building in Rome in its day. But, in
general, the architecture of the city was far inferior to that
of the great cities of the Greek world, Alexandria, Antioch,
Pergamum, and Syracuse—inferior, even, to the more prosperous Hellenized cities of Campania like Pompeii.

Philosophy, which lay at the heart of Greek culture, had
an uphill struggle at Rome. When Diogenes the Stoic and
Carneades of the New Academy lectured there in 155 b.c.,
they met with very different receptions. Diogenes made
a good impression with a modest and sober speech. So did
Carneades when, in his first lecture, he maintained that
justice exists by nature. Next day, with equal brilliance,
he maintained that it exists by convention. The Senate did
not appreciate the tour de force, and ordered him out of the
city. Plainly, the new masters of the world were likely to
judge a philosophy by its usefulness to the state. Because he
saw this, and because his intimacy with Scipio Aemilianus
and his friends gave him an insight into Roman conditions,
Panaetius of Rhodes (c. 185–109 b.c.) won some very
important successes with his own version of Stoicism, re-
styled, as it were, for the Roman market. By replacing the
Ideal Wise Man in the Cosmopolis by Scipio in the Roman
Republic, he enabled Stoicism to take out nationalization
papers at Rome. Critics have rightly pointed out that his
system is marked by a decline in intellectual force and
by a lack of coherence. But it appealed to what was best in
Roman character and institutions. The *antiqua virtus* of the
old Roman morality was incorporated into a new system of
ethics; the Roman constitution was extolled as the most perfect of all political systems; the traditional Roman religion
was left untouched. But the convert to Stoicism was faced
with rigorous demands—the complete subordination of
personal ambitions to the good of the state, the suppression
of greed and luxury, conformity to a code which regulated
conduct in every situation of private and public life. Himself
an aristocrat, Panaetius provided a philosophical justification for the traditional standards of the Roman aristocracy.
By educating them to a sense of their duties, he hoped to
provide for the good government of the world.

CHAPTER V

The Decline and Fall of the
Roman Republic: 133–78 b.c.

Stability derived from its mixed constitution, Polybius thought, was the great virtue of the Roman Republic. Certainly the long period of senatorial supremacy after the Second Punic War was marked by unusual tranquillity in internal politics. But it was the lull before the storm—a storm that would last a century and not die down before the Republic itself was swept away.

By 140 b.c. it was obvious that a challenge would be made to the growth of the great estates and to the senatorial monopoly of political power. Equally it was clear that this would meet with bitter resistance. That the challenge should be so revolutionary, the counterattack so violent and unprincipled, is explained by the personal qualities of the two great champions of reform, the brothers Tiberius and Caius Gracchus. These men belonged to the inner circles of the aristocracy whose power they confronted. Their grandfather had done good service before he was killed in the Second Punic War. Their father had been one of the most distinguished generals and colonial administrators of his time, with a fine record in that graveyard of Roman reputations, Spain. Their mother Cornelia, daughter of Scipio Africanus, was a great Roman lady; beautiful, intelligent, a devoted wife and mother, she saw to it that after her husband's death her sons were educated by the best Greek tutors of the day. Tiberius married Claudia, the daughter of Appius Claudius; Caius married the daughter of Crassus Mucianus, consul in 131. Their sister Sempronia married Scipio Aemilianus.

Tiberius Gracchus himself fought gallantly under Scipio at the capture of Carthage, and again in Spain in the siege of Numantia. His experience in Spain determined his career. On the way out, he passed through Etruria, and saw a land cleared of its peasant farmers to make way for the great estates with their gangs of brutalized slaves. In Spain he was involved in a military disaster, when an ill-disciplined Roman army under its incompetent commander Mancinus had to surrender. Worse still, he saw a treaty which he had personally negotiated with a generous but simple-minded enemy repudiated by the Senate. He got back to Rome when the urban poor were seething with discontent. Soon afterward the appalling Slave War broke out in Sicily, and was only put down after three years' fighting. To Tiberius the troubles of the state—the low morale of the army, the discontent of the poor, the danger from foreign slaves—were all due to the great estates. And the remedy was obvious. Redistribute the land, and restore a sturdy peasantry. But a program of agrarian reform could only be put through on a basis of popular support. So Tiberius stood for the tribuneship, and was elected for the year 133 B.C. The Roman people had had no such leader for a century. Even from the fragments of his speeches, it is clear that Tiberius was one of the greatest Roman orators. "Wild beasts have their lairs, but the men who fight and die for Italy can call nothing their own except the air and the sunshine. . . . Your generals exhort you to fight for hearth and home. You have neither. . . . You fight to defend the luxury of the rich. They call you the master of the world, but you have not a foot of land you can call your own. . . ." Moving words, even today, in their sincerity and passion.

In the Senate he had a group of supporters, chief among them Appius Claudius and Crassus Mucianus. Among his personal advisers was Blossius of Cumae, a Stoic and a member of a family which had long been connected with the democratic party in that city. Blossius may have been his guide to the agrarian problem in Greek politics. The Agrarian Law he brought forward in the Assembly proposed to revive the old *Lex Licinia Sextia* of 367 B.C., which had limited to 500 *iugera* the amount of public land that any citizen could hold. A further 500 *iugera* was to be allowed for two grown-up sons, making a maximum holding of 1,000. Land in excess of this was to be surrendered for distribution to the poor in lots of 30 *iugera*. There would be compensation for land surrendered, and land retained would become the property of the occupant. The whole operation would be supervised by a board of three land commissioners.

Like the issue of freeing of slaves in America before the Civil War, or the emancipation of serfs in Tsarist Russia, agrarian reform in the classical world might be just but was certain to be political dynamite. And the opponents of the bill had their case. It was unlikely that compensation would cover improvements. In some cases the land had been accepted as security for mortgages. There were family graves on some of the land to be confiscated. The Italian allies had a real grievance, for their excess holdings would be confiscated, but only Roman citizens would get new lots. Above all, there was the formidable concentration of power in the hands of the land commissioners. But what a tribune introduced, a tribune could veto; the tribune Octavius was induced by the Senate to veto the bill in the Assembly. According to Roman practice, this should have been the end of it, but Tiberius had his Greek advisers to point a way out. In Greek democratic theory, the will of the people was sovereign; a tribune was elected to carry out the will of the people; if he opposed it, he was failing in his duty and should be removed. But, in the Roman view of the equal standing of magistrates, the one exercising a veto must prevail. Tiberius chose Greek theory rather than Roman practice. Octavius was deposed. The bill was passed, and the commissioners—Appius Claudius, Tiberius, and his brother Caius—got to work. But they needed money, and they needed time. The first, in ample measure, fell into their laps with the bequest of the kingdom of Pergamum to the Roman people. Tiberius passed through the Assembly a bill setting up the province of Asia, and converting the royal revenues for the use of the Land Commission—two grave blows at the Senate's prerogatives. To provide time, he proposed to stand for re-election as tribune for 132 B.C.—an ominous departure from Roman custom. The senators began to reflect that Greek political institutions included tyranny, and that tyrants usually won their place with the support of the people. On the day of the elections there were riots, and a mob of senatorial supporters, headed by Scipio Nasica, his cousin and the chief pontiff, caught and murdered Tiberius and some of his followers by the Temple of Jupiter. "So perish all who do such deeds" was the comment of his brother-in-law Scipio Aemilianus from Spain, which he later amplified: "If he was aiming at seizing the government of the state, he was rightly killed."

The work of the Land Commission lasted for fourteen years, from 133 to 120 B.C. It was stripped of its judicial powers by Scipio Aemilianus in 129 at the instance, it would seem, of the Italian allies. But its personnel was remarkably stable. Only eight names appear during the whole period; three of them, Caius Gracchus, Marcus Fulvius Flaccus, and

Papirius Carbo, held office continuously from 129 to 121. Small wonder that the Commission was able to act with energy and to good effect. Tenney Frank has estimated that at least 50,000 men received not less than 1,000,000 *iugera* of redistributed land, which would be 7 per cent of the *ager publicus*—10 per cent may be nearer the true figure. A hard blow had been struck at the great estates, though not so crippling as Tiberius would have liked. Archaeology has recovered eight of the boundary stones set up by the Commission—six in southern Italy, one in the North, one near Carthage. They have been used by the French scholar Carcopino for a fascinating piece of research that throws new light on the whole problem of the Gracchi.

Two years after the murder of Tiberius, Scipio Aemilianus died, whether by violence is uncertain. But rumor had it that he was about to be given some extraordinary position in the state, and he was found dead in bed, having seemed in perfect health overnight. The official verdict was death by disease, but it remained the great mystery of the age. In him were exemplified the virtues of a passing type, the Roman noble of the age of aristocratic supremacy. In Caius Gracchus were to be seen the qualities of a new age.

It was with all deliberate speed that Caius Gracchus moved to take up his brother's legacy, knowing that it would be fatal to himself. He worked as a land commissioner and served in the wars in Sardinia. Not until 124 B.C. did he stand for the tribuneship, but his program and his support had been carefully prepared. Tiberius thought of agrarian reform; only when opposed did he pass on to wider measures. Caius from the start seems to have planned a frontal attack on the whole position of the Senate. To launch it, he had built up a vast coalition of the *equites,* the financial and business interests, the urban poor, and the Italian allies. These interests would surely clash in the long run, but they all had an immediate stake in the destruction of senatorial supremacy. Since the re-election of tribunes had been made legal in 131 B.C., Caius was in a better position than Tiberius to carry through a large program of reform. So 123 and 122 were years of such hectic legislation as Rome was not to know again until the dictatorship of Julius Caesar. Sources do not allow the dating of all the laws of Caius: they are best understood in terms of the interests they were meant to serve. Lucrative prizes went to the businessmen. There was a great program of roads, harbors, and public works in Italy, for which they got the contracts. But the biggest killing of the financial world was to be made from the contract for the collection of the Asian taxes. Gracchus saw to it that this was put up to auction in Rome, for terms of five years. The contractors (*publicani*) who landed this prize had in their hands a private financial empire comparable to that of the East India Company in the eighteenth century, or to the big oil interests in the Middle East in our own day. And Gracchus further ensured that their opportunities for profit should not be hampered by any mere concern for the rights of provincials. Special extortion courts (*de repetundis*) already existed to try charges against Roman provincial officials. By the *Lex Acilia*, the text of which still survives on bronze fragments in the Naples Museum, it was laid down that the juries for these courts should be drawn from the *equites*. So a governor who had defied big business in his province was to be tried by big business on his return. The way was open to that exploitation of the provinces which was one of the worst features of the later Republic.

For the benefit of the urban poor, Caius strengthened the Land Commission by restoring its judicial powers. Then—a wholly new measure—he provided for the public distribution of grain at less than half the market price (*Lex frumentaria*). For the poor of Rome it was a long step to the welfare state, though it hardly helped the Italian farmer. The distribution of grain at Rome, first at a reduced price and then free, lasted until the end of the Empire, and profoundly affected the whole of Mediterranean agriculture.

Side by side with these measures went enlightened schemes for colonization, some of them of a kind new to Rome, and designed too for commerce rather than for agriculture. Such were the proposed colonies of Neptunia at Tarentum, and Junonia on the accursed site of Carthage.

For the Italians there were generous proposals for an extension of the franchise, which would have given Roman citizenship to all Latins and carried Latin rights through Italy to the Alps—something that was not brought about until the time of Julius Caesar.

Such, in outline, was the legislation of Caius Gracchus. It was unprecedented for a tribune to exercise such powers. But the Senate, too, had learned something since the days of Tiberius. Once again it used a tribune against a tribune —but this time not to veto but to outbid. Marcus Livius Drusus proposed not three but twelve colonies, all in Italy or Sicily, the settlers in which should pass no means test and pay no rents. This drew some popular support from Caius, and he lost more ground when he went on a tour of in-

spection to Carthage. Senatorial propaganda made great
play with the horrible portents which followed his disregard
of Scipio's curse. Even more effective were the reminders to
the Roman people of the folly of sharing their privileges with
the Italians. The coalition was split, and Caius was not re-
elected as tribune for 121 B.C. The elections had been held
in an atmosphere of feverish excitement and were followed
by riots. The Senate declared martial law; an attack was
made on the Gracchan party in their stronghold on the
Aventine; Caius was killed as he tried to escape from the
city, and more than three thousand of his supporters were
liquidated in the purges that followed. A grateful Senate
dedicated a new temple, to Concord.

A statesman has the right to be judged in the context of
his own age, but the sources are too late and too biased for
a fair verdict on the motives and policy of the Gracchi. Yet
there can be no doubt of the enduring mark they left on
the Roman Republic. From this time on the divisions in the
state were deep and unbridgeable. Party strife was incessant:
civil war carried on party politics by other means. Moreover, the aim of each party was to win complete supremacy
and to annihilate its opponents. This led to the concentration of extraordinary powers in the hands of party champions
—the six consulships of Marius, the dictatorships of Sulla
and Caesar. At first it was the parties who made the champions, but later the champions used the parties for ends of
their own. So the hundred years between the death of
Tiberius Gracchus and the Battle of Actium was a hundred
years of revolution, at the end of which the Republic had
passed away.

This last century of the Republic is the most difficult
period of Roman history. For part of it the sources are
defective; for others, fuller than for any period of European
history before the seventeenth century. Only a survey, and
that of the most important topics, will be attempted here.
It falls into two periods, the Gracchi to Sulla (133–78 B.C.),
then from Sulla to the Battle of Actium (78–31 B.C.).

The period of senatorial supremacy which followed the
death of Caius Gracchus is obscure. Two achievements call
for notice: first, the ending of the Land Commission and the
gradual winding up of the Gracchan agrarian laws, finally
ended in 111 B.C., and second, the creation of a new province, Gallia Narbonensis, in the Rhone valley, with the
great colony of Narbo (118 B.C.) as its capital. The two were
connected. The Gracchan reforms had done much to appease
genuine land hunger among the Roman poor. When there

was added to these the steady opening up of the Po valley, and the new opportunities for settlement in Narbonensis, it was appeased for many years to come. The problem as it existed in the days of Tiberius was solved, though not by the full restoration of a peasant economy in Italy. When we hear of land distribution again, it is for discharged soldiers.

The war against Jugurtha in Africa, the other main event of these years, though not dangerous, was long drawn out and harmful for the prestige of the stronger party, as was the Boer War to that of Britain. But it led Marius to the consulship and to the first great career in Roman politics wholly dependent on control of the army—ominous for the future. Caius Marius was of peasant stock from Arpinum. He had served with Scipio at Numantia and had caught the eye of that martinet by his personal courage and the excellent condition of his weapons and animals. Tribune in 119, he later did good service as praetor in Spain. Elected by the democrats as consul in 107 to finish off the endless African war, he achieved this in two years, thanks to a new volunteer army raised from the Roman poor and trained by him in new tactics. This was the first stage of the great reforms by which Marius transformed the Roman army from a militia to a professional long-service force.

Before the war in Africa was over, a new and appalling danger burst on the northern frontiers—a gigantic invasion of northern barbarians, like those of the later Goths and Vandals. The Romans knew nothing at this time of the peoples and politics of central and northern Europe, and such incursions were as unexpected as they were alarming. The Cimbri and Teutoni—for such were the names of the chief peoples concerned—seem to have come from Scandinavia, and their memory is preserved by place names in the Danish peninsula. By slow stages they had made their way up the Elbe to the Danube (113 B.C.), and thence north of the Alps to Gaul, where they annihilated a Roman army in the terrible disaster of Arausio (Orange) in 105 B.C. The worst might have happened if they had then attacked Italy. But they made for Spain instead, where in the free Celtiberians outside the Roman province they found warriors as tough as themselves.

Rome had a respite, and Marius used it well. Throughout the Roman army, tactics were overhauled and weapons standardized. All infantry now used the stabbing sword (*gladius*) and the javelin (*pilum*). The old maniples disappeared: a newer and larger unit, the cohort, took their place, ten of which made up the legion. As a focus for regimental

loyalties, the legions now had their silver eagles or standards. Since the legion was an engineering corps as well as
an infantry assault force, all soldiers carried their own trench-
ing tools. With eighty pounds of equipment on his back, and
trained to march forty miles a day, the Roman legionary had
a right to call himself "Marius' mule" (*mulus Marianus*),
and to keep green the memory of that animal which had once
paraded before the gratified eyes of Scipio. The troops
served with the colors for sixteen years, and their loyalties
inevitably went to the men who led them in the field. The
Roman army, as remodeled by Marius, is the army of the
late Republic and early Empire.

In 102 the Cimbri and Teutoni reappeared in Gaul, this
time bent on the invasion of Italy. The barbarian host was
divided into two armies, the Teutoni to attack from the northwest, and the Cimbri from the northeast. Marius was ready
for them. The western army was utterly crushed by him
near Aix-en-Provence (Aquae Sextiae) in a great battle still
commemorated by the people of those parts. A few months
later he was with Catulus to win an equally decisive victory
against the Cimbri near Vercellae in the Po valley. The
barbarian menace had come and gone like some great catastrophe of nature.

Now Rome was menaced by her deliverer. There was no
precedent for the four successive consulships Marius had
held from 104 to 101; they were tantamount to a military
dictatorship. They had been justified by the danger from the
Cimbri, but now that that was over, Marius was not willing
to step down. His personal ambition was inordinate, and
he relied on a prophecy that he was to have seven consulships. Unfortunately, his political abilities were small;
of all the great soldiers who have shown themselves inept
in politics, Marius has a fair claim to be considered the
most inept. He allied himself with the extreme democrats
Saturninus and Glaucia to gain his sixth consulship in
100 B.C. Before the year was up he had abandoned them
and was hunting them as the tool of the Senate. In less
than two years after the defeat of the Cimbri, Marius was
out of office, with nothing but his reputation, his ambition,
and his dreams of revenge.

Meanwhile, the question of the Italian franchise was
coming to a head. A quarter of a century earlier the selfishness of the Roman plebs had prevented Caius Gracchus from
a generous solution of this problem. Since then nothing had
been done, and the Italians were in no mood to wait. They
had always had the sympathy of the more enlightened

senators, and in 91 B.C. Marcus Livius Drusus, son of the
contemporary of Caius Gracchus, as tribune brought forward a complex series of laws. These provided for Italian
emancipation, and also for the restoration of the extortion courts from the *equites* to the Senate. The need for
this had been strikingly shown two years earlier by a
cause célèbre, the trial of Rutilius Rufus, who had ven-
tured to withstand the business interests when he was governor of Asia. Condemned by a scandalous verdict, he went
into exile as the honored guest of the people he was supposed to have exploited. Drusus hoped, then, for a coalition
of the liberal wing of the Senate and the democratic party
to break the power of the *equites*. In the event, he roused
against himself the most powerful coalition in Rome—that
of the selfish elements of all parties. Drusus was murdered,
and the Italians had to rely on themselves. A confederation
of central and south Italian peoples was formed, and an
embassy was sent to Rome to put their demands. The Senate
refused them a hearing.

Roman selfishness had accomplished what Hannibal had
failed to do. The Roman Confederacy was at an end; the
allies seceded, and a bloody civil war followed. Comparison
with the American Civil War is inevitable and just. Both
wars were fought with desperate valor between kindred peoples who believed in the same political ideals, however their
economic interests might clash. The political institutions of
the Italian Confederacy were modeled on those of Rome;
there was a Senate of five hundred, two consuls, and a board
of twelve praetors. The town of Corfinium, renamed Italica,
became the federal capital. For three years (91–88 B.C.) the
Italian armies held the field against Rome. But the end of
the Social War was very different from that of the American
Civil War. The cause of the secessionists was so just that
Rome was forced to recognize it. First the citizenship was
given en bloc to all Italian communities which had joined the
revolt and laid down their arms. Next, by the *Lex Plautia
Papiria*, it was extended to all individual Italians who withdrew from the revolt and appeared before a praetor in Rome
within sixty days. These concessions, rather than military
force, broke the Italian resistance. Only the Samnites, ir-
reconcilable under their great leader Pontius Telesinus,
fought on. Rome had won the war, but Italy had won the
peace. At a fearful and unnecessary price, Roman citizenship had been extended to the whole peninsula.

Nor was it only in Italy that some ugly fowls came home
to roost at this time. In the east the whole Roman position

was challenged by the most formidable foreign enemy she had had to face since Hannibal—Mithridates VI, King of Pontus. In the fifty years since the bequest of the Attalid kingdom Roman penetration of the finance and commerce of Asia and the eastern Mediterranean had been deep and far-reaching. Since the decline of Rhodes, the free port of Delos had become the first port of the Aegean and the chief center of the slave trade. A study of the inscriptions of Delos shows the presence at this time of large numbers of traders, bankers, and shippers from Italy, especially from the south. There were Romans living in Athens, and Roman or Italian traders are found at Delphi, at Argos, and on many of the islands. Roman citizens, as we have seen, had made a corner in the great financial deal—the contract for the Asian taxes. Only in the governorships of Rutilius Rufus had any attempt been made to stop them from draining their milch cow dry. Their agents, Italian or native, were to be found in every Asian city, for alongside the tax farming went a vast and lucrative system of loans and mortgages, public and private. The tentacles of this financial octopus stretched beyond the Roman province to neighboring kingdoms such as Bithynia. There was plenty of raw material for a great explosion of anti-Roman feeling.

The old kingdom of Pontus occupied the middle southern shore of the Black Sea. It was rich in the sinews of war. The pine forests on the Pontic hills produced the best ship timbers of antiquity; it had perhaps the first iron deposits ever worked by man, those of the half-legendary Chalybes of Greek tradition. A line of monarchs bearing the dynastic name of Mithridates and claiming descent from the old royal house of Persia had ruled it since the time of Alexander. Their capital was the Greek colony and trading post of Sinope, and there were other Greek cities along the coast. Mithridates V had been a friend of the Romans since they first appeared in Asia, and had thus been able to enlarge his kingdom at the expense of his neighbors. His son, Mithridates VI, the Great, had larger ambitions than his father. Campaigns on the north shore of the Black Sea brought him extensive lands in the Crimea and southern Ukraine, manpower for his army, and control of the grain trade from southern Russia and the fisheries of the Sea of Azov. With Syria in the last stage of decline, and before the rise of Parthia, Mithridates VI was in control of the most powerful kingdom in the east.

Rome took alarm, and encouraged the King of Bithynia to move against him. But then came the Social War in Italy,

and Mithridates' hour of opportunity. To evict the Romans
from Asia would leave him the greatest of Asiatic rulers
since Antiochus III of Syria. His agents were in touch with
the democratic and anti-Roman parties throughout Syria and
Greece, and in 88 B.C. he attacked Asia with a huge army.
The small forces of the Roman governor were soon swamped,
and Mithridates was in control of the province. His next step
was to organize one of the largest and best coordinated mas-
sacres prior to modern times. On a given day, throughout
Asia, all Romans and Italians, men, women, children, and
slaves, were murdered, with every kind of atrocity. Estimates of the dead vary between 80,000 and 150,000. Their
estates were confiscated for the royal treasury. With them
perished many of the Asiatic rich, for a royal proclamation
said that any debtor killing his creditor should have half his
debt remitted—a novel stimulus to action. Asia was lost.
Deprived of the Asian taxes, the Roman treasury was nearly
empty; cut off from their Asian connections, many business
houses went bankrupt. To defeat Mithridates had become as
urgent as to end the Social War. Who was to have the vital
eastern command?

The choice of the Senate was Lucius Cornelius Sulla, one
of the consuls of 88 B.C., then with his army in Campania.
He had served with distinction under Marius against Jugurtha and the Cimbri, and was the most successful Roman general in the Social War. But Marius, of course, wanted the
command for himself, though he was by then physically
unfit, alcoholic, more than half mad, and nearly seventy. The
tribune Sulpicius passed a bill through the Assembly trans-
ferring the command from Sulla to Marius. Things then
moved fast. Sulla fled to his troops in Campania, led them
against Rome, captured the city, ousted the democrats, ex-
ecuted Sulpicius, and drove Marius into exile. Then, with an
army of only 30,000, he sailed for Greece to fight Mithridates. In a few months the democrats regained power, and
Marius was back, striking down his enemies right and left.
It was a reign of terror, but short-lived, for he died a few
days after entering on his fated seventh consulship. But the
democrats were firmly in control, and Sulla, cut off from supplies and money, was in Greece facing an enemy in overwhelming strength. It needed a bold man to persevere in
such circumstances, but Sulla had faith in his star.

Now that the traditional mold of the Roman aristocracy
was broken, the characters of the men who wielded great
power had become important factors in history. Fortunately,
the masterly biographies of Plutarch give us an insight into

some of the men of this last age of the Republic—Marius,
Sulla, Pompey, Crassus, Cicero, and Caesar. The *Life of
Sulla* is one of the best. It shows a man of a type rare today,
but not uncommon in Roman history, who combined in almost equal proportions the life of the man of action and the
voluptuary. On a campaign he was indifferent to hardship,
personally fearless, a man the troops would follow anywhere.
Off duty, he liked the company of actors and prostitutes.
"He could never take anything seriously," says Plutarch,
"once he had sat down to dinner." But, affable though he
might seem, he had a cold ferocity about bloodshed that no
Roman had yet shown except to Rome's enemies. In an emergency no scruple, human or divine, could stop him. Hard
pressed for money in Greece, he confiscated temple treasures, not shrinking from the most venerable shrine of all,
that of Apollo at Delphi. The temple treasures, he explained
in a letter to the priests, would be safe with him (if he kept
them); if he sold them, they would be replaced. Meanwhile,
he was sending his agent to weigh and value them. Even
the agent hesitated to touch the holy objects: the priests
hinted at evil omens. The sound of a lyre had been heard,
the god was in his shrine. . . . Precisely, said Sulla, but they
had misread the signs. Music was a mark of joy, not of
anger: the god was only too delighted with the proposal. Let
them press on without fear. Sulla's life was ruled, above all,
by his belief in himself as the darling of fortune, the favorite
of destiny. He was Sulla Felix, the Lucky, (as he later called
himself): whenever he acted boldly, he was right.

All the luck was needed in the war against Mithridates.
Athens had declared for him, and a Pontic force had seized
it as a bridgehead. The Pontic fleet controlled the Aegean,
most of the islands were lost, Delos had been attacked and
destroyed. Athens fell to Sulla after one of the most famous
sieges in antiquity, which ended in great loss of life and the
destruction of many of the city's historical monuments. Relieving armies, coming by the historic invasion route used in
the Persian Wars, were shattered in two great battles in northern Greece. Then, to complicate matters, a second Roman
army arrived, sent out by the democratic government. Nobody quite knew what its role was to be, but it looks as
though a secret agreement was reached between Sulla and its
commander, Flaccus, who thereupon did useful service by
pushing the Pontic forces out of Macedonia and invading
Asia. Later, under a new general, Fimbria, this same army
captured the city of Pergamum and nearly caught Mithridates himself.

This was too much for Sulla. He had no understanding with Fimbria, and he could not let a democratic army win the credit for the recovery of Asia. Mithridates, too, needed a pause; he had lost two great armies and most of his conquests. So Sulla and the king negotiated the Treaty of Dardanus (84 B.C.), according to which the king renounced all his conquests, paid an indemnity, but retained Pontus and was recognized as the friend and ally of Rome. There was much criticism of its terms, but it was the best Sulla could do at the time. And it gave him what he wanted—the chance to get the credit for the recovery of Asia. For when Sulla appeared in Asia and camped next to the troops of Fimbria, the two armies became one by a sort of osmosis, and the deserted Fimbria had no choice but suicide. So it was Sulla who, at a general conference held at Ephesus, negotiated the new settlement with the cities of Asia. These could hardly be light, and were in fact a demand for the payment of a large indemnity and five years' taxes—at once. To the wretched Asiatics this fell on top of the extortions of the Roman *publicani* and of Mithridates, who had not been a light taskmaster. And further than that there were the demands of Sulla's troops, who, besides the other arts of war, had a thorough mastery of all the means by which an occupying force can enrich itself. Small wonder that the province of Asia entered on an economic decline that lasted until the early empire.

There now remained the question as to the terms on which Sulla should return to Italy. For a while the situation was fluid: everyone distrusted everyone else; the only constants were the need for each other of Sulla and his troops, and the undying hatred of the Samnites, still in the field, for Rome. But negotiations for an unopposed return broke down. Sulla re-entered Italy as the declared enemy of the democrats and the protagonist of the Senate. There followed yet another round of civil war. It ended in the hardest battle of Sulla's career, fought under the very walls of Rome outside the Colline Gate against the Samnite army under Pontius Telesinus (82 B.C.). For long it looked as though the Samnites would win; had they done so, Rome would have been destroyed. When victory went at last to Sulla, all Samnites not killed in battle were butchered as prisoners of war. So perished the last of all the valiant Samnite armies.

Sulla and his supporters were now the absolute masters of Rome, and proceeded to show it with a cruelty and ferocity that served as models for all future attempts of the kind. His position was legalized by reviving in his favor the old office of dictator, which had lain in disuse since the Second Punic War. Ominously, no limit of date was set, and the dictator was indemnified for all his actions, past and future. Then the Sullan Terror was unleashed. Murder of political opponents was to be expected: Marius had set a precedent for that. But Sulla went much further. Men were murdered who had taken no part in politics at all, and it was soon clear that the real motives were financial. Sulla's henchmen were to enrich themselves on the goods of his victims. An attempt to curb him was met with a sinister innovation, that of the proscription list. In a kind of official Gazette, published in the Forum, appeared the names of the intended victims. Men on this list were outlawed, they could be killed without penalty, their estates were confiscated, and their descendants were excluded from the citizenship. Some forty senators and sixteen hundred *equites* are said to have been proscribed by Sulla. Many great fortunes, including that of the multimillionaire Crassus, were built up by men who bought the estates of the victims at knock-down prices. Metella, Sulla's wife, was a constant bidder at such auctions: hers must have been a difficult bid to beat. Proscription remained one of the most terrible threats of the later civil wars. Besides private individuals, Italian communities, especially in Etruria, who had opposed Sulla lost their lands, which went to discharged soldiers. These made bad farmers and were a dangerous element in the countryside, always ready to promote disturbances. Sulla picked out and liberated ten thousand men from the slaves of the proscribed and gave them full citizenship; they took the name of "Cornelii," and were ready to act as his agents when required. Sulla now had the largest personal following ever known in Rome, men who owed everything to him. He had become a kind of gangster chief, on an enormous and legalized scale.

A dictator in Rome was appointed for a purpose. That of Sulla was to set up a constitution (*dictator reipublicae constituendae*). It does not seem likely that the ideas underlying the constitution of Sulla were his own. Through his marriage to Caecilia Metella he was linked with some of the most powerful families of the old aristocracy—the Metelli, the Aemilii Scauri, the Lutatii. They were probably the brains behind a program whose obvious intention was to restore and make permanent the supremacy of the Senate as it had been before the Gracchi. The office of censor was abolished, and with it control of the list on which depended entry to the Senate. Instead, entry to the Senate was to depend on the holding of a magistracy. The tribunes were drastically reduced: they lost all power of initiating legislation, and became ineligible for any future office. No more great careers should be built up on the tribuneship, like that of Caius Gracchus. The Assembly was confined to the discussion of proposals referred to it by the Senate. The grain dole was abolished—an attempt to cut down the numbers of the urban *plebs*. The *equites* lost their control of the extortion courts, which were restored to the Senate; indeed, Sulla's reform of the higher judicial arrangements was both useful and lasting. Even among senators, excessive ambition was to be discouraged. Offices were to be held in regular order, no one could enter his official career before the age of thirty, and there was to be a gap of ten years before re-election to an office for a second term. No more great power should rest on successive consulships, as it had with Marius. Finally, no army was to be stationed in Italy, and all returning generals should lay down their commands and enter as private persons. No more Sullas, to hold up the government at the point of the sword. Thus was Rome made safe for oligarchs to live in.

Having turned back the hands, Sulla waited for a few months to see if the clock would go. Then he laid down his office for the pursuit he had always preferred—dissipation. He did not long enjoy his retirement, for he died within a year at the age of sixty (78 B.C.). He was given a state funeral, and on his tomb was an inscription he had chosen for himself, proclaiming that no man had ever done more good to his friends, or more harm to his foes. Such were indeed the political ideals of Sulla and his times. If it had also said that no man had done more harm to the state, the whole truth would have been told. One further judgment on Sulla should be quoted. Julius Caesar—the dictator who did not retire—said of Sulla that "he didn't know his ABC." The modern world may view the retirement of a dictator with more indulgence. Certainly, of all the lost works of Latin literature, few would be more interesting to have than the *Memoirs* of Sulla.

CHAPTER VI

THE DECLINE AND FALL OF THE ROMAN REPUBLIC: 78–30 B.C.

The constitution of Sulla was intended as a final solution of the political problems of the Roman Republic. Within ten years of his death it had collapsed in ruins. That it would be challenged sooner or later was inevitable; neither the *populares* nor the *equites* would have acquiesced for long in the powers given to the Senate. But between 79 and 70 B.C. it was the pressure of events outside Rome that was decisive. In the East, Mithridates seized his chance of renewing the struggle with his hated enemy. In the West Sertorius, a follower of Marius and a provincial governor of genius, gained control of Spain and ruled it for many years as an independent province. In Italy the feebleness of the central government was thrown into high relief by the terrible Slave Rebellion led by Spartacus. On the high seas, an alarming development of piracy threatened to bring the commerce of the Mediterranean world to a standstill. Extraordinary commands were needed to deal with these dangers, and there was no lack of able men to fill them. To such men, the most striking lesson of Sulla's time was the career of Sulla himself. He had come back from a great command with an army behind him and made himself master of Rome. Others could do the same. Political history from the death of Sulla to the dictatorship of Caesar is best understood in terms of the careers of three great figures—Pompey, Crassus, and Caesar—each of whom was able to win a concentration of powers great enough to challenge those of the state.

Pompey had already made his mark in Sulla's time. Success came to him easily and early, and he already bore the title of "Magnus." But when greater responsibilities came his way, he had the talents to meet them: he could have established a personal autocracy if he had been as ruthless as he was vain.

Immense wealth was the foundation of Crassus' career. He added to a large inherited fortune by shrewd speculation at the time of the Sullan proscriptions and afterward, and became the greatest Roman capitalist of his day. His estate was estimated at one period at $16,000,000. He used the prevalence of fires at Rome to increase his holdings of metropolitan real estate. Since there were no public fire brigades, Crassus organized one of his own, and would send it, together with his estate agents, to the scene of a conflagration. An offer would be made for the burning property and property adjacent; if it was accepted, the fire brigade got to work. If refused, they stood by and watched it burn; another and lower offer would be forthcoming when devastation was complete. It is not to be supposed that so well-organized an enterprise lacked its own incendiary department. Crassus was naturally the head of the business interests in Rome; he could have been successful among the tycoons of nineteenth-century America. It was a strange fate that was to drive him to death at the head of a lost army in the Syrian desert.

Caesar, the youngest of the three, was as yet notable chiefly for his family connection with Marius, for the size of his debts, and for the way in which he could display charm or ruthlessness as the occasion demanded. The penetrating eye of Sulla had seen his qualities and marked him down for liquidation; he allowed him to be begged off with the grumble, "Say what you like, in that young fellow is many a Caius Marius."

There was no lack of able men who based their careers on the normal working of the Republic. Lucullus had military gifts as great as any of his time. A young man from the country town of Arpinum, Marcus Tullius Cicero, with no powerful political connections, was making his way through his brilliant oratory. The prosecution in 70 B.C. of Verres, the notorious governor of Sicily, was his great chance. Cato, a descendant of the great censor of the preceding century, was quixotic enough to rely on rigid virtue (and extreme narrow-mindedness); it brought him to suicide and a lasting reputation as the champion of a lost cause. Some of the great noble houses—the Metelli, the Lutatii—produced men not inferior to their ancestors who had once ruled Rome. But the times favored men who could be disloyal to all ties of party or class and think only of themselves.

Pompey won his first major laurels in the war against Sertorius, an episode which provided a telling indictment of the republican system of provincial government. Quintus Sertorius was sent out by the democratic party as governor of Hispania Citerior, but was immediately superseded by a senatorial governor and forced to retire to Africa. In 81 B.C. he was invited by the Lusitani (modern Portugal) to head a native rebellion. Back on Spanish soil, his movement became a focus for refugees from the rule of Sulla, and in 77 B.C. he was reinforced by a democratic Roman army from Sardinia under Perperna. Now a native rebellion was granted the intelligence and discipline of a first-rate Roman commander, for Sertorius was one of the ablest men of his time. He formed a small, highly mobile Romano-Spanish army, uniting Roman discipline and Spanish genius for guerrilla warfare, which could beat a good Roman general like Metellus Pius, and confront a great one like Pompey. Sertorius' policy toward the Spaniards was liberal and enlightened, endowed with insight and sympathy toward their characteristics. No Roman before him was so successful in enlisting Spanish loyalties. He fully grasped the importance of religion as a unifying force among the native peoples, and represented himself as under the special protection and inspiration of Diana, the great goddess whose cult was the most widespread in Spain. As a sign of her protection he was accompanied by his famous white fawn. A senate of three hundred members provided his Roman followers with the chief political institution of the Republic. At his most successful, he dominated central Spain, and there was serious talk of a possible invasion of Italy. Alliances with Mithridates and with the pirates on the Mediterranean foreshadowed an antisenatorial coalition on a world-wide scale. But in the long run the coalition of Sertorius collapsed through the conflicting political aims of its components. The Spanish allies wanted independence, the Roman political refugees a triumphant return to Rome of the antisenatorial party: there was personal rivalry for leadership between Sertorius and Perperna. Sertorius could hold the coalition together by his personality so long as it was successful; checked by Pompey, it fell apart, and Sertorius was assassinated (72 B.C.). But he had given a foretaste of what, in better days, Roman civilization was to achieve in Spain.

The renewal of the war with Mithridates in 74 B.C. followed another "bequest" to Rome—that by Nicomedes IV of his kingdom of Bithynia. It was not surprising that the King of Pontus should dislike the idea of a new Roman province on his doorstep; he already had cause to complain of breaches of the treaty he had made with Sulla. He accordingly overran Bithynia, pushed the Romans out of the Black Sea, and besieged the great fortress of

Cyzicus. He allied himself with the pirates to cut Roman communications with Asia, and was in diplomatic contact with
Sertorius, who sent him officers to train the Pontic army in
Roman tactics. Another Sulla was needed for another great
eastern command. In Lucullus, who had been a lieutenant of
Sulla's in the first war against Mithridates, the right man was
found.

Lucullus stands up well in the company of the great
generals and administrators of the last fifty years of the
Republic. He was given an extraordinary command—the
three provinces of Asia, Cilicia, and Bithynia, with a general
commission to finish the war against Mithridates—and he put
it to effective use. Between 74 and 67 he cleared Bithynia,
pushed Mithridates out of his own kingdom of Pontus,
and pursued him to the heart of Armenia, where he had
taken refuge with his son-in-law Tigranes. That monarch
had greatly extended his ancient kingdom and had assumed
the old Persian title of King of Kings. The pinnacle of
Lucullus' success was the capture of his splendid new capital
of Tigranocerta, built near the headwaters of the Euphrates
to revive the lost glories of Babylon and Nineveh. He also
found time to reorganize the finances of the province of
Asia, relieving the distress into which the cities had been
plunged in trying to pay off the Sullan indemnities, and
curbing the Roman tax collectors and moneylenders.

But Lucullus had enemies more dangerous than the foe in
the field. Pompey begrudged his success in a command
greater than any he had yet held; the *equites* hated his
curbing their activities in Asia; his own soldiers increasingly
resented his strict discipline and above all, his attempts to
deprive them of what they considered legitimate opportunities
for loot and plunder. There were intrigues against him in
Rome and in his own camp. Finally his army mutinied; he
suffered the humiliation of seeing Mithridates return to
Pontus, and was himself forced to hand over his command
to Pompey and return to Rome. He would have been a great
success a century earlier, when a Roman commander could
count on discipline in his troops and support from his government. In his own times, he won his lasting reputation in
retirement in his splendid palace on the Pincian Hill—as
a gourmet.

The war with Spartacus (73–71 B.C.) was no ordinary
slave rebellion. It began when Spartacus, a Thracian gladiator,
and some of his fellows broke away from their training camp
near Capua; they were joined by others, and there were
mass break-outs from the slave barracks throughout southern

Italy. Many of these deserting slaves were Cimbric and Teutonic prisoners from the wars of Marius—excellent fighting material. With the gladiators, highly trained professional swordsmen, as their nucleus, and a leader of genius in Spartacus, they made up a formidable force. Moving up and down the Apennines, they made rapid descents on the towns in the plain for plunder. Roman armies sent against them were shattered; their numbers grew with success, and for two years they terrorized Italy. Spartacus formed the remarkable plan of leading them north so that they could disperse and return to their own homes. They actually reached Cisalpine Gaul, but turned back into Italy, whether through lack of provisions or through a liking for brigandage. There Crassus, holding his first important command, brought them to bay in Lucania and crushed them. The last embers of the rising were stamped out by Pompey on his way back from Spain. Characteristically he claimed credit for the whole victory. Spartacus, so far as our information goes, seems to have been a remarkable man with a capacity for winning the devotion of his followers; Communist historians, from Marx onwards, have regarded him as a kind of patron saint of proletarian risings.

Soon after these events Pompey and Crassus stood as joint candidates for the consulship of 70 B.C. By the strict rules of the Sullan constitution neither was eligible; Pompey had not held the proper sequence of offices, and both had failed to disband their armies as required. None the less, they were elected, by the votes of the popular party and against the wishes of the Senate. Not much survived of the work of Sulla by the end of the year. The tribunes had been fully restored to their old powers. The office of censor had been revived, and the new censors began by clearing some of the more notorious Sullan adherents out of the Senate. A proposal to restore control of the extortion courts to the *equites* met with stiff resistance. It might not have passed at all but for the alarming revelations, at the trial of Verres, of the way in which the Senate had abused its judicial powers. In the event, the *Lex Aurelia* set up mixed courts, with the *equites* holding two places for every one held by the Senate. For another decade, the Senate was nominally in control of Rome, but the legal provisions on which Sulla had sought to base its powers were gone forever.

The word "pirate" has something of a comic ring to the modern ear, a suggestion of *Treasure Island* and the Jolly Roger. But piracy has been a grim reality in the Mediterranean at many periods of history. The pirates of the Bar-

bary Coast had been a terror to sailors for centuries before
they were exterminated, as late as the nineteenth century,
in a series of actions which saw some of the earliest exploits
of the United States Marines. In the early years of the first
century, the pirates, especially those of Cilicia and Crete,
had built up a power of that order. Since the collapse of the
sea power of Rhodes in the second century, police duties
had devolved upon Rome, but she had neglected them, possibly because of the links between the pirates and the supply
of slaves to the market at Delos. Both Mithridates and
Sertorius formed alliances with the pirates, who by 70 B.C.
were bold enough to patrol the approaches to Ostia and
Puteoli, make raids on the coasts of Italy, and menace the
grain trade on which the life of Rome depended. Pompey
was given command against them, and was invested with
extraordinary powers by the *Lex Gabinia* (67 B.C.). He had
five hundred ships, twelve thousand soldiers, and a sphere
which included the whole Mediterranean and fifty miles
inland from all coasts. This conception of *imperium infinitum aequum*—power not limited to any province, and
equal to that of the governor of any province—was to be
important in the future. Equally notable was Pompey's speed
of action and the nature of his settlement. The pirates were
crushed as an organized force in three months. But captured
pirates were not crucified or sold into slavery: they were
settled in deserted regions of Cilicia and elsewhere and
turned into useful citizens. One of them survived to be
immortalized in the *Georgics* of Virgil as a virtuous old
gardener notable for his success with early blooms.

When Lucullus met Pompey to hand over his command,
he made the bitter comment that Pompey was like a carrion
bird, preying on the corpses that other men had slain. Years
before, Crassus, referring to Pompey's premature assumption of the title "the Great," had asked, "Great in relation
to what?" There was force in these strictures on the easy
successes of Pompey's early career. But he had done well
against the pirates, and he was to do better in his greater
command against Pontus and Armenia. The powers he now
held were unprecedented in Roman history, for by the *Lex
Manilia* of 66 B.C. the great command of Lucullus in Asia
had been added to the *imperium* he already held against
the pirates. In a few months Mithridates was expelled from
Pontus and his kingdom annexed for Rome and added to
the province of Bithynia. Mithridates sought refuge in the
Crimea. The reduction of Armenia quickly followed, but
it was not annexed, for Pompey saw that its real value to

Rome was as a glacis against the Parthians. So Tigranes became a client-king, with the title of Friend and Ally of the Roman people. Pompey then led his army beyond Armenia into Transcaucasia, and made war on the Albani and Iberi. Here, nearly a thousand miles from the Aegean Sea, he was in a region which belonged to romance rather than to sober geography. This was the land of the Golden Fleece, of Prometheus, and of the Amazons. Amazons, indeed, were reputed to have fought with the Iberians against him; it was disappointing that no women's corpses were found on the battlefield! There was talk of an expedition to the Caspian Sea, then thought to be the eastern boundary of the world: the western boundary Pompey had seen on the Atlantic coasts of Portugal and Africa. The parallel with Alexander is obvious.

These plans he dropped in favor of more serious tasks. First the affairs of Asia Minor were reorganized. The dynastic arrangements of all the surviving native kingdoms were overhauled, and Roman nominees put in power; the old Celtic kingdom of Galatia was enlarged. Several new cities were founded in Pontus and Bithynia, and a vigorous stimulus was given to municipal life throughout the Roman provinces. Then, in 64, Pompey crossed from Armenia to Syria, and proceeded to reorganize the whole region as far as the frontiers of Egypt. At Antioch he deposed the last feeble Seleucid king and declared Syria a Roman province; a momentous acquisition, this, for Syria under the Empire was to be the richest part of the Roman East. In 63 he captured Jerusalem, to put it into the hands of a Roman nominee; this was the first contact between Rome and the Jews. There followed an expedition to Jericho and Petra, interrupted by the news of the death of Mithridates. The indomitable old king had planned yet another attack on Rome; this time it was to be a drive up the Danube valley and an alliance with the Gauls. Balked in this, he tried to poison himself, but earlier he had all too successfully acquired immunity by taking small doses. Finally, he asked a mercenary to kill him, lest he should be taken alive and figure in Pompey's triumph. So perished one of the most implacable of Rome's enemies.

By 62 B.C. Pompey had completed his mission in Asia. Three new provinces had been acquired—Pontus, Syria, and an enlarged Cilicia. A glacis of client kingdoms protected them on the east. The western termini of the great caravan routes across Asia to India and China were now in Roman control, as was the route along the south shore of the Black

Sea to the Caucasus and the Caspian. The royal estates of
Mithridates were a huge addition to the public lands of Rome.
Pompey had shown himself the greatest of all Roman procon-
suls. His settlement had been made on his own authority
without the usual senatorial commission, and its main features
were to last for centuries. Such was the achievement that
Caesar, a few years later, set himself to rival in the west.

Roman politics from 66 to 62 B.C. were overshadowed by
the absence of Pompey in the East, and by speculation as to
what he would do when he came back. But they did not lack
excitements of their own. Caesar and Crassus worked hand
in hand for a while. They were thought to be behind a revolutionary land bill put forward by a tribune, which might
have produced another Gracchan crisis—for there was again
the possibility of a great bequest to Rome, that of the kingdom of Egypt. The bill was defeated, largely through the influence of Cicero, who began to play the part of leader of
the conservative forces. Elected consul for the year 63, it fell
to him to deal with the famous conspiracy of Catiline.
Thanks to the speeches of Cicero and the monograph of
Sallust, this episode is known in great detail, and is usually
given a larger place than it deserves in Roman history. An
Italian scholar has well said that it belongs to the police records rather than to political history. But it gave an alarming
insight into the forces of violence and revolution that were
at large in Roman society, and of the way in which they
might spread if given a start. To Cicero it seemed one of the
great crises of Roman history, and he attached inflated importance to the title of *Pater Patriae* (Father of His Country)
which he received for suppressing it. All such distinctions
paled at the return of Pompey in 62 at the head of such
power as Rome had never seen. Would he be another Sulla?
The answer was soon seen to be No; Pompey had an odd
liking for observing the rules from time to time. He dis-
banded his army and asked for two things only—ratification
of his doings in Asia and land for his veterans. On the part
of the Senate, relief soon turned to abuse. Pompey was not
forgiven for what he had done as consul in 70; Lucullus resented the way in which he had snatched his own laurels.
Soon after celebrating the most magnificent of all triumphs
yet seen in Rome, Pompey found himself humiliated and
impotent.

It was Caesar who showed him the way out, proposing in
great secrecy a political alliance of Pompey, Crassus, and
himself. Each wanted something: Caesar, the consulship for
59; Crassus, on behalf of the *equites*, a reduction of the sum

due from the Asian taxes; Pompey, the two demands mentioned above. With Pompey's army, Crassus' money, and Caesar's popularity with the Roman people, they would be irresistible. So was born the First Triumvirate (60 B.C.)—the Three-headed Monster, as its enemies called it. Livy was right in calling it a standing conspiracy.

Caesar's consulship was a year of decisive importance. The other consul, Bibulus, was reduced to a cipher; there was talk of "the consulship of Julius and Caesar." The Senate itself was not much more, for Caesar did not hesitate to go above its head and the Assembly's if need be. No wonder Cicero in his letters spoke of a *regnum,* a personal monarchy. The bargains with Pompey and Crassus were kept. Crassus got a reduction on the Asiatic contracts for 61 B.C.—a scandalous piece of jobbery. Pompey got confirmation of his eastern settlement, and his veterans their lands—mostly from the Ager Campanus, the last big holdings of public land in Italy proper, and noted for good farming. Yet another land bill provided for the urban poor, in the manner of the Gracchi, and there was a useful law to curb extortion in the provinces by governors and their staffs.

The Senate's hopes were now fixed on reducing Caesar to insignificance after his consulship, and a derisory "province" was worked out for him—the care of public forests and drove roads in Italy. Caesar took the matter to the Assembly; a *Lex Vatinia* gave him Cisalpine Gaul and Illyricum for the unusually long term of five years, three legions, and the right to choose his own legates and to plant colonies. It was a dangerous command, for these three legions would be the nearest striking force to Italy. The Senate, perhaps hoping to mollify Caesar, added Transalpine Gaul and a fourth legion. Caesar was soon to show that the potentialities of this command were greater than the glittering prize that had fallen to Pompey in the East. It was the governorship of Transalpine Gaul that enabled him to undertake the momentous conquest of Gaul itself.

Gaul in Caesar's day stretched from the Rhine to the Pyrenees, from the Atlantic to the boundaries of the Roman province of Narbonensis. It was a densely populated country —some French scholars accept a figure as high as twenty million—divided into sixty states (*civitates*) politically independent, but speaking a common Celtic language, and observing common religious cults, especially that of the Druids. There was no ethnic unity—Iberian strains were strong in the Southwest, Ligurian in the Southeast, Germanic in the Northeast. But everywhere, more or less strong, was an ad-

mixture of people calling themselves Celts and recognizing a
common Celtic ancestry. Gaul was, in fact, the Celtic country par excellence, the most powerful part of that huge Celtic
area which extended from Ireland to the kingdom of Galatia
in Asia Minor.

Classical historians and modern archaeology agree in plac-
ing the homeland of the Celtic peoples by the sources of the
Rhine and the Danube. The first people in central Europe
to use iron, they spread from this diffusion point as a con-
quering aristocracy between 500 and 250 B.C. At the height
of their power, they held southern Germany, France, northern Spain, the Po valley, part of Yugoslavia, and much of
Britain and Ireland. Throughout this area, Celtic society con-
stituted a brilliant "heroic" culture of rich warrior chiefs,
skilled agriculturalists and pastoralists, artists and metal-
workers, lawmakers, poets, and priests. For centuries there
had been trade relations with the classical world, first with
the Greeks and Etruscans, then with Massilia and Rome.
Archaeologists have excavated the burial mounds of the Celtic
chieftains with their rich grave goods—chariots, torcs, armor,
mirrors, wine jars—at such sites as Hallstatt in Austria, Vix
in France, and Lexden in Britain. In essence, this is the society portrayed centuries later in the heroic literature of
Wales and Ireland.

Such was the material condition of Gaul in 58 B.C. Politically, it was an age of confusion. About 150 B.C. it seemed
that the powerful confederacy of the Arverni of the Cev-
ennes and their allies of the Rhone valley might unify the
whole of Gaul. This was the age of great kings like Luernus
and Bituitus, whose authority was undisputed in their tribes.
But the power of the Arverni was smashed by Rome when
Narbonensis was established, and there were no successors.
By the time of Caesar strong monarchies had almost everywhere given way to oligarchic rule, with power in the hands
of great nobles divided among themselves. "Every tribe was
divided into two factions," is Caesar's comment. This hin-
dered the growth of confederacies and made them more
transient. Before Caesar the rivalry of the Aedui and the
Arverni affected the policies of almost every Gallic tribe;
his presence in Gaul meant that almost every tribe divided
into pro- and anti-Roman. These were the conditions in
which Caesar carried out his conquest.

The story of Caesar's eight years of fighting in Gaul should
be read in his *Commentaries*. But it should not be forgotten
that these are the memoirs of a general and—as is well known

nowadays—generals write memoirs to justify themselves. There was much that needed justification in Caesar's conduct in Gaul. For these conquests, so fruitful, in the long run, for the civilization of Europe, were undertaken solely for Caesar's personal aggrandizement. Treachery, cruelty, and ruthlessness make his Gallic command one of the ugliest chapters of imperialist aggression. Beneath the limpidity of the *Commentaries* and their apparent candor lies some very special pleading, designed to convince the reader that there had been no breach of the old rule that Rome undertook only defensive wars. Hence the Aedui are cast for the role of threatened ally who turns to Rome for help; one recalls the Mamertines in the First Punic War, and Saguntum in the Second.

The campaigns of 58 B.C. were creditable enough, in which Caesar pushed back the Helvetii into the Alps, and the Germanic Suebi across the Rhine. In 57 he attacked the powerful tribes of the Belgae around the Meuse and the Rhine. He devoted 56 to the southwest and west, where the navy of the Veneti (Morbihan, in Brittany) was annihilated. There followed years of adventure: in 55 a crossing of the Rhine and a short stay on the German bank; in 55 and 54 the two famous but puzzling expeditions to Britain, in the second of which Caesar crossed the Thames and captured the *oppidum* of the great British king Cassivellaunus, near the modern St. Albans. On the military side these expeditions were badly planned, and their political results were negligible. But they make sense as a counter to Pompey's fabulous exploits in Transcaucasia and toward the Caspian. As Pompey had reached the ocean at the eastern edge, so had Caesar crossed it on the west, and with an army had entered the mysterious island at the farthest boundary of the world. The year 53 was again taken up with the Belgae, who had allied themselves with the Germans beyond the Rhine and started rebellions that shook Caesar's hold on Gaul.

In the winter of 53–52 the course of politics in Rome took Caesar to Italy. In his absence there broke out the great national uprising under Vercingetorix, "the war," said Caesar, "that was different from all other wars." Vercingetorix, the son of a great chief of the Arverni, was by birth, education, and family tradition the heir to all that was best in the native culture. But he also knew Rome and Roman military methods; the Arverni had so far held aloof from the anti-Roman movement, and Vercingetorix himself had served for six years in Caesar's camp throughout his campaigns. But the growing

harshness of Caesar's methods and the brutality of the
Roman *negotiatores* had brought all Gaul to the edge of
rebellion.

The rising was planned at the annual meeting of the council of the Gauls in the territory of the Carnutes, the headquarters of the Druidic cult. The war both began and ended
with religious ceremonies. It opened with the most solemn
rites in support of the Carnutes, who had volunteered to make
the first move—the massacre of Roman *negotiatores* at the
supply base of Cenabum. This looks like a ritual shedding
of Roman blood, though no doubt there was reason enough
for it on the secular plane. The war ended in the personal
surrender of Vercingetorix in full war panoply to Caesar—
an act of *devotio* to appease the anger of the gods. These religious ceremonies at the beginning and end of the war suggest that the Druids took part in what was regarded as a
holy war for the common safety of Gaul.

By the time the war was well under way, Vercingetorix
was at the head of a powerful confederacy which included
all the chief tribes of central Gaul and Armorica. Even the
Aedui deserted Rome for a time. Vercingetorix' position was
that of war leader, and the strategy he adopted called for
guerrilla warfare and a scorched-earth policy: deprived of
supplies, the Romans were to exhaust themselves in assault-
ing the great Gallic hill forts. This worked well at Avaricum
and again at the more famous siege of Gergovia, where
Caesar took heavy losses. But in an attempt to invade the
Roman province there took place a battle near Dijon in
which the Gauls lost nearly all their cavalry. The last event of
the war was the grim siege of Alesia—the modern Alise-Ste.-
Reine, Côte d'Or—whose details are known from Caesar's
narrative and from the excavations of modern times, beginning with those of Napoleon III. In this great fortress and
sanctuary of the goddess Epona, Vercingetorix with 80,000
men was besieged by a Roman army of 65,000. The Roman
circumvallation shows their military engineering at its most in-
genious. Later, a huge Gallic relieving force (perhaps 250,000
men) appeared and besieged Caesar in turn. Through two
terrible months (August–September, 52 B.C.) the position
was in doubt. But the strength of the relieving army, perhaps
because of divided command, was never effectually de-
ployed, and the attempt to relieve Alesia ended in disaster
and the collapse of the last and greatest confederacy of free
Gaul.

The uprising had brought to the brink of defeat the greatest Roman general and the finest Roman army, and this was

above all the achievement of Vercingetorix. In the field he had trained the Gauls in new tactics, including the complicated techniques of siegecraft. In policy he stood above all intertribal jealousies for the conception of a free and independent Gaul, which he believed could resist any power in the world. He became the embodiment of his country's cause, and when he surrendered, it was lost. It is worth pausing to note the capacity of native societies to produce, from time to time, leaders of outstanding ability—a Pontiac, a Vercingetorix, an Arminius. The difference in intellectual and moral power between such men and the general run of their society is far greater than is found in the civilized world. Such men can lead their peoples to triumphs which might be thought far beyond their scope.

Caesar's work in Gaul was nearly done. There followed a few mopping-up operations in Aquitania, but in 51 B.C. he left a Gaul conquered, pacified, and bled white. In these years he had forged a magnificent Roman army, united to him by a personal devotion as strong as that of the Old Guard for Napoleon, resting on common memories of the famous battles and sieges, the great marches, the expeditions to Britain and Germany. With this Army of Gaul Caesar was to win the mastery of the Roman world.

Caesar's absence in Gaul had placed a strain on the Triumvirate. Pompey and Crassus had always been jealous of each other; when their younger colleague entered the limelight, they became disgruntled with him. It was easy for the Senate to exploit the situation. Cicero, in particular, worked hard to detach Pompey as the best means of breaking up the coalition. In these circumstances Caesar invited his colleagues to a conference at Luca in 56 B.C., from which the Triumvirate emerged renewed and strengthened. Pompey and Crassus were to be consuls in 55, Caesar got five more years in his Gallic command, Pompey a five-year command to Spain, and Crassus one of the same length in Syria. Ostensibly, Crassus got the biggest prize—a great eastern command, in emulation of Alexander. The prospect of a war against Parthia was an *ignis fatuus* that was to haunt Roman foreign policy for long years to come. The Parthian kingdom had grown up in the vacuum caused by the collapse of Seleucid power in central Asia since the middle of the second century B.C. In a sense, it was a revival of the old Persian Empire, and its kings, of the Arsacid line, had revived the proud title of "King of Kings." They controlled the great caravan routes from China, India, and the Persian Gulf to the Black Sea and the Mediterranean, traffic on which had recently increased very greatly. It has been suggested that Roman financial interests had taken a hand in this lucrative trade since Pompey's eastern conquests, and now saw a chance of getting complete control. That would at least supply a rational motive for the campaign of Crassus, which otherwise seems lacking. For, reading the story of that campaign in Plutarch's *Crassus*, one gets the sense of a great force stumbling on under incompetent leadership to a terrible doom. For Crassus and his seven legions the disaster was final. Caught on a march in summer through the Syrian desert, without food or water, the Roman infantry was surrounded near Carrhae by the terrible Parthian armed cavalry and horse-archers and cut to pieces in the worst Roman defeat since Cannae (53 B.C.). Seven eagles were lost, 20,000 men killed, and 10,000 taken prisoner. Crassus' head was cut off and sent to the King of Kings, then a guest at the court of Armenia. It chanced that the *Bacchae* of Euripides was being performed; the head of the Roman triumvir was seized and brandished as the head of Pentheus in the play. Such was the philhellenism of the Eastern kings.

Revenge for Crassus was a cry in Roman politics for thirty years. Horace pictured the disgrace of the Roman prisoners, married to barbarian wives, and forgetting the very name of Italy and Rome. Their fate may have been stranger than he knew. Recent scholarship has found evidence in Chinese sources of Western mercenaries being employed at this time in what is now Turkestan. Some of these may well have been Crassus' men, sold by the Parthians to the Chinese.

Now Caesar and Pompey were face to face. A year before Carrhae, the death of Julia, Caesar's daughter and Pompey's wife, had removed a bond between them. Crassus' death left them rivals; within a few years they were open foes. By the terms of the conference of Luca, Pompey should have taken up his command in Spain after his consulship in 54 B.C. But he chose to stay in Rome and to govern Spain through legates. This made it possible for the Senate to use him as a counterweight to Caesar and to the growing political anarchy in Rome, caused by the private armies of thugs and gladiators, like those which harassed Germany in the last years of the Weimar Republic. One gang under Clodius operated for Caesar, another under Milo for Pompey; from 57 to 52 these gangs ruled the streets of Rome; finally Milo's men murdered Clodius. Pompey was then called in by the Senate to put them down with troops, and made sole consul. From this time on he moved away from Caesar to the position of champion of the Senate, whose hostility to Caesar gained strength during the crisis of the rebellion of Vercingetorix. Caesar had earned the undying enmity of senatorial extremists by the use he had made of the Assembly when consul in 59 B.C. They were alarmed by the prestige he had won in Gaul, and the use he might make of it when he got back. Somehow, Caesar must be brought back to Rome as a private individual; then he could be attacked and his political career brought to an end. Caesar, for his part, wanted to stand for the consulship of 48 B.C., and after that to be given another great command. He knew exactly what his opponents wanted, and had no intention of walking into the trap. Eighteen months of tortuous negotiations failed to produce conditions for his return. Finally, meetings of the Senate on January 1 and 7, 49 B.C., decided to recall Caesar, to hand over his army to his enemy Domitius Ahenobarbus, and to arm the consuls with powers of the *senatusconsultum ultimum*, the terrible weapon which had destroyed the Gracchi and Catiline. There was no doubt who was the public enemy this time.

Caesar, with one legion, was waiting for the news at Ravenna. On January 12 he left his province and entered Italy under arms, crossing the little river Rubicon at the boundary and making its name forever after proverbial for the decision that cannot be revoked. The die was cast, and the Civil War had begun. Caesar's was the nearest army to Rome, and he exploited this advantage with his usual boldness. Within a week Ariminum and Ancona were occupied. Pompey saw he had no chance of holding Italy, and decided to cross the Adriatic and organize resistance in Greece. Caesar made a dash to Brundisium to cut him off—perhaps even to try to come to terms—but it failed. By the end of March, he was master of Rome and all Italy.

But this was only the first round. The republican position was still immensely strong. Pompey's lieutenant held Spain and Africa. With his prestige in the east, he could himself mobilize all its forces for a return to Italy. But in the Civil War, even more than in Gaul, Caesar relied on speed for victory. In a six-week campaign he smashed the republican position in Spain and had won over the defeated army to his side. By the end of 49 B.C. he was ready to challenge Pompey. Early in 48 B.C., in winter and in the face of superior sea power, he crossed the Adriatic and landed an army south of Dyrrachium (Durazzo), the great Pompeian base. Reinforced soon afterward by Mark Antony, he boldly besieged a larger Pompeian force. In mid-June he was forced to raise the siege, and drew off southeast toward Thessaly,

followed by Pompey. On August 9, near Pharsalus, there took
place the decisive battle between the two greatest Roman generals of their day. Thanks to the steadiness of his Gallic veterans, it ended in a victory for Caesar. "They would have it
so" was his comment as he gazed on the faces of the republican dead after the battle.

The great victory which in effect made Caesar master of
the world was followed by tragedy and farce. Pompey
escaped from Pharsalus, took ship, and finally reached
Egypt. But the rulers of Egypt had no taste for a losing
cause. He was assassinated as soon as he landed—the second
of the great triumvirs to die by the sword. Following hard
after him with a small body of troops, Caesar got involved
in the dynastic quarrels of Cleopatra, queen of Egypt, and
her brother. The conqueror of Vercingetorix and of Pompey
was in danger of being killed in street fighting by Egyptians.
From this predicament he was rescued by a son of Mithridates of Pontus. There followed a lightning campaign in
Asia, and a stubborn one in Africa, where the last big republican forces were crushed (46 B.C.), and Cato committed
suicide. In the autumn of 46 Caesar celebrated a magnificent
fourfold triumph over Gaul, Africa, Egypt, and Pontus. All
were foreign foes; there was no mention of Pharsalus. But
in 45 there was a last flare-up of civil war in Spain, crushed
in Caesar's last battle at Munda. News of this victory
reached Rome at the time of the Palilia of 45—an auspicious
event, showing Caesar as a second Romulus. Less auspicious-
ly, his fifth triumph, in October, 45 B.C., was over the defeated rebels in Spain—a Roman foe. He had only six
months to live.

No estimate of Caesar's dictatorship can overlook the
brief time he had for political affairs. Between Pharsalus
and his death he never had six continuous months in Rome.
His personal agents, Oppius, Hirtius, Cornelius Balbus,
were an excellent team, and must be given credit that so
much was achieved. But it was all improvisation, to settle
immediate problems; we do not know what form Caesar's
mature plans would have taken, if indeed he had any. Reconciliation was certainly in his mind. There were no proscriptions. It is true that many of the leading republicans
had died on the battlefield, but at least he won over—for
a time—men like Cicero, Cassius, Marcus Brutus, and his
old enemy Marcellus, consul of the year 50 B.C. But for the
political feelings of his opponents he showed no regard.
The institutions of the Republic were reshaped for his con-

venience. The Senate was increased to 900 and packed with his adherents, chosen from the provinces as well as Rome and Italy. It became a rubber stamp for measures put forward by Caesar. The magistrates were those of his choice. His agents controlled the treasury, and his image appeared on the coins. In his own person were concentrated all the effective powers of the state. The armies owed obedience to him, and he took the title of *Imperator* as part of his own name. The office of dictator had been granted to him by the Assembly early in 49 B.C.; for some time he combined it with the consulship. In 46 B.C. he was made dictator for ten years; in January, 44 B.C., for life. By a vote of the Assembly, he held tribunician power, though not a tribune, and he also held powers that had belonged to the censors. He was *pontifex maximus*, and a member of all the priestly colleges. Besides all this, he was granted many honorific titles and distinctions, such as the right to wear the purple robes of a *triumphator*, to vote first in the Senate, and so on. We do not know whether this personal autocracy would have been his final solution for the political problems of Rome. What is certain is that its unprecedented nature roused the hostility of a group of men—some republicans, some former followers, but all senators—who decided to kill him.

His plans for extending the franchise are the most important features of Caesar's legislation. Roman citizenship was extended to Cisalpine Gaul, a region that brought a great addition of strength to Italy with its flourishing agriculture, sturdy peasantry, and growing urban life. The same was planned for Narbonensis, though it did not mature. But Gades (Cadiz), with which he had ties since his Spanish governorship, became a town of Roman citizens. There was a big program of colonies, in Spain, Gaul, Africa, and Illyricum, and around the Black Sea. Notable among them was the refounding of Carthage and of Corinth, a revival of the plans of Caius Gracchus. Many towns in Sicily received Latin rights. The constitutions of the municipalities of Italy were revised and standardized, a measure attested by archaeology as well as the literary sources. There was a proposal for a new codification of Roman law. The calendar—by now three months wrong—was reformed with such accuracy as not to need further revision until the sixteenth century. The month of July—formerly Quintilis—received and still bears Caesar's name. Great engineering projects were entertained—a canal for the Isthmus of Corinth, the channeling of the Tiber at Rome, and the building of a new harbor at its mouth. There were splendid plans for new developments in Rome, some of which were later carried out by Augustus. An absolutist regime may be expected to foster great designs in engineering and architecture. But one looks for signs that Caesar was getting to grips with the central problem of the Roman world—the securing of political stability at Rome and good government for the provinces. It is not reassuring to find his energies bent on a great war against Parthia due to begin in 44 B.C. It would, no doubt, have revenged Crassus and rivaled Alexander; perhaps it would have placed Rome's eastern frontiers on a sound footing: certainly it provided an excuse for shelving political problems to which, perhaps, he had no answer. At all events, sixteen legions had been assembled in Illyricum for this grandiose project, and Caesar was due to join them when he was assassinated on March 15, 44 B.C.

For centuries, there has been controversy about the Ides of March and the motives of the "Liberators." Did Brutus act from Stoic principles, or from a family tradition of tyrannicide? What was the role of Cassius? Was Caesar aiming at a monarchy on the Hellenistic model? That can never be known. What is certain is that the deed followed two months after the assumption by Caesar of the dictatorship for life, a complete breach of Roman tradition and, of itself, the death knell of the Republic. Republican sentiment and Roman political tradition account for—though they do not excuse—the motives of Caesar's murderers.

No Roman, and few men of any age, show such a brilliant combination of gifts as Caesar. He ranks among the greatest of the world's generals, with Alexander, Hannibal, and Napoleon. He was a consummate politician, and a great provincial governor. He had brilliant qualities of mind, allied to an avid thirst for knowledge; one of the best-educated men of his day, he was a splendid orator and a fine writer. His influence on the world has been great—especially his work in both Cisalpine and Transalpine Gaul—and still endures. In the unlovely company of the men of power, his is much the least unattractive figure. He did not like cruelty for its own sake, and he knew the value of clemency and of humor. Yet the picture of Caesar the superman, the paragon above fault or reproach, invented by Mommsen and followed by many German and Italian scholars, is quite unhistoric. No doubt he had a deeper insight than any man before him into the pathology of the Roman Republic, but there is no evidence that he had any better cure for it than personal absolutism. It was left to others to learn and apply the lessons of Caesar's life and death.

The main events from the death of Caesar to the battle of Actium are perhaps better known to the educated layman than those of any other period of Roman history—the Second Triumvirate, the defeat of Caesar's murderers at Philippi, the loves of Antony and Cleopatra and their great designs in the East, the growing estrangement between Octavian and Antony, the final rift and the battle of Actium, the suicides of Antony and Cleopatra in Egypt and, at the end, Octavian sole master of the Roman world. But, whether we know it or not, we see these events through the eyes of Shakespeare, at least in the English-speaking world. The dramatist must select and simplify: so in *Julius Caesar* the speech of Antony turns the Roman people against the Liberators, and in rapid succession follow the proscriptions, the quarrels of Brutus and Cassius, and the battle of Philippi. Reality was different. Only slowly did the rival forces coalesce and form up for the second round of the Civil War. Indeed, it was for a time doubtful whether there would be a contest at all. The Liberators do not seem to have planned beyond the murder of the dictator—once that was done, they considered the Republic restored. But there was still a Caesarean party, and there was still an army that had been loyal to Caesar. Whoever could succeed to that loyalty would be the victor at last. Thus early, the one who seemed most likely to do so was Marcus Antonius (Mark Antony), one of Caesar's ablest marshals and the surviving consul for 44 B.C., and Lepidus, who had been Caesar's Master of Horse. On the republican side, the prestige of the Liberators was a wasting asset in Rome and Italy, but there was Cicero, the only Republican statesman of the first rank, and Sextus Pompeius, son of Pompey the Great. Finally, there was an outsider, a young man of eighteen called Caius Octavius, great-nephew of Caesar. Making his will before setting out for Parthia, Caesar had adopted him as his son under the name of Octavian, and declared him heir to his estate. He was now said to be on his way from Illyricum to Rome to take up his dangerous legacy. It was not clear what he took that legacy to be.

Meanwhile, there was an uneasy truce. Immediately after the murder, the acts of Caesar were confirmed, but his murderers were pardoned. The arrangements he had made for provinces for the consuls of 44 B.C. were broken when Antony claimed Gaul, the base of Caesar's power, and for a term of six years. Here was the first breach, and it was widened by a series of bitter speeches—the *Philippics*—by Cicero against Antony. Brutus and Cassius went to the East to gather an army to counter the Caesarean forces in the West. Octavian appeared in Italy, and for a time was the Senate's champion in open warfare against Antony (April, 43 B.C.). "The young man must be flattered, used, and pushed aside," was Cicero's judgment. But the young man had other ideas. At the critical moment he marched against Rome rather than Antony, and became consul for 42 B.C. In November 43 B.C. there was a reconciliation of the Caesarean leaders, and Antony, Octavian, and Lepidus were recognized as triumvirs for five years. Their first act was to organize a proscription on a truly Sullan scale. Among the many victims of this new terror was Cicero; he met his end with courage and dignity. The proscriptions were followed by something new in Roman history, the proclamation of the divinity of Julius Caesar. It met with an enthusiastic reception from the people. It also gave to Octavian a novel distinction: he was now *"divi filius,"* son of the deified Caesar. Then Antony and Octavian followed the Liberators to Greece. Once again the forces of the West, in the name of Caesar, met those of the East, fighting for the Republic. In the two engagements of Philippi (42 B.C.), the West was again successful. Brutus and Cassius committed suicide, and two more names were added to the list of republican martyrs.

The victory of Philippi left the Caesarean party triumphant. But it still had three leaders, and there was an ugly precedent for the rivalries to which that might lead. For the moment, Antony's reputation stood highest, much enhanced by his conduct of the campaign of Philippi. That of Lepidus was on the wane. Octavian had consolidated his position with the army and the people, but he had not done well in the war. So it was natural that Antony should take up the major task after the defeat of the republicans—the re-establishment of order in the East and the projected war against Parthia. Octavian got what seemed a thankless task —control of Italy, and supervision of demobilization and land grants for veterans, together with a watching brief against Sextus Pompeius. The land grants could only be invidious. The eighteen Italian cities whose lands were to be confiscated resisted; with the encouragement of Antony's partisans in Rome there broke out the confused and confusing War of Perusia, which resulted in the destruction of that ancient Etruscan city. With a large force, Antony sailed for Italy. To the universal horror, the third round of the Civil War seemed imminent. But the situation was resolved by diplomacy, not by arms. By the treaty of Brundisium (October, 40 B.C.), the Triumvirate was renewed. Antony got all the provinces east of Illyricum, Octavian the West, except Africa, which went to Lepidus. To complete the reconciliation, Antony married Octavia, sister of Octavian. Men could hope for peace again, and hope and relief found expression in the *Fourth Eclogue* of Virgil, a messianic vision of a new Golden Age.

A year later, the Triumvirate was extended to include Sextus Pompeius, who got three provinces and control of the fleet. But the hopes of the *Fourth Eclogue* were premature. Universal peace still lay ten years in the future, beyond fresh civil wars. It was a decade marked by the rivalries of the dynasts, and also by the personalities of three remarkable women. Octavia was devoted to her brother and to her husband, and so long as she retained her influence with Antony she was a force for peace. No other woman won such widespread respect, even love, from the Roman people. In 38 B.C. Octavian married Livia Drusilla, a young matron whose husband divorced her to allow him to do so. It proved an ideal match. A member of the great house of the Claudii, beautiful, intelligent, and clever at handling her husband, Livia's influence had much to do with the transformation of the cold-blooded and ruthless young Octavian to the wise and benevolent Augustus of later years. Cleopatra, the last ruler of independent Egypt, united in herself the traditions of the Macedonian and the native rulers of the land. The Macedonian dynasty had produced many remarkable princesses, and Cleopatra was very conscious of her role as the last heir of Alexander and his ideas. But she spoke Egyptian as well as Greek; she was also the heir of the Pharaohs, and like them, daughter of Ra, the sun god. Her land was wealthy but weak, the beauty and charm of its queen among its greatest assets. She had won Caesar's favor when he came to Alexandria and had borne him a son; later she followed him to Rome and perhaps hoped for marriage. Caesar was dead—but there was a Roman in the East more biddable yet, Antony, "whom ne'er the word of 'No' woman heard speak." It was as a move in the game of high politics that Cleopatra in 40 B.C. made her famous journey to Cydnus to meet Mark Antony. She won him, as she had Caesar, and after her return to Egypt bore him twin children. But then came the marriage to Octavia, to cut across all the ambitions of the queen of Egypt.

From 39 to 37 B.C. Antony ruled the East from Athens, with Octavia at his side. Frontiers were strengthened, client kingdoms reorganized, an invasion of Syria by the Parthians repelled. In 37 he met Octavian again, at Tarentum, and

the Triumvirate was renewed for five years. Then he set out
for the long-delayed war against Parthia. Octavia did not
go with him, but Cleopatra was summoned to meet him in
Syria.

Between 37 and 33, their own ambitions and the course
of events opened a wide breach between Antony and Octavian.
They were years that Octavian put to good use. In 36 he
defeated Sextus Pompeius at the battle of Naulochus. Soon
afterward he eliminated Lepidus, winning over his troops by
persuasion to his own side. By now he had solid support in
Rome and Italy, and had found ministers of high quality,
for Agrippa was a great marshal, and Maecenas a first-rate
administrator and diplomat. For Antony, these were years
of decline, caused, above all, by the failure of his two campaigns in Parthia (36 and 35 B.C.). All he could salvage was
a triumph over Armenia, and he made the mistake of
holding this in Alexandria. He was coming to depend more
and more on Cleopatra, and on the wealth of Egypt. He
had contracted some sort of marriage with her—though a
legal Roman marriage it could not be—and assigned Roman
provinces and cities to the queen and her children.

A clash between the old Caesarean leader and his younger
rival could not be long delayed. It was preceded by a bitter
war of propaganda, from which came the stories of the
grandiose plans of Antony and Cleopatra for a new universal monarchy, of which the capital would be Alexandria,
not Rome. Octavian won the war of pamphlets as de-
cisively as he was to win the war of arms. Consul for 31 B.C.,
and reinforced by an oath of personal allegiance from the
people of Rome and Italy, he was able to take the field
as the constitutional champion of the West in a war declared against Cleopatra. Antony mustered against him all
the Roman forces of the East, reinforced by the fleet of Egypt.
In September of 31 B.C. the two naval forces confronted
each other off the Adriatic coast close to Actium, the site
of a famous temple of Apollo. The accounts of this mysterious
battle maintain that, before action was joined, Cleopatra's
squadron hoisted sail and made away. Antony went in a
pinnace to her flagship, boarded it, and for two days sat
in the bows and would speak to no one. Deserted by their
leader, the Antonian forces fought on long enough for honor,
then surrendered to the mercy of Octavian. The last struggle was fought a year later on Egyptian soil. When it went
against him, Antony committed suicide. Cleopatra followed
him a few days later, some accounts say after an attempt
to seduce Octavian.

The story is told of a Spanish brigand admonished on his deathbed to forgive his enemies. "Father," was his reply, "I have no enemies. I have shot them all." Such was the position of Octavian, at the age of thirty-two. He was the sole master of a world longing for peace, deeply conscious of the blood guilt of three sets of civil wars in less than twenty years. The writers of the time often recur to the legend of Romulus and Remus—Rome had been founded in the shedding of brother's blood. War weariness and guilt were to be among Octavian's greatest assets as he worked for a lasting settlement of the problems of the Roman world.

CHAPTER VII

SOCIAL AND CULTURAL LIFE OF THE LATE REPUBLIC

It is scarcely possible to give a full and balanced account of the economic life of Italy in the last century of the Republic. No uniform, regular statistics were kept of even such elementary factors as production, wages, and prices. In their place, we have a mass of individual instances, often highly detailed, but hard to fit into a coherent picture. Yet certain generalizations can be made. First, it is clear that the conquest of the Mediterranean world brought an enormous increase of wealth to Rome and Italy. Not even the incessant civil wars could make serious inroads on a standard of living that was constantly rising—for some. For this new wealth was very unevenly distributed. There were fortunes to be made from banking, moneylending, tax farming, war contracts, building, real estate, and the import-export trade. The great wars in Gaul and the East gave booty and gratuities to all who took part, from the commander to the common soldier. The proscriptions offered a quick way to wealth for astute operators on the winning side. So the first century B.C. was marked by the appearance, for the first time in Roman society, of a new class of super-rich, men like Pompey, Crassus, Sulla, and Lucullus. And of course such multimillionaires could only arise from a much larger number of wealthy or merely well-to-do.

For the first time, after about 80 B.C., Rome became familiar with the economics of conspicuous waste. Huge country houses were built—still called by the old rustic name of "villa"—in favored places such as Tivoli, the Alban hills, and the fashionable watering places around the Bay of Naples, and there was a boom in real estate like that of Florida in the 1920's. But the owners of these houses would also maintain great palaces in Rome, where, in Cicero's time, there were a hundred town houses finer than anything in the previous century. Precious marbles were brought from all parts of the world for these houses, their ceilings were coffered and inlaid with gold, they had elaborate mosaics and wall paintings and costly furniture. Private libraries were kept, and the masterpieces of Greek sculpture, both copies and originals, were displayed. Large staffs of highly trained and expensive servants were needed to run them, especially for the elaborate banquets which became a fashionable entertainment. On the country estates vast sums were spent on laying out parks and gardens, growing exotic plants and trees, and breeding oysters and other delicacies for the table. Blooded horses, smart carriages, yachts, expensive mistresses with their jewelry, clothes, and cosmetics, helped the Roman playboy to squander his father's wealth. All this may be read in the Latin authors of the time, who never tire of contrasting it with the simplicity of the old ways by which Rome had grown great.

But not all the new wealth of Italy went into extravagance. Much of it was used to try out the new methods in farming and stock breeding; such new experiments brought benefits to Italian agriculture as a whole. Under scientific management, the production of wine and olive oil outstripped that of cereals to become the most lucrative forms of agriculture. In full production, a good vineyard would give an annual return of 18 per cent on capital invested. It was now that vintage wines such as Falernian established their reputation, and Italian wines in general began to dominate the home market and to be in demand for export. The olive and its products were basic to the economy of the Mediterranean world. The cheaper grades of oil were used for lamps, the finer for cooking, in the absence of butter; a great variety of fine olives were eaten raw. It was of great importance that the Italian olive merchants now entered the export market on a large scale. But cereals continued to play an important part. Despite the import of grain from the provinces for the Roman grain dole, it was still necessary to draw on Italian sources. Outside Rome, the needs of the growing population of the Italian towns were met almost wholly by the Italian grain harvest. Etruria was the great grain land, though Apulia and Campania were also important. While much of the labor was done by slaves, there is evidence of free tenants on some of the big estates. But in general these were bad times for the small farmer, tenant, or proprietor in Italy itself; there were still prospects for him in the Po valley and Gallia Narbonensis, but many preferred to leave the land for the cities.

Pedigreed strains of horses, sheep, and cattle were evolved at this time, and the great ranchers of the South grew rich on the increased yield of wool and hides. The huge urban market of Rome encouraged the growth of specialized lines such as beekeeping (in the absence of sugar, honey was the universal sweetener), market gardening, fruit growing (apples, pears, figs, cherries), and the rearing of game birds and poultry. The domestic fowl played little part in this; the hen was valued for its eggs rather than the table. But pigeons, ducks, thrushes (fieldfares), guinea fowl, and peacocks were all reared for the poultry market. The economics of these operations were studied, with careful attention to cost. For example, it was found that thrushes fattened more quickly when they were fed on dates. But the experiment of giving them dates premasticated by slaves turned out badly—too much was swallowed by the human intermediary! On such small margins do profit and loss depend.

Industry also benefited from the prosperity of Italy and the new markets of the West. Agriculture and war needed the iron of Etruria. At Arretium (the modern Arezzo), this period saw the beginning of the famous pottery industry which was soon to enjoy boom conditions. Earthenware pottery was used as the container for every kind of liquid. Its production may be called the canning industry of the ancient world. The bronze and silverware of Campania were the most flourishing of Italian industries; they combined with a prosperous agriculture to make this the richest part of Italy. Pompeii provides archaeological evidence of this in no uncertain manner. From about 150 B.C. to the Social War, building in Pompeii, public and private, was on a lavish scale. The splendor of the wealthiest Pompeiian houses, from which came the superb wall painting to be seen in Naples Museum, far exceeded anything that had yet been built in Rome. The Social War brought a check to this prosperity, but did not end it; a lesser but substantial amount of building went on until the end of the Republic.

In Rome there was a steady growth in population, which by the end of the period had probably reached one million —the figure for London in 1800, New York in 1860. A big total for a city by any standards, for those of the ancient world it was prodigious. To feed, clothe, house, amuse—and bury—so large a population called for many big undertakings. The supply of grain to the capital from overseas, though not perfected until the early Empire, was probably the most complex operation continuously maintained until modern times. New aqueducts were built to meet the growing need for water, for both use and ornament: Rome became a city of fountains, as it is today. The public markets were enlarged, and there was supervision of weights and measures. Street traffic was regulated, and heavy delivery wagons were allowed into the city only at night. For housing, a cheap type of building was evolved, six to ten stories high, let off in apartments. Since they often stood on island sites, such houses were called *insulae*. Many of them were badly built and maintained by landlords interested only in quick profits. Such tenements were the usual dwellings of the Roman poor. The poorer quarters of the city, and notably the Subura, just off the Forum Romanum, had become squalid slums. Even in the better quarters, there was a lack of many of the services that would be thought indispensable in a modern city. There was no street lighting, no public transport, and, as yet, no proper police force.

Nor was the public architecture of the city worthy of Rome's position as a world capital. From the aediles, who held office for a year only, no great schemes of town planning could be expected. Some improvements, it is true, were made during this period. Sulla, as dictator, restored many temples and built the *Tabularium,* or record office, whose plain and noble façade still rises above the west end of the Forum. In 62–60 B.C. the temple of Aesculapius on the Tiber Island was repaired and adorned with frescoes, and the platform of the temple modeled into the shape of a ship, while two new bridges were built to the island itself. From his eastern spoils, Pompey carried out a really notable project of urban development, which included the first stone theater in Rome, modeled on the Greek theater at Mytilene and seating twenty-five thousand people, a temple of Venus Victrix, and a great colonnaded square enclosing a garden, the first public amenity of its kind in Rome. In the Curia of Pompey, part of this group of buildings, Caesar met his death.

The dictatorship of Julius Caesar offered conditions under which architecture thrives. We hear of the commission of a Greek architect and approval of a master plan to regulate future development. The Tiber was to be channeled and straightened, leaving the Campus Martius free for building purposes, with its sports activities transferred to the Campi Vaticani on the other bank. A great new basilica was constructed in the Forum, and more space for public business was to be provided by a new Forum, to be built around a temple of Venus Genetrix in discharge of a vow made at the battle of Pharsalus. Caesar did not live to complete these schemes. Had his life been longer, there is no doubt that he, not his successor, would have carried out the great transformation which "found Rome a city of brick, and left it a city of marble."

But although, for much of the period, Rome kept its old-fashioned look, the racial make-up of its population was radically transformed. For a century there had been large-scale immigration to the city, from Italy and from all parts of the Mediterranean. By the end of the Republic, Rome had become a cosmopolitan city, as it was to remain under the Empire. Many of the new inhabitants were slaves—Asiatics, Greeks, and Syrians after the Mithridatic wars, Celts and Germans from the wars of Marius and Caesar. It is hard to estimate the number of slaves in Rome at this time, but perhaps they formed between a fifth and a third of the total population, employed in a wide range of domestic, business, and industrial occupations, and especially on the labor force of public contractors. Their condition, though hard, was not hopeless. They were allowed to accumulate money, to own property, and to buy their freedom by the process of manumission, which was widely practiced. As freedmen, *liberti*, they would become shopkeepers, artisans, or petty clerks, though some found openings as builders, teachers, and doctors, and a few made large fortunes (like the baker Eurysaces, whose costly and vulgar tomb still stands by the Porta Maggiore). The *libertus* was subject to some legal restrictions, but his children became full citizens (the poet Horace was such a one). This constant reinforcement of the citizen body by non-Roman and non-Italian elements was a very important factor in the social life of Rome.

Slaves and freedmen apart, trade with the provinces caused the growth of sizable foreign communities in Rome, notably from Asia, Syria, Egypt, and, by the end of the period, Spain. It is often said that the competition of slave labor deprived the free urban poor of work, but the truth seems to be that it depressed wages rather than produced unemployment. So long as most manufacturing trades were carried on by a system of small owners, selling products made on the premises by a few workmen, there would be plenty of employment, though profits would be small. There were no doubt guilds for each trade, as at Pompeii and other Italian towns, though there is little evidence for Rome itself.

Greek philosophy continued to expand the influence it had won in the days of Scipio. Young Romans followed their studies, at the university stage, in the intellectual centers of the Greek world. Many studying at Athens were swept into the armies of Brutus. But, increasingly, Rome itself was a magnet which attracted Greek savants in search of lucrative fees and a wider reputation. Philo of Larissa, founder of the New Academy, taught there after 88 B.C. Antiochus of Ascalon, afterward head of the Academy in Athens, and Posidonius, the greatest thinker of the age, visited Rome to lecture. Philodemus of Gadara came in 75 B.C. and settled down to teach Epicureanism at Herculaneum, in a magnificent villa presented to him by the wealthy family of the Pisones. Another Epicurean, Siron, taught there and at Naples; to him went the young Virgil, anxious to free his mind from care, and ready to bid the Muses farewell. Fortunately for the world, he returned.

It was not an age of original thought. The great systems of Plato and Aristotle were still expounded by the schools they had founded, the Academy and the Peripatetics. The Epicureans remained faithful to the words of, their master and hostile to all other schools. But the prevailing interest in ethics was drawing the other schools closer together; Antiochus taught that there was little difference between the Academic, Peripatetic, and Stoic systems. The dominant influence at Rome was Stoicism, with its doctrine of a beneficent providence, the law of nature, and the possibility of progress toward virtue even for the layman. But this was Stoicism as modified by Panaetius; a few Romans preferred the earlier austerity and rigidity of Zeno (335–263 B.C.). Its influence can be seen in such men as Marcus Favonius, who dared to rebuke Octavian after Philippi, and above all, in Brutus and Cato the Younger. Their deaths in the Civil War began the association between Stoicism and extreme republicanism which was to be such a feature of the Empire.

Posidonius is the one great name of the age, the last first-rate mind among the Greek philosophers. Born at Apamea on the Orontes, about 130 B.C., he worked for many years with Panaetius, and then set up his own school at Rhodes. His reputation attracted many Romans, among them Cicero and Pompey. Although his works survive only in fragments, there can be no doubt of their far-reaching influence. At the center of his system lay a belief in the harmony that pervades the cosmos. In man, this is to be seen in the "sympathy" between the stars and our souls, which are also parts of the divine fire, to which they will return after death. In nature, it is seen in the influence of the moon on the tides, a brilliant discovery which Posidonius made from his observations of the Atlantic on the shores of Africa and Spain. He was a great traveler, deeply interested in the barbarian peoples of northern and western Europe. These were the peo-

ples destined to be conquered and civilized by Rome, and
Posidonius taught that the universal empire of Rome corre-
sponded to the universal state of all mankind postulated by
the law of nature. The Roman statesman who governs this
empire with justice and virtue is fulfilling the highest of
earthly missions, to be rewarded after death by personal im-
mortality. This is the idea expounded by Cicero in the famous *Dream of Scipio*. On the scientific side, Posidonius'
interests led him to the study of astronomy, geography, and
meteorology; he was also interested in mathematics, rhetoric,
and history. He wrote a history of Rome from 146 to 70 B.C.,
as a continuation of Polybius. Few Roman writers of the next
two generations escape his influence.

Nor should the importance of Cicero be underestimated.
Although he describes his philosophical works as mere com-
pilations (the only activities of his about which he is so modest!) they have had an influence seldom attained by works of
popularization. Essentially, they deal with problems of personal and political conduct from the standpoint of a civilized
and kindly gentleman. Without profundity, they are informed
by a humanity which deeply impressed not only his contemporaries, but all European thought from the Renaissance
to the eighteenth century. The modern world, which has deserted Cicero as a philosopher, has followed some much
worse masters.

But Greek philosophy, as a guide to life, could satisfy only
a section of the educated class. Far wider, and in the long
run of much greater import, was the appeal to all classes of
the mystery cults of Greece and the Orient. We are not so
well informed on Roman religion in this period as in that of
Augustus and later, but there can be no doubt that the spread
of these cults was its chief feature, and the reasons for this
are clear. In part, it was due to the large number of Greeks
and Orientals in the population of the city, in part to Roman
contacts with Asia and Syria, but, above all, to a deep need
for religious and spiritual guidance in the terrible times of
the later Republic. The Bacchic and Orphic mystery cults
had come to Rome from the Greek cities of southern Italy by
the beginning of the second century B.C. The attempt of the
Senate to put down the orgiastic features of the Bacchic cult
in 186 B.C. seems to have had no lasting effects. The Villa of
the Mysteries and the Villa Item at Pompeii display famous
frescoes of the rites of the Bacchic initiates. These date from
the early part of the first century B.C.; Rome itself has nothing
comparable before the early Empire. But the symbols of the
Bacchic mysteries are frequent in Arretine pottery and on

other *objets d'art,* and the literary references to Bacchus
gain in significance when we remember how widespread the
cult was. All these mysteries, of Eleusis, Bacchus, or Orpheus,
promised initiates a life beyond the grave, with rewards or
punishments according to their conduct on earth. Their rich
ceremonial and profound symbolism satisfied a need for personal religious experience in a way that the formalism of the
state cults could never do. Small wonder that they won so
many adherents at this time.

The Oriental cults made slower progress, and often met
with official hostility. Although Cybele had been brought to
Rome in the Second Punic War, the Romans still loathed her
eunuch priests and their lewd rites. They were strictly confined to their temple on the Palatine except for an annual
procession which took the cult image to be washed in the
waters of the Anio. The Megalesia, the ceremonies at which
Rome discharged her debt to the Great Mother, were organized on strictly Roman lines. When, in the consulship of
Pompey, the High Priest of Pessinus came to complain of
some disrespect to the cult, he was very coolly received by
Senate and people. Not until the reign of Claudius was the
cult encouraged to proselytize. Again, when Sulla's soldiers
brought back the worship of the goddess Ma from Cappadocia,
Roman opinion was horrified by her dancing dervishes and
their bloody gashings. But the Egyptian cult of Isis and
Serapis met with widespread popular support. This cult,
which united Egyptian beliefs with Greek ritual and liturgy,
had appeared in Sicily and southern Italy about 300 B.C.
The temple of Serapis at Puteoli was founded about the
same time. The first temple in Rome belongs to the age of
Sulla. Five times in the next forty years did the Senate order
the destruction of the temples of these Egyptian divinities;
in 48 B.C. the shrine pulled down was on the Capitol itself.
In the years before Actium there was official hostility to all
things Egyptian, but popular support maintained the cult into
the Empire. It will be more convenient to describe it when
we come to consider the conflict of religions in the Empire,
but it is important to note that the seeds of that conflict were
laid by the spread of Greek and Oriental religions under the
late Republic.

Along with its religions came two more dubious imports
from the East, astrology and magic. Astrology derived from
Babylonia and Persia, and spread widely in the Hellenistic
world. The Babylonian priest Berosus (c. 290 B.C.), who wrote
in Greek, was important in its transmission. So was the
collection of writings under the name of Petosiris, sum-

ming up the astrological and magical lore of Egypt, and probably made in Alexandria about 150 B.C. The prisoners taken in the wars against Antiochus are said to have brought astrology to Italy. As early as 139 B.C. the praetors banned from Rome the "Chaldaei"—itinerant astrologers selling horoscopes and telling fortunes. But astrology reached higher social levels than this. It is fundamental in Posidonius' doctrine of "sympathy"—he was, after all, born at Apamea —and the Stoics played a leading part in familiarizing Roman society with the doctrines of the seven planetary divinities, the twelve signs of the zodiac and their influence, and the fatalism that derives from these beliefs. Under the Empire the influence of astrology became all-pervading. Even under the Republic there were men like Nigidius Figulus, senator and occultist, who foretold the future greatness of Augustus at the hour of his birth. As for magic, there was—and still is—a flourishing indigenous tradition of witchcraft in Italy. The wise woman of the Marsi and the Sabines could dispense love potions, cures and curses, and look into the future. But the Orientals brought with them magic of a more potent and sinister kind. In the *Epodes* of Horace we get a glimpse into a sub-world of filthy midnight hags in the slums of Rome, robbers of graveyards and raisers of ghosts, dealers in poisons and infant sacrifice. It is close to the Black Magic of the Middle Ages and the Voodoo of modern times, and its presence in the world of Cicero and Lucretius is a reminder of the wide span bridged by the culture of a single society.

The literature of the late Republic shows what that society could achieve at its highest levels. The portion of it which we possess gives a misleading impression of discontinuity, of a gap between the writers contemporary with Scipio Aemilianus and those of the age of Cicero. To correct this, we must take account of the reasons for the survival of some authors and the loss of others. Chief among these is the eclipse of lesser names by a greater—of his friends among the "new poets" by Catullus, of his famous rivals in oratory by Cicero. The latter example is particularly striking. How rich Roman oratory was in its greatest days can be seen from the fact that a bare list of orators and speeches which can be dated to the years 81–42 B.C. covers more than three printed pages. How misleading, then, the silence which for us surrounds the mighty voice of Cicero! So too with the historians: Caesar and Sallust appear now as isolated peaks, but they were really part of a continuous Roman tradition of historiography going back to the third century B.C. One would indeed expect the political struggles of this period to produce a harvest of contemporary history, memoirs, and propaganda, like the great "war of pamphlets" of the time of the Gracchi, and of the rivalry between Octavian and Antony. In the fifty years before the death of Sulla, we hear of the memoirs of Cornelia, Rutilius Rufus, and Aemilius Scaurus, as well as those of the dictator himself. The times of Sulla produced an historian of some stature in Claudius Quadrigarius: his *Annales* were drawn upon by Plutarch for the *Lives* of Marius and Sulla and gave—not unnaturally—a favorable picture of the dictator which it would be interesting to have. But, in this same period, literature was not confined to the two great Roman traditions of oratory and history. Lutatius Catulus, the colleague of Marius in the defeat of the Cimbri, was a man of all-round culture, philhellene, connoisseur, orator, lyric poet, and the patron of poets. It has been said that with him Alexandrianism enters Rome. His contemporary, Afranius (C. 150–94 B.C.), the best-known writer of *fabulae togatae*, plays dealing with Roman life, had a vogue which lasted until the reign of Nero, and is known to us by the titles of forty-three plays and a few fragments, unfortunately too short to give any real idea of this highly individual genre. But there were no writers of tragedy and comedy in the line of Ennius and Plautus. Changing taste had led to a decline of popular interest in the theater; in its place, the cheaper thrills of the gladiatorial contests and the chariot race held sway. But there was still a faithful public to support revivals of the old repertory of plays, and to provide actors like Roscius with a handsome reward. Laevius was the most notable poet of Sulla's time; his *Erotopaegnia* seems to have been a forerunner in subject of Ovid's *Heroides*, and his style, with its archaisms, neologisms, and Alexandrianism, offers parallels to that of Catullus and his friends.

These last were a group of young poets, mostly from Cisalpine Gaul, who were writing in Rome about 60 B.C. They took their poetic models not from early Latin literature nor from classical Greece, but from the poets of Alexandria, with their insistence, in style, on lightness of touch and a high polish; and in subject, on personal experience or the unfamiliar reaches of mythology. Thus Caecilius of Novum Comum wrote a poem on Cybele, Cinna on Zmyrna, and Cornificius on Glaucus. Their new doctrine made a stir at the time and left a mark on later writers such as Virgil and Propertius. So little of them survives that we can only judge the movement by Catullus, though there is

no reason to think that any of the others were of his stature
as a poet. Catullus himself was born in Verona in 84 B.C.,
of parents rich enough to own a villa on Lake Garda and another at Tivoli. In 62 he went to Rome, probably to follow
Clodia, the wife of the governor of Cisalpine Gaul. She was
the Lesbia of his poems and the passion of his life. Women
like Clodia were new in Rome. She was a great lady, a beauty,
and a bitch. Cicero calls her "the farthing whore" for her
promiscuity, and "the Medea of the Palatine" from the
suspicion that she poisoned her husband. Out of this liaison
came some of the most direct and moving love poetry ever
written—the poetry of which Yeats spoke as

> the lines
> That young men, tossing on their beds
> Rhymed out, in love's despair,
> To flatter beauty's ignorant ear.

Finally, after extremes of rapture and debasement, Catullus
broke with her. Later he spent a year in Asia on the staff
of the governor of Bithynia, cruised among the Isles of Greece,
and came back to Lake Garda and to Rome. He died at the
age of about thirty. The Lesbia poems are those on which
his fame rests, and which set him beside Sappho, Burns, and
Dafydd ap Gwilym. But it is quite wrong to neglect the
longer, mythological poems, or to set up the "learned poet"
(*doctus poeta*) of Alexandria against Lesbia's lover. Catullus'
experience informs almost all he wrote. The *Attis* shows the
disasters to which love's frenzy can lead, and ends with a
plea for freedom from its madness; the *Marriage of Peleus
and Thetis* shows Ariadne, deserted and betrayed, finding
consolation at last in the mystic rites of Bacchus. Such a
peace the poet himself may have found before his early
death.

To read Catullus after any other Latin author is like coming, in the Uffizi Gallery in Florence, to the *Primavera* of
Botticelli after a surfeit of madonnas. That the world can
enjoy this experience is due to the survival of a single manu-
script in Verona, the city of his birth—the city, too, of
Romeo and Juliet.

Lucretius (c. 94–c. 50 B.C.), the other great poet of the
Republic, belonged to no poetic school and says almost
nothing about himself. It seems likely that he was a Roman
and an aristocrat. His poem *De Rerum Natura* (*On the Nature of the Universe*) was written to expound the philosophy
of Epicurus to a Roman audience. It must be remembered

that Epicurus sought scientific knowledge as a missionary rather than as a scientist. He is concerned to show that all natural phenomena can be explained by reason, rather than with the true explanation of any one. Hence the uneven quality of the scientific theories in his system. Its physics —that of the earlier atomists Leucippus and Democritus— was a brilliant piece of scientific insight, anticipating the atomic theory which held the field from Newton to the discovery of nuclear fission. Its astronomy was childish, far below the best thought of the day, and could not have survived the test of even the simplest observation and experiment.

The evangel that Lucretius propounds is that the universe consists solely of atoms and the space in which they move. The world as we know it is the chance product of atomic motions that have gone on from infinite time past, and will continue to an infinite future. The gods, though they exist, have neither the wish nor the power to intervene in this mechanistic process. Our souls are no more than a combination of atoms, which will dissolve at death to leave nothing behind. Once men grasp this truth, they can emancipate themselves from fear of the gods and of punishment after death, the two great sources of crime and misery in life. True happiness is now in their reach. It lies in the simple satisfaction of bodily needs, and the use of the intellect to contemplate the world of nature.

If this is an evangel, it has been said, it is one of the gloomiest ever offered to mankind. Certainly, Epicureanism was a selfish and defeatist creed. Perhaps—like Clodia!—it did not deserve to become the subject of great poetry. Yet there is nothing gloomy about Lucretius' exposition of the triumph of the human intellect, which can range beyond "the flaming ramparts of the world" to watch the workings of nature through an infinite but intelligible universe. The intellect, too, will carry us back in time to the evolution of the earth with its seas and mountains, to the origins of vegetable and animal life, to see how their generations "like runners in a relay race hand on the torch of life," and to watch the progress of man from a life of primitive squalor to civilization, by his own efforts and without any supernatural aid. "All this they learned by practice and the inventiveness of the eager mind, as they went forward step by step." The great forces of nature are the heroes of this epic of science—"the moon, night and day, and the stern signs of the night, night-wandering torches and the flying fires of heaven, clouds, the sun, storms, snow, the winds, lightning

and hail." . . . Yet he has for the particular the keen eye
of the old naturalist, undimmed by microscopes. He shows
the cow lowing for its lost calf, the motes in a sunbeam,
the hound twitching in his sleep as he dreams of hunting,
"the hawks and ospreys and shags, seeking life and liveli-
hood in the salt waters." For human life Lucretius has both
scorn and compassion. No other poet can match his satiric
picture of the ennui of the idle rich, or the pathos of his
description of the wife and children, bereaved by death.
Lucretius was known and admired by Virgil; apart from
that, he left little mark on Latin literature or thought. In
the Middle Ages his poem was placed on the list of banned
books. Since the Renaissance he has been recognized as
among the very greatest of the world's poets, and his theme
should commend him above any other Greek or Roman author to the mind of the modern world.

Cicero dominates, in every sense, the prose of the late
Republic. The Ciceronian corpus—fifty-eight speeches, seven
works on oratory, nearly twenty on philosophy, and the
epistles—crowds the works of Caesar, Sallust, and Varro
into a small corner of the shelf. What is left of Varro, that
is, for he was in fact the most voluminous of Latin writers,
and his fifty-five titles and some five hundred separate books
covered history, archaeology, linguistics, philosophy, education, and agriculture. His *Disciplinae* was the most important
Latin encyclopaedia, from which derive the seven liberal arts
of medieval education. The *Imagines,* biographies of distinguished Romans, was the first illustrated book in the world.

That Cicero has survived, while most of Varro is lost, is
due above all to his incomparable mastery of the Latin language. Like Shakespeare in English, he could play on all the
notes; passionate, persuasive, or humorous to suit the occasion in his speeches, lucid and easy in philosophy, graceful
and familiar in the letters. He perfected Latin prose, and
made it one of the world's great instruments of thought and
expression. Ciceronian Latin was the chosen model of the
Renaissance, and so came to have a far-reaching influence
on modern European languages, especially Italian, English,
and French. Molière's character who found that he had
been talking prose all his life was in debt to Cicero—as
are we all, whether we know it or not.

The generation of Cicero saw the high noon of Roman
oratory. In politics and at the bar great rewards awaited
forceful and persuasive speech. Cicero is said to have made
not less than $45,000 a year from his legal practice; his
rival Hortensius was wealthier still. The study of oratory

now took a leading place in Roman education. The old and honorable tradition of Roman eloquence, which went back to Appius Claudius Caecus, was brought into contact with the latest Hellenistic fashion. For the Greeks had turned rhetoric—like everything else—into a "science"; having established its principles and analyzed its effects, the great Greek schools of rhetoric at Pergamum, Athens, and Rhodes were equipped, for a fee, to teach its practice. Some of the leading Roman orators put themselves to school with Greek masters and did not disdain, even in their prime, to take refresher courses. Gesture, delivery, diction, the marshaling of arguments, the production of emotional effects, were carefully practiced. There was much argument over the merits of the rival "styles" of oratory, the Asiatic with its rich vocabulary, rhythmic prose, and highly charged emotionalism, the Attic with its easy lucidity and grace. An elaborate technical vocabulary came into use, as translators of Roman handbooks on oratory know to their cost. The form and performance of leading speakers were criticized by an audience as knowledgeable as that which now concerns itself with the doings of a great athlete. It is easy to understand the fascination of Roman politics for Cicero, the greatest orator of the day. To take a leading part in debates in the Senate, such as those on the conspiracy of Catiline, was not only to serve the state and to advance personal ambition, but to know the rewards of a virtuoso performing before an audience of connoisseurs. No wonder he was dismayed, in his later years, to find that men of his stamp were struggling *"contra arma verbis"* —with words against arms—and that, worse still, the generals also had their professional pride.

Caesar, the greatest of them, had a reputation as an orator second only to Cicero himself. None of his speeches survive, and he is known to us by the *Commentaries*— seven books on the Gallic wars, three on the wars against Pompey. Supplements to these histories, dealing with the campaigns in Egypt, Spain, and Africa, were written by his lieutenants and published after his death. It has been said earlier that Caesar wrote to justify himself, and the reader must be on guard against the apparent candor of the Attic style. But no student of Roman history—and no serious student of military affairs—can neglect the *Commentaries*. They allow us to see the Roman army in action through the eyes of its greatest commander. Like the sculptures on Trajan's Column, they give an invaluable psychological insight into the Roman conquest of barbarian people. There are two ways of reading Caesar—fast, for the sake of the narrative—slowly, as an analysis of the art of propaganda. A high British intelligence officer has told how useful he found his knowledge of Caesar in interpreting German communiqués in the Second World War. But it is a pity that he has been used to provide the first Latin reading of schoolboys, who find either method quite beyond them.

They would do far better with the biographies of Cornelius Nepos (c. 100–c. 25 B.C.), of which those we have include nineteen lives of Greeks, one of a Persian, and two of Romans—Cato and Atticus. He was a Gaul from Gallia Cisalpina, the friend of Catullus and Cicero, and seems to have written for a popular audience. Simple and unpretentious, his biographies are notable chiefly for their freedom from Roman nationalism and their interest in the great men of other nations.

Sallust (86–35 B.C.), of Amiternum in the Sabine country, is a much weightier author. His chief work was the *Histories,* dealing with the decade after Sulla, but this survives only in fragments. We must judge him by the *Catiline* and the *Jugurtha*—the first historical monographs, it would seem, in Latin. A supporter of Caesar and a man of great wealth, Sallust settled down to write history after a career in which his morality, public and private, met with censure. His object was to uphold the views of the democratic party to which Caesar had belonged. In the account of the war against Jugurtha, he sets up Marius as a hero in contrast to the incompetent generals of the aristocracy. In the *Catiline* his purpose is more subtle. He has first to clear Caesar from the suspicion of sympathy with the conspiracy in its early stages, then to show him as taking the only sensible line among Catiline's opponents. It has been said that in Sallust we find an advance toward scientific history, but this claim can only be accepted with reserve. It is true that he used many sources (including Punic ones for Jugurtha), and that he was an ardent student of Thucydides, with an insight into political intrigue that he had no doubt gained for himself. But he is not scrupulous about dates or events, and he looks through the fixed frames of a "philosophy of history." History, for him, was determined by the characters of the leading men of action. In his hands it becomes a drama, but the characters are typed and do not evolve. From this it soon follows that the chief business of a historian is to produce a literary masterpiece. This was a view that had a dangerous fascination for the Romans, and Sallust had much influence on later writers, notably on Tacitus, a far greater historian than himself.

Greek influence was strong on the Latin writers of the late Republic. But they assimilated it and turned it to their own ends, often with results that far surpassed their models. In art things were different. Greek influence—through classical Greece or Sicily, through Pergamum or Alexandria—was overwhelming, and almost swamped the native Italian style. Almost, but not quite; the native tradition of realistic portraiture survived, and the funeral monuments of the late Republic show us the Roman face in uncompromising, sometimes alarming, realism. In this respect Greek artists working in Rome had to come to terms with Roman taste. Otherwise the vogue was for all things Greek, as it has been at times in England for all things Italian. Greek sculpture, acquired by loot or purchase, adorned the public squares and temples and the great villas. Dealers set up in Rome and Campania and the great art centers of the Greek world, and an international art market very like that of modern times was established. An eloquent commentary on this is the famous treasure ship of Mahdia, discovered as a wreck off the Tunisian coast in 1907. It contained some sixty marble columns from the quarries of Attica, and a miscellaneous cargo of works in bronze and marble, some of them repaired antiques. It may have been a consignment to a Roman art dealer, or else purchased en bloc for some great villa. Underwater archaeology is now making such progress that more such discoveries may lie ahead.

The career of Pasiteles shows what Rome had to offer to an artist. A Greek from South Italy, but a Roman citizen, he is known to have been working in the city in 62 B.C. His reputation was built up on metalworking, especially silver mirrors, but he later turned to statuary. He also wrote a book in five volumes on famous works of art of the whole world —the equivalent of the connoisseurs' guides of modern times. In art, then, the Republic was a province of the Hellenistic world, though a great and wealthy one. Not until the time of Augustus was there evolved a national art on Hellenistic models.

CHAPTER VIII

AUGUSTUS

Few statesmen in history have faced such problems as those which confronted Octavian on the morrow of Actium. Fewer still have solved them with such an imposing measure of success. While there is much that is obscure about his policy and motives, there is no doubt that his cardinal aim was that expressed in the famous prayer quoted by Suetonius in the *Life*: "May it be mine to build firm and lasting foundations for the government of Rome. May I also attain the reward for which I hope, and be known as the author of the best possible constitution, taking with me when I die the hope that these foundations will endure." He achieved his aim. The foundations of the system he laid lasted for two centuries, making possible the *Pax Romana,* Rome's greatest service to the world.

Fortune played a part by granting him a long reign. The forty-five years of Augustus were as important to Rome as the reign of Queen Victoria to England, of Louis XIV to France. But the credit must go, above all, to his own political gifts. If politics is the art of the possible, he was a supreme artist. The elaborate attempts of modern scholars to analyze and classify the Principate according to the categories of political science do not get us very far. Syme, in one of the most penetrating of recent studies, has said that "the Principate eludes definition." Augustus intended that it should. He was not interested in political science; he was a practical politician. He knew what he wanted, and he knew what Roman opinion would stand. The two could be reconciled by the skillful use of names to disguise political realities, an art brought to perfection in the *Res Gestae,* compiled in his last years. Nor is it always helpful to treat his reign under headings, such as the constitution of the Principate, social legislation, and so on. We must try to see his problems as he met them—in order of time. But always we must bear in mind the saying of Dio Cassius, that under the Republic the great issues were debated in public; under the Empire decisions were taken in secret by a few men. There is much about the Empire that we may divine but never know.

Octavian had defeated Antony as leader (*dux*) of a confederacy of all Italy—the famous *conjuratio totius Italiae.* As such he was virtually military dictator. But he was also the leader of a party, that of Caesar, the only political party left in Rome. It was time to liquidate the problems of the Civil War and to find the basis for a new order. But first, a settlement of the East, where Antony's arrangements were confirmed whenever possible, and of Egypt. The death of Cleopatra left in his hands a prize of immense value, which he did not mean to let go. "Egypt," it is stated in the *Res Gestae,* Augustus' own account of his career, "I added to the empire of the Roman people." But it did not become a province of the ordinary kind. Octavian ruled Egypt as the successor of the Ptolemies, as they had done as heirs of the Pharaohs. The revenues of the land had always belonged to its ruler. Immediately, the treasure of Cleopatra gave him money to buy lands for the settlement of veterans, for the army was to be reduced from sixty legions to twenty-eight. On August 13, 14, and 15, 29 B.C., Octavian celebrated a threefold triumph—"Before my chariot walked nine kings or children of kings."

There followed acts designed to show the character of the new regime. There was an amnesty for the followers of Antony. Arrears of taxes were canceled and the records destroyed. The Senate was purged and reduced in numbers. The splendid temple of Apollo on the Palatine was consecrated, in discharge of a vow made at Actium. The Temple of Janus was closed as a sign of general peace. Eighty-two other temples in the city were put in hand for repairs. But harmony was disturbed by an awkward incident. Marcus Crassus, grandson of the triumvir, had fought successfully on the frontiers of Macedonia and earned a triumph. More than that, he had killed an enemy chief with his own hands, on the strength of which he claimed the right to dedicate the *spolia opima* in the Temple of Jupiter Feretrius. This was the rarest of military distinctions. It had been won only three times; a fourth, just now, would never do. The reply to Crassus was that the honor was reserved for commanders fighting under their own auspices; he had been fighting under those of Octavian. But, retorted Crassus, one of the three

previous holders, Cossus, had only been a military tribune.
Archaeology came to Octavian's rescue at this point: the
restoration of the Temple of Jupiter Feretrius discovered
Cossus' dedication, and showed him to have been consul.
There was no precedent for Crassus' claims; and at Rome,
what was unprecedented could not be allowed. Crassus and
his pretensions disposed of, Octavian addressed himself in
earnest to find bases for his own unprecedented position.

In January, 27 B.C., at two meetings of the Senate, the solution was disclosed. What conferences or discussions preceded them, we do not know; but obviously the meetings
themselves were most carefully stage-managed. At the first,
Octavian resigned all his powers to the Senate and people.
Cries of protest—he must not abandon the Republic which
he had saved. Would he be willing to accept proconsular
imperium for a term of ten years over Gaul, Spain, and
Syria? He would; but the Senate, people, and magistrates
must resume their old functions. Three days later came the
quid pro quo. A grateful Senate voted him a laurel wreath
for saving the lives of citizens, a golden shield inscribed
with his virtues of clemency, valor, justice, and piety, and
the name of Augustus. The month Sextilis was renamed in
his honor—August to follow July.

This was the operation described, on the coins and in the
Res Gestae, as the "restoration of the Republic." "In my
sixth and seventh consulships, after I had brought to an end
the Civil Wars, . . . having attained supreme power by the
consent of all, I transferred the state from my own power to
that of the Roman Senate and People. . . . After that time I
excelled all in authority (*auctoritas*) but of power (*potentia*)
I possessed no more than those who were my colleagues in
each magistracy." The operation was masterly, and so are
the terms in which it is described. Such emotive titles as *rex*
or *dictator* are avoided—no more Ides of March! And the
truth is told. The magistrates of the Republic continued to
function, under the same names, and Augustus was a Republican magistrate, elected by the Senate for a limited period of years to a large but not unprecedented command. But
it is not the whole truth. Gaul, Spain, and Syria gave him
command of most of the armed forces, which already looked
to him as their *imperator.* He had held the consulship every
year since 31 B.C., and so could control the proconsular
governors of senatorial provinces. He disposed without check
of an immense revenue, hardly less, perhaps, than that of
the state. The Senate was filled with his adherents, and all
patronage was in his control. It might be true that in any

one magistracy he held no more power than his colleagues, but his agglomeration of powers, though all derived from magistracies of long standing, put him in a position that no one could challenge. *Auctoritas* on this scale was *potentia* in the highest degree. Moreover, there were the supernatural connotations of his position as *divi filius,* son of the deified Julius, and of the name Augustus, a term of majestic import and good omen—for Romulus had founded Rome *augusto augurio.* Here, it could be inferred, was another Romulus for a second foundation. But, formally, Augustus described his position by no loftier a title than *princeps,* another word deliberately left vague, but in such contexts as *princeps senatus* implying primacy among equals. Such, in outline, was the first Augustan settlement.

Good authorities are lacking for the next four years. But it is clear that they were difficult for Augustus, and at the end of them he felt the need for new powers. In the summer of 27 B.C. he left for a tour of Gaul and Spain. He led in person the campaign that was to add the still unsubdued Cantabri of northwestern Spain to the Roman province. It turned into another grim Spanish struggle that was not to end until 19 B.C. Augustus' health, never robust, was unequal to Spanish campaigning, and in 25 B.C. he had to recuperate at a spa in the Pyrenees. Meanwhile, in 26 B.C., there had been bad news from Egypt. Cornelius Gallus, Virgil's friend and the first Roman governor, was publicizing his successes in a war against Ethiopia beyond what was allowable in a holder of that office. He was recalled, and committed suicide. Then Augustus, on returning to Rome in 23 B.C., fell desperately ill again and seemed likely to die. Cold baths and a good doctor pulled him through, but now the problem of his successor had to be faced, although he was only forty. Livia had borne him no children—the first of many domestic griefs. His nearest male relative was a dearly loved nephew, Marcellus, son of his sister Octavia; Augustus himself had a daughter, Julia, by his first marriage. In 25 B.C. the cousins were married; from their union Augustus hoped for grandsons, though it was uncertain, as yet, whether Roman sentiment would accept a dynastic succession. There were also Livia's sons by her first marriage, Tiberius and Drusus. But immediately, Agrippa, the great marshal and administrator, whose unselfish loyalty had sustained so many tasks, was the obvious successor, and to Agrippa Augustus had given his signet ring when the end seemed near. But he had recovered, and things changed again. Marcellus could be brought forward and Agrippa kept in reserve.

His own illness, and a conspiracy in 25 B.C., caused Augustus to revise his own powers. Refusing in 23 B.C. what would have been his twelfth consulship, he was given proconsular power over the whole empire—*imperium proconsulare maius*. He thus had overriding powers in every province, for the governors of even the Senate's provinces were under his control. So important was this *imperium* that the Res Gestae passed it over in silence! In addition, the grant of tribunician power for life gave him the right of veto and a direct link with the people. Tacitus, who neglects the settlement of 27 B.C., saw in the union of proconsular and tribunician power the real bases of the position of the *princeps*, and modern historians have claimed that this marks the true end of the Republic. Yet, at the same time, proconsular power was conferred on Agrippa for five years, since he was shortly to be given a major task in the East. This made him at least deputy leader, and some have seen in it a move toward rule by syndicate. But soon an unexpected blow shattered Augustus' plans. Marcellus died of malaria, his marriage still childless. Virgil's famous lines in the Sixth Book of the *Aeneid* have made him forever the archetype of promise cut short by early death. Yet another dynastic marriage was needed, and his young widow became the wife of Agrippa, a man of her father's age.

Many problems in the East called for solution, and Agrippa's diplomatic mission was followed by a tour of inspection by Augustus in the years 22–19 B.C. The death of Amyntas, king of Galatia, had caused a large and amorphous area east of Asia to be incorporated as a new province. The arrangements with the client-kingdoms on the desert frontiers of Syria needed overhaul. In Judaea, King Herod the Great was trying to transform that stubborn theocracy into a Hellenized client-kingdom and the loyal agent of Rome. Above all, there was Parthia. The mirage of a great Parthian War to avenge Crassus still loomed large, as can be read in the literature of the time. And at a more practical level there was the question of Armenia, where Roman influence had been at a low ebb since the campaigns of Antony.

The leisurely and dignified approach of Augustus to the East suggests that a good deal of the diplomatic spadework had been done by Agrippa. Sicily was the first province to be visited, where Sextus Pompeius had left a trail of damage. Augustus founded no fewer than six colonies in the island, the most important being at Tauromenium (Taormina) and Panormus (Palermo). In Greece, too, there were new foundations. Nicopolis in Epirus, founded to commemorate Actium,

1. The Tiber Island and the Pons Cestius.

2. The Capitol. What is seen is mostly the work of Michelangelo, but the classical layout, a piazza surrounded by buildings on three sides, is preserved. In the center was the Tabularium, on the right, the Temple of Jupiter Capitolinus, and on the left, that of Juno Moneta.

3. The Forum Romanum looking west. On the right are the foundations of the Basilica Aemilia, the Senate House, and the Arch of Septimius Severus. In the center was the Tabularium and on its left was the Temple of Saturn.

4. The Temple of Castor and Pollux.

5. Statue of a Vestal Virgin, and behind, the Basilica of Constantine.

6. The Arch of Titus, commemorating the capture of Jerusalem.

7. The Mausoleum of Hadrian, now the Castle of Sant' Angelo.

8. Aerial view of "campaigning country" on the borders of Wales. The Roman road runs through the valley. The forts of the Celtic tribes were on the hills. Air photography has given the archaeologist a new and powerful tool. Crop-marks visible from the air show up earthworks and buildings which are invisible on the ground.

9. Aerial view of some streets and buildings at Wroxeter.

10. Aerial view of a fort.

11. Aerial view of about eight miles of the Fosse Way near High Cross.

12. Christ as a youthful, beardless figure, in the tradition of Apollo or Hermes.

Anderson

13. Coins were the most useful medium of mass propaganda in the Roman world. Consequently there were frequent new issues, especially under the Empire, and coins and their legends are valuable evidence of official propaganda and policy. A few historic issues of the Republic and early Empire are shown. a) Denarius of Augustus. Reverse, trophy: IMP. X. ACT(IUM)—The victory of Actium. b) Aureus of Claudius. Reverse, triumphal arch: DE BRITANN(IS). The conquest of Britain. c) Denarius of the civil wars. Reverse, IUDAEA. The capture of Judea.

14. a) Denarius of the early Republic—Bellona. Reverse, Castor and Pollux—ROMA. A long-lived Republican design. b) Denarius of Julius Caesar. Caesar was the first to portray himself on a Roman coin. c) Denarius of Brutus. Reverse, Cap of Liberty, daggers: EID(IBUS) MAR(TIIS). The assassination of Caesar. d) Denarius of Q. Labienus: Q. LABIENUS PARTHICUS IMPERATOR. Reverse, horse. Labienus is the renegade general who served with the Parthians. The horse stands for the Parthian cavalry.

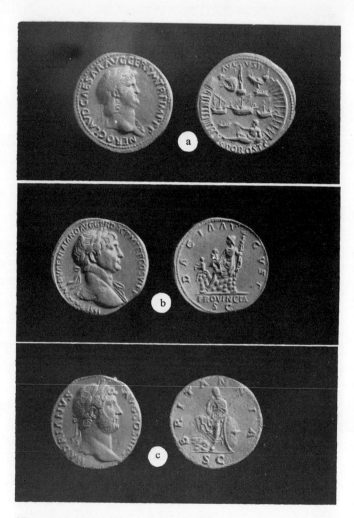

15. a) Sestertius of Nero. Reverse, AUGUSTI PORT(US) OST(IA) SC. The
opening by Nero of Claudius' new harbor at Ostia. b) Sestertius of
Trajan. Reverse, DACIA AUGUST. PROVINCIA. Dacia as a Roman
province. c) Sestertius of Hadrian. Reverse, BRITANNIA. One of
Hadrian's series showing provinces. Britannia guards her frontiers
(Hadrian's Wall?).

16. Catacomb inscription with the Christian formula, GERONTI VIBAS IN
    DEO (Gerontius may you live in God). Early Christian art borrowed
    forms and motifs from the classical tradition, as in this portrayal of
    Christ as the Good Shepherd.

17. This sarcophagus (c. 350 A.D.) is a brilliant adaptation of classical
    motifs to Christian use. In the center is the Trophy of the Cross.
    The letters Chi-Rho, the monogram of Christ, and the Roman laurel
    wreath, form the Trophy. Under the cross the Roman soldiers sit in
    the attitude of defeated barbarians. Christ is victorious over Death
    and the powers of this world.

18. Foundation of a colony (Aquileia).

RVINIS·SERVATAM·IVL·CAER·SIX·TI·IIII·PONT·NEPOS·HIC·STA

SIXTO·V·PONT·MAX·
ORD·MIN·CON
IVSTITIAE·VINDICI

Alinari

19. Imperial Eagle, perhaps from Trajan's Forum (from the Church of SS. Apostoli, Rome.)

20. Cippus from the Roman Forum—the oldest inscription in Rome (sixth century B.C.).
Alinari

21. Celtic warrior from Vacheres.
Alinari

Museo Civiltà Romana

22. Aeneas' escape from Troy (from Pompeii).

23. Trajan distributes *alimenta* to the cities of Italy (from the Arch of Beneventum).

Alinari

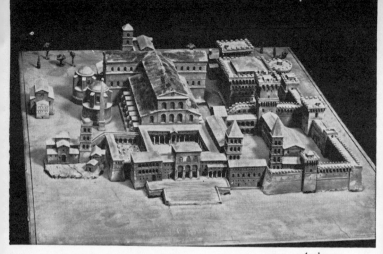

Anderson.

24. Reconstructed model of St. Peter's. It was built in the pontificate of Silvester (314-335) and destroyed by Julius II (1503-1513). It had been built over a cemetery of the first and second centuries, and excavations in 1945 revealed the modest *memoria* directly beneath the shrine of St. Peter.

25. Reconstruction of the Praetorium at Lambaesis.

Museo Civilta Romana

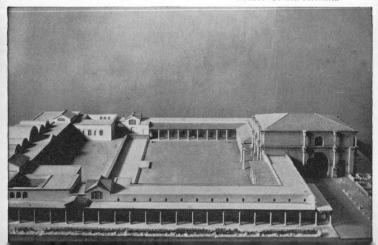

26. Reconstruction of the Acropolis at Baalbek.

27. Imperial Rome—reconstruction of the district around the Circus Maximus. Behind the Circus is the Palatine, with the imperial palaces, the Colosseum, and the Temple of Venus and Rome.

Museo Civilta Romana

28. Rome—reconstruction of the Imperial Fora.

29. Reconstruction of Hadrian's villa at Tivoli.

Alinari

was to become an important center of Roman culture in
Greece; Patrae (Patras) grew into a busy port for the crossing to Italy. After visiting Athens and Samos he went to Asia
to take up the grave problems of Parthia and Armenia. The
circumstances were favorable to Rome, since the Parthian
throne was in dispute. King Phraates was glad enough to
return Crassus' standards and what was left of his men if
the Romans dropped diplomatic support of his rival. Armenia
was a little more difficult and called for a show of force, but
in the end a Roman nominee was imposed as king. In both
these events a leading part was played by the young Tiberius.
The Armenian settlement was not to last, but nothing shows
Augustus' sagacity better than the rejection of grandiose
plans of eastern conquest in favor of a sensible arrangement
with Parthia, by which the Euphrates was recognized as the
boundary between the two empires. One other outcome of
Augustus' visit to Syria should be noted—the foundation of
a military colony at Heliopolis, the modern Baalbek, whose
gigantic temples are amongst the most imposing Roman
buildings in the world. The Temple of Zeus perhaps belongs
to a later period, but probably, as Paribeni suggests, Heliopolis was from the first planned on a lavish scale to rival the
grandiose works of the Seleucid kings in Syria. On his return
journey Augustus visited Athens for the second time, and
was initiated into the mysteries of Eleusis. He reached
Rome in 19 B.C.

There followed (17 B.C) a program of social legislation
which tried to arrest the decline of Roman morals and restore the domestic virtues of an older day. The *Lex Julia de
adulteriis* made adultery (defined in Roman Law as the sexual intercourse of a married woman with a man other than
her husband) into a criminal offense. There were heavy penal-
ties—even death, in certain cases—for the guilty parties; nor
were complacent husbands exempt. The *Lex Julia de maritis
ordinandis* was aimed at celibacy and childless marriages.
Marriage, and with a partner of suitable social standing, was
made almost compulsory for Roman citizens: benefits were
provided for parents, increasing with the size of the family:
disabilities were imposed on bachelors. At the same time,
other laws restricted luxury and extravagance, and the granting of citizenship to freed slaves. Measures of this kind, hit-
ting at everybody, cannot be popular, and a good deal of
ridicule has been directed at the social legislation of Augustus. The mordant verdict of Tacitus is that they led to a
growth in the number of informers rather than of children
—"now the country suffered from its laws, as it had done

earlier from its vices." But Augustus was surely right to think that a sound human stock in Rome and Italy was needed to hold the empire together. And his efforts met with some response—seldom, perhaps, on such a scale as that of the citizen of Faesulae recorded by Pliny, who visited the Capitol with his eight sons, thirty-five grandsons, and eighteen great-grandchildren. He set a high target of production.

In 17 B.C. the Principate had lasted for ten years. Augustus determined to mark the occasion by a ceremony which should leave an indelible impression on all who saw it—that of the Secular Games (*Ludi Saeculares*). The reappearance of the comet which had followed the death of Caesar gave supernatural sanction. According to Etrusco-Roman occult belief, a *saeculum* is a period of 100 or 110 years—it is not certain which—during which the entire human race is renewed. No one had ever seen such a ceremony before; no one would see it a second time. The details of the ceremonies of 17 B.C. are known from a huge inscription which is the official record of the Board of Fifteen, headed by Augustus and Agrippa, responsible for their conduct. Their chief features were the performances of prayers and sacrifices on three successive days and nights to certain carefully chosen deities. On the night of May 31, in the Campus Martius, the Fates were invoked to maintain the majesty and empire of the Roman people. That night the matrons offered a banquet to Juno and Diana. On June 1 there were sacrifices to Jupiter Optimus Maximus on the Capitol by day; at night, to the goddesses of childbirth. On June 2, Juno Regina was honored in the Capitol: at night, Terra Mater. The ceremonies of June 3 belonged to the Palatine. During the day there were sacrifices to Apollo and Diana: at night, outside the new Temple of Apollo, and close by the house of Augustus, choirs of twenty-seven boys and twenty-seven girls sang the *Carmen Saeculare,* composed by the poet Horace. The Roman people, triumphant over its foes, restored to its old morality, and in good standing with the divine powers, was ready to enter a new and more glorious cycle of existence. Such were the hopes behind the celebration of the *Ludi Saeculares*.

In 16 B.C. Augustus set out for the West in what was to be the last of his major provincial tours. Again Agrippa had preceded him; in Gaul he had planned a great network of roads, in Spain he had wound up the Cantabrian War (19 B.C.). Augustus spent most of his time in Gaul. The taxes were revised, and new arrangements were made for provincial and local administration. The new Gaul was to comprise three provinces besides Narbonensis—Aquitania, Lugdunensis, and Belgica, the last three under governors responsible to the emperor. At a local level, the old tribal communities (*civitates*) were to continue in these new provinces, for urban life proceeded more slowly here than in Narbonensis. The national spirit of the Gauls, which Vercingetorix had evoked, was to be won for Rome by setting up a Council of the Gauls, and as a new capital for it to meet in, Lugdunum (Lyons) was the city chosen to be the Washington or Canberra of Gaul. As the seat of the cult of Rome and Augustus, the center of the road system, an imperial mint, and the emperor's headquarters when in Gaul, it grew rapidly into the greatest city beyond the Alps. In Spain there were three provinces, Baetica in the Southeast, Lusitania in the Southwest, and the huge province of Tarraconensis covering almost the whole northern half of the peninsula. Tarraco played the same role in Spain as Lugdunum in Gaul, and there were new colonies at Emerita (Merida) and Caesaraugusta (Saragossa). The Spanish mountaineers were encouraged to enlist in the new auxiliary units of the Roman army (compare the Highland regiments raised for the British army after the '45).

It was probably during these years in the West that Augustus perfected the grand design of a new northern frontier for the Roman Empire. To its execution he committed the best troops and commanders for the next quarter-century, and his successes and failures alike have been crucial for the history of Europe. Rome was now responsible for the defense of Gaul as well as Italy, and Julius Caesar had fixed the frontier of Gaul on the Rhine. But communications between Gaul and Italy, and indeed the defense of Italy itself, called for control of all the Alpine passes. Farther east, there was the question of Illyricum and Macedonia. If access could be had to the Sava valley, a short route would be gained from the Rhine to the lower Danube, outflanking all the Balkan mountains (it is roughly that of the modern Orient Express through Zagreb to Belgrade). The campaigns of Crassus twelve years earlier had already extended Roman control into Moesia on the lower Danube.

Near Monaco, the Trophy of Augustus at La Turbie records the campaigns of Tiberius and Drusus in the western Alps, which subdued forty-four tribes and added the province of Rhaetia, the modern Switzerland and part of Bavaria, to the Empire. It was protected by two legions based on Augusta Vindelicorum (Augsburg). At the same time, the old Celtic realm of Noricum, long an ally, was made a prov-

ince, to complete the Roman hold on the upper Danube as
far as Vienna. A northern frontier seemed to be taking
shape—the Rhine-Danube line. But a bolder plan was in Augustus' mind, put there, perhaps, by Tiberius and Drusus. A
Rhine-Danube line is long—at least 750 miles from the
mouth of the Rhine to Vienna—and there is an awkward re-
entrant where the Rhine turns at a right angle beyond Basel.
And the upper Danube is uncomfortably close to the head of
the Adriatic, as NATO strategists must be painfully aware.
But an advance from the Rhine to the Elbe would give a
firmer position and a much shorter line. Hamburg-
Magdeburg-Prague-Vienna is not much more than 500 miles.
The geographer of today will point to the Oder-Dniester
line, only 900 miles from the Baltic to the Black Sea; but
this was far beyond the Roman horizon. So, in the years
after 13 B.C., as part of the same plan, operations were
started in Illyricum (Yugoslavia) and in western Germany.
Little is known of the fighting in Illyricum, but by 9 B.C. the
Roman forces—led for most of the time by Tiberius—had
reached the middle Danube and established the province of
Pannonia (western Hungary). It was now that Carnuntum
—later the chief town of the province—was first used as a
base. At first brilliant success attended the campaigns of
Drusus in Germany. Operating in conditions unknown to a
Roman army—the shores of the North Sea, the swamps of
Batavia, and the forests of Germany—the young commander
advanced in successive years to the Weser, the Ems, and the
Elbe itself near Magdeburg (9 B.C.). The outlines of a German province took shape. But in the late summer of his
third year's campaigning, he met with an accident from
which he died. His body was brought back to Rome and
buried in the Mausoleum of Augustus—another and more
poignant loss than that of Marcellus. For this was the high
tide of Roman success in Germany: had Drusus lived to
consolidate it, the history of the world might have been very
different. What if Russia had stayed in Alaska?

It is best to complete the story of the northern frontiers
here, although it will take us into the early years of Tiberius.
The decade after the death of Drusus is obscure, but since
the winter quarters remained the forts he had established
along the Rhine, with the chief bases at Vetera and Moguntiacum (Mainz), it does not look as though there were any
gains east of the river. But there were at least three expeditions north of the Danube, for a strong Germanic kingdom—
that of Maroboduus, king of the Marcomanni—was building
up in the Bohemian quadrilateral, a position from which

Napoleon once said it would be possible to dominate Europe. Certainly Maroboduus and his allies might soon be able to attack the Rhine and the Danube at once, and it became Roman policy to isolate him by diplomacy and then crush him. After the return of Tiberius to a Rhine command in 4 A.D. the policy was put into motion. In 6 A.D. all was ready for the final phase. Twelve legions were assembled for a three-pronged drive against the Marcomanni, the combined forces of the Rhine, Rhaetia, and Illyricum. But a great rebellion in the rear of the Danube army brought the plan to nothing.

The rebellion in Pannonia and Illyricum in 6–9 A.D. was one of the greatest dangers Rome ever faced, and an alarming proof of the risks of having all the military forces on the frontiers, with no strategic reserve for emergencies. It began with two risings, one among the Celtic tribes of Pannonia, a land already familiar with Roman culture and full of Italian traders and settlers, the other among the primitive hill tribes of Dalmatia. In each, a chief called Bato led a native confederacy; could they have joined their forces before the Romans had concentrated in their path, they might have swept down into Italy, and the whole frontier along the Rhine and the Danube might have gone up in flames. But they did not do so until each had been checked by the Romans; then at last they took up a strong position on the Mons Almus above the Roman base of Sirmium. In 7 A.D. they almost defeated a Roman army of five legions and auxiliaries. But Tiberius kept a firm hand on the Sava valley, and had concentrated 150,000 men at Siscia by the end of the year. The Pannonian Bato abandoned his cause and was murdered by his namesake in 8 A.D.; the Dalmatian rebellion lasted until the next year.

No sooner was the great rebellion in the Danube lands over than there was a disaster to the Rhine army—the defeat and massacre of three legions under Varus by Arminius, chief of the Cherusci. The site of the battle is unknown, but it was probably near the modern Osnabrück. Arminius had served in the Roman army, and turned his knowledge to good account as the great champion of German independence. Tacitus accords to him a higher praise than to any other barbarian leader, saying that he lost battles but never lost a war. By his massacre of three legions he had destroyed a tenth of the Roman forces and crippled the Rhine Army.

Augustus was now seventy, and he took the disasters in Germany and Illyricum very hard. There was no question of another offensive while he was alive, and his dying testament was to keep the Empire within the existing frontiers.

With this advice Tiberius agreed, and he must have known more about conditions across the Rhine and the Danube than anyone else. And, amid all the disasters, there had been one constant, encouraging factor—German disunity. Maroboduus made no move at the time of the rebellion in Illyricum; he made none after the victory of Arminius, who sent him the head of Varus to induce him to do so. "Long may the Germans persist, if not in loving us, at least in hating each other," wrote Tacitus, "for the imperial destiny drives hard, and Fortune no longer has any better gift for us than disunion among our foes." That disunion prevailed for the half-century after the defeat of Varus. Arminius died in battle with a German foe, Maroboduus in exile in Italy. For Tiberius, then, the problem was to provide the setting for an honorable withdrawal from Germany. Hence the campaigns of Germanicus, Drusus' son, in 14 and 15 A.D. They bulk large in the pages of Tacitus; they gained Rome some prestige and Germanicus a triumph. After this, it was decently possible to organize a permanent defensive frontier along the Rhine. So it was the Rhine-Danube after all: the vision of an Elbe frontier and a Roman Germany had vanished. Yet it might well seem that, of Augustus' great design, the better half had been secured. The Danube lands were worth more to Rome than the forests of western Germany; the two halves of the Empire were now firmly knit together, and Illyricum itself was to be a tower of strength in men and resources in years to come. So was solved, for the time, the problem of the northern frontiers.

When Augustus came back from Gaul in 13 B.C., the Principate had lasted for twelve years, for almost half of which he had been away from Rome. It was decided to mark his return by setting up an altar to peace—the peace which he had secured throughout the Roman world. This altar—the high-water mark of Augustan art and a superb graphic illustration of the nature of the Principate—was consecrated in 13 B.C. and dedicated in 9 B.C. In these four years a heavy change had come over the imperial family: Agrippa died in 13, Octavia in 12, and Drusus in 9 B.C. For so many of the figures of the Augustan age fate gave either early death—Marcellus, Drusus, Caius and Lucius Caesar, the grandsons of Augustus—or death in the prime of life—Agrippa, Horace, Virgil. Only to Augustus and Livia was longevity given. The last twenty years of Augustus' life were touched with the sadness of a man who has outlived his friends.

Agrippa's death brought up again the problem of the succession. Once more Julia's widowhood was cut short by a dynastic marriage—to Tiberius, who had to divorce a well-loved wife. Their marriage produced a boy who died in infancy. Augustus then turned to Caius and Lucius Caesar, Julia's elder sons by Agrippa. Though Tiberius was made consul in 13 B.C. and granted tribunician power for five years, he was not to be the heir, only the workhorse, and the protector of the young Caesars should Augustus die. It was a poor reward for his splendid service; that, and the growing unhappiness of his marriage with Julia, caused him to throw up public life and retire to Rhodes in 6 B.C. Behind all these events, as Syme has said, lie the rivalries and intrigues of court factions whose secrets we cannot unravel. Such must have been the case with the famous scandal of Julia, which blazed up in 2 B.C. and caused her to be banished to an island. Julia was a beautiful, gay, and brilliant young woman; Augustus had cast her as a brood mare. She had had six children, so she cannot be said to have failed, but it is easy to believe that it was not her favorite role. Perhaps it was natural for her to look for lovers, but that one of them should be the son of Mark Antony was too much. Their mother's disgrace did not involve Caius and Lucius Caesar; both were advanced in honors beyond their years. But again death struck at Augustus' hopes: Lucius died in 2 A.D., Caius in 4 A.D. Tiberius had seen all his rivals into the grave. In 4 A.D. he was adopted by Augustus and given tribunician power. Augustus' words were true but hardly gracious. "This," he said, "I do for the sake of the country." In 13 A.D. a special law passed by the Senate gave Tiberius proconsular power and placed him on a par with Augustus, who had only a year to live.

During the long reign of Augustus, innovation and reform transformed every organ of the state. Nowhere is this clearer than in the case of the Senate. It continued to function, it was honored, it was consulted. It renewed the grants of powers to the *princeps* and his deputies for terms of five or ten years. At the end, it confirmed Tiberius as his successor. It controlled Italy and some of the most important provinces. It even gained judicial powers, compared with the Senate of the Republic. Yet it was never strong enough to be an equal partner with the *princeps* in a joint rule of the Empire. If that is what is meant by the term "dyarchy," used by many modern scholars to describe the Augustan Principate, it is misleading. Through his control of the army, of finance, of questions of war and peace, Augustus possessed overriding powers which he could exercise without reference to the Senate and through which he was able to control their activities in a variety of ways. Election to the Senate still lay through the magistracies chosen by the people, and the published list of candidates favored by the *princeps* seemed to coincide with the people's choice. The *princeps* also controlled the exits from the Senate: at the periodic revisions of the senatorial list a contumacious individual could be removed. More than that, he controlled the business brought before them, for the practice grew up of preparing the agenda through an advisory board, made up of the *princeps*, the consuls, two other magistrates, and fifteen senators chosen by lot for periods of six months. At the end of his reign, it seems that the decisions of this body might have the force of *senatusconsulta*, thus making it an executive committee. And of course, Augustus as a member of the Senate could speak and introduce legislation. It is obvious that no real opposition could develop in the Senate, although that body never became a rubber stamp like the Reichstag of Nazi Germany. To be a senator was still a coveted distinction, partly because of traditional prestige, but more because it opened for the individual prospects of a splendid career in the public service.

It is said that great empires cannot exist without an efficient civil service. The Republic had tried to govern the Roman world with the institutions of a city-state, and this was one of the chief reasons for its failure. Under Augustus the outlines of an imperial civil service were blocked out with a firm hand, and his testament to his successors enjoined them to employ all men of intellectual and practical ability in the service of the state. A systematic organization of the civil service was undertaken by Claudius. In imperial provinces, the officials were the representatives of the *princeps* and were selected by him. The governors (*legati*) were usually senators, although Egypt, always exceptional, had a *praefectus* of equestrian rank. The financial officers (*procuratores*) of the higher ranks were *equites*; those of the lower, *equites* or freedmen. Now that the great corporations of *publicani* had lost their lucrative tax contracts, it was a good idea to use the acumen of members of that order in the public service. The governors were often given long terms of office, so that they could become experts in the problems of their province in a way that had not been possible earlier. Good salaries were paid to all grades of officials, the tax yield went to the imperial treasury, and there was machinery to investigate and redress complaints from provincials. Regular and detailed census returns were made in the provinces to form a basis for taxation. Naturally, these good standards were reflected in the senatorial provinces; in any case, the *princeps* could take a hand in their affairs in an emergency. The Edict of Cyrene (discovered in 1927) shows him intervening, tactfully but firmly, to settle a long-standing quarrel between Greek and Roman citizens in that senatorial province. While provincial misgovernment could and did occur under the Empire, the reforms of Augustus set the general level of administration very much higher than under the Republic.

Besides these reforms in the provinces, a number of great departments were set up in Rome and Italy. The *cura annonae*, which supervised the collection, storage, shipping, and distribution of provincial grain to the populace of Rome, became an imperial department. It was in charge of a *praefectus*, who held one of the most responsible posts open to the *equites*. The city of Rome was divided into fourteen districts, and was provided—at long last—with a fire service and a police force. At the end of the reign of Augustus, these were controlled by the city prefect (*praefectus urbi*), always a high officer. His post became very influential in the early Empire. Important functions were also entrusted to senatorial commissions, one of which had charge of aqueducts, another of the care and maintenance of temples in the city. This last was the outcome of the great program of urban development and conservation which made Rome a worthy capital of the Empire, and to which we shall return. A third was a highway commission, responsible for the upkeep of the great trunk roads throughout Italy. Perhaps under Augustus, certainly under Tiberius, a Tiber River Board had charge of the embankments and channel of the river. On all sides there is evidence of investigation, planning, and control. On his death, Augustus left to his successor a *Breviarium totius Imperii*—a digest of the resources of the whole Empire.

Nowhere is there a clearer contrast between the system of the Principate and the haphazard methods of the Republic than in Augustus' treatment of the armed forces. Strictly speaking, the Republic had never had a regular army, only a succession of expeditionary forces raised *ad hoc*. It is true that the incessant civil wars had meant that there was little risk of unemployment for those with a taste for a military life. But with no regular terms of service or pension, the troops were wholly dependent on their commanders for good treatment on their discharge. Moreover, Rome and Italy had to shoulder an undue share of the burden of military service, since the Republic never dared to enlist provincials on any large scale.

All this was changed by the reforms of Augustus. First, the army itself had to play a different role. Warfare within the Empire having come to an end, its task was to police the provinces and man the frontiers. The legions remained the core of the army, but their service and pay were improved and regularized. The legionary soldier served with the colors for sixteen, later for twenty years. On discharge, he received a pension from a special pension fund (*aerarium militare*) financed from death duties. Recruiting was mostly from Italy, Narbonensis, and Baetica, though the eastern legions recruited locally, especially in Galatia. The army thus became a professional long-service force, and the legions themselves developed the *esprit de corps* of the great regiments of a modern army. Even today, in such parts of the Empire as the military districts of Britain, one is conscious of the personality of the legions, the Twentieth Valeria Victrix at Chester, the Second Augusta at Caerleon, the Sixth Victrix at York, and so on. Besides their value in battle, the legions provided a reservoir of trusty officers, used to handling men, who could fill administrative posts on their retirement. Especially was this true of the senior centurions (*primipilares*): the evidence of inscriptions shows a wide variety of posts open to them. Each legion was under the command of a *legatus* of senatorial rank, who was the emperor's nominee, and the troops took an oath of allegiance to the emperor as commander-in-chief.

For Rome and Italy Augustus raised a new force, the famous Praetorian Guard, nine cohorts of 1,000 men each, enjoying very favorable terms of pay and service. Inevitably these troops and their commander came to play a decisive role in many crises in the early Empire. Their great barracks, the *Castra Praetoria,* was built under Tiberius, and the site is still used by the Italian army for the garrison of Rome.

Besides this new-model legionary army, Augustus set up another of equal size, but recruited from the provinces. Probably he was influenced by the example of Caesar, who had used Gallic troops to great effect. From Augustus onward, the auxiliary troops became an important part of the Roman forces. Recruited from imperial provinces, and commanded either by their own leaders or by *primipilares* from the legions, they were organized in units of 500 infantry (*cohortes*), and 500 or 1,000 (*alae*) of cavalry. At first it would seem that they were meant for local service—Gauls on the Rhine, Pannonians on the Danube—and their units often bear the names of the districts in which they were first raised. Later, transfers became common, and such titles have little meaning. But these auxiliary units became one of the most powerful factors working for Romanization, for they gave the provinces a share in the defense of the Empire, and —though probably not until after Augustus—Roman citizenship was granted to the auxiliary soldier, his wife, and his children, on his discharge. Archaeologists are familiar with the *diplomata*, the bronze tablets on which such grants were recorded. More than 150 are known, and they make it possible to reconstruct the army list of the Empire at certain times.

As reorganized by Augustus, the strength of the Roman army was some 300,000 men: a small force for so huge an empire, and a sure proof that Roman policy was not one of aggression. Troops were continually on the move in his reign, but under Tiberius the normal posting of the legions was: on the Rhine, eight legions; on the Danube, seven; in Syria three; Egypt one; Africa two; Spain four.

Augustus also reorganized the navy, establishing an Adriatic command operating from Ravenna, and a Tyrrhenian command from Misenum. But there were no rival naval powers in the Mediterranean, and these forces were really meant as a safeguard against piracy. There were also flotillas on the Rhine, Danube, Euphrates, and, later, the English Channel.

To the civilian Augustus was head of the state, to the soldier commander-in-chief. Yet something further was wanting as a focus for that loyalty which large cosmopolitan empires always need to evoke. It was found in the ruler cult, a device which had been employed by Hellenistic monarchs since Alexander the Great. The Seleucid kings had their temples and high priests; the Ptolemies inherited the divine status of the Pharaohs. Eminent Romans had been accorded divine honors in Greece and the East since Flamininus, and the worship of the goddess of Rome (*Dea Roma*) was already widespread. All that was needed in the East was to link the worship of Augustus with hers and to regulate the cult. Hence temples for the cult of Rome and Augustus became established at Pergamum for Asia, at Nicomedia for Bithynia, at Ancyra for Galatia; the priests were drawn from the local aristocracy, and the worship was associated with meetings of the provincial council. This Asiatic model was followed in the newly won provinces of the West—Gaul, Spain, and Germany—though as yet only altars and not temples were built. Besides these official cults at a provincial level, it was open to cities, client-kings, and individuals to express their loyalty by setting up cults of their own, and inscriptions show how widely this was done. Herod of Judaea, for example, founded the new city of Caesarea and built in it a temple of Rome and Augustus.

In Rome and Italy things were rather different. Public opinion would not tolerate the worship of a living man. But Julius Caesar had been deified after his death; Augustus bore the title of *Divi filius* and might expect divine honors in his turn. Meanwhile, there was no objection to the worship of the *genius Augusti*, the life force of his family. After 7 B.C., organizations devoted to this cult, linked with the *lares publici*, sprang up in all the city districts (*vici*) of Rome. A similar cult of the *lares Augustales*, with its own priesthood, became widespread in the towns of Italy. Besides all this, there were public celebrations of important anniversaries in the life of the emperor and his family. A calendar from Cumae (about 4 A.D.) lists sixteen in the course of the year, and at least one in every month except February and June. The most important was the two-day celebration of the birthday of Augustus (September 23–24), but anniversaries of Julius Caesar, Tiberius, and later, Germanicus were also observed.

Fate, which dashed so many of Augustus' hopes, did not deny him the reward for which he had prayed, that of taking with him to the grave the hope that the foundations he had laid for the government of Rome would long endure. In fact, they were to last for some two hundred years, surviving many bad emperors. Not until the economic and military disasters of the third century were they superseded by the orientalized despotism of the late Empire. When Augustus died at Nola in Campania in his seventy-sixth year (14 A.D.), the Principate had become part of the order of things. The Civil War had faded to a memory: very few at Rome had seen the Republic. The murder of Caesar was nearly sixty years in the past; the issues that had stirred the Liberators would raise faint echoes now. In Italy and the provinces the Republic was remembered with dislike and the Principate accepted with content or even enthusiasm. All human achievement is won at a price, and the price in this case was loss of political freedom. The bill was not due yet; but some features of Augustus' rule, such as provisions for prosecuting offenses against the dignity of the emperor (*laesa maiestas*) showed how unpleasant it would be. But meanwhile, men had found in Augustus the savior to give them peace,

prosperity, and good government. Looking forward from
Actium, that would have seemed achievement enough.

Augustus was also granted time to arrange for the smooth
transfer of power to Tiberius, and to compose his own memorial to posterity. This last is the famous *Res Gestae* or
Monumentum Ancyranum, so called from the bilingual copy
found in 1555 at Ancyra (Ankara) in Turkey. Suetonius
speaks of this document as intended to be set up outside the
Mausoleum of Augustus in Rome; presumably copies were
distributed to the provinces. After reciting the honors
granted to him, it goes on to detail the money he spent on
public objects from his own funds, then summarizes his
conquests, and ends by explaining and justifying his position in the Roman state. At once an epitaph, a triumphal
inscription, and an apologia, it projects his career in the
light in which he wished it to be read. It can never be
neglected, nor accepted without qualification.

The personal character of Augustus is hard to grasp;
Suetonius' many anecdotes do not form a coherent picture.
Perhaps Syme is right in seeing as the key to it his family
background, that of a small Latin country town. This would
account for his religious conservatism and puritanical outlook, and indeed for his simple tastes and dislike of affecta-
tion. It is significant that his great building schemes in
Rome did not include a palace for the *princeps*. It was his
successors—from Tiberius to Domitian—who turned the Palatine into a kind of Escorial. Augustus was content to live
in a modest house, which was later preserved as a national
monument, and whose remains under the name of "The House
of Livia" can still be seen today. There are certain things
about his career that must strike any fair-minded observer.
First, here is a man who actually improves with power.
Personal ambition and the desire to avenge Julius Caesar
had ruled the young Octavian. In a desperate and ruthless
struggle for power he held his own and reached the top. But
once there, he bore himself with the self-abnegation and
devotion to duty of a philosopher-emperor. Like Marcus
Aurelius, he saw the Roman *princeps* as posted to a station
from which only death could bring release. Virgil sensed
this quality in Augustus, and made of Aeneas a man who
grows greater as his responsibilities grow, and who comes,
in the end, to accept the terrible burden placed on him by
destiny. Yet Augustus seems to have avoided petrifying
into the inhumanity of the man with a mission. He liked the
company of children, he could relax with his friends, he
could find humor even at public ceremonies—as when he

said to a nervous petitioner, "You look as though you were trying to offer a small tip to an elephant." And, on his death-bed, he could ask his friends whether he had acted well in life's comedy—"If so, applaud me and send me on my way."

In dedicating to Augustus his work *De Architectura,* Vitruvius remarked that he had cared for the common life of men. The same tribute, in a rather different way, was paid by the passengers and crew of a ship from Alexandria, which his yacht passed on his last voyage. Dressed in white and wearing garlands, they lined ship and called out that thanks to him they enjoyed life and prosperity, and were free to sail the seas.

Yet, for all his incessant care for the world he ruled, the great emperor knew nothing of the most important event of his reign. In what seems to have been 8 or 6 B.C.—although by our calendars it should be 1 A.D.—Quirinius, governor of Syria, held a census in Palestine. Among the crowds going back to their native villages to register were a carpenter and his wife. They were going from Nazareth, but the young wife was pregnant, and her time came upon her when they were in Bethlehem. There was no room at the inn, and so, in a manger, was born the child whose life was to transform the Roman Empire and the world.

To the mind of the Middle Ages, which saw the birth of Christianity and the establishment of the Roman Empire as part of the same divine plan, it was not to be believed that Augustus knew nothing of Jesus. So grew up one of the most affecting of Christian legends—how Augustus, through the Sibyl of Tibur, had been granted a vision of a fair maid carrying a babe, and standing on an altar . . . "and a voice said, This is the altar of the Son of God. And straightway the emperor fell down and worshipped the Christ that was to be." This vision is said to have taken place on the Capitol, where now stands the church of Santa Maria in Aracoeli.

CHAPTER IX

AUGUSTAN LITERATURE AND ART

Few periods in history can match the creative achievements of the age of Augustus in literature and the arts. The age of Pericles in Athens, of Elizabeth in England, and of Louis XIV in France—it would not be easy to add to the list, for the Renaissance in Italy was a more complex phenomenon and spread over a longer period of time. And the term "Augustan" has been appropriated for those periods in a nation's culture which truly deserve to be called classical, periods in which the arts are in sympathy with the aims and ideals of the government. That great writers should support the Establishment may well seem a paradox in the modern world, where from the time of the Romantics they have almost always been rebels. But the program of Augustus could provide themes to enlist idealism and enthusiasm: peace after war, the destiny of Rome and Italy, the grandeur of the past, and the moral regeneration of the present through a return to its virtues. Some or all of these ideals find expression alike in the *Aeneid,* the *Odes* of Horace, the history of Livy, and the sculptures of the Ara Pacis (Altar of Peace). But, in a narrower sense, Augustus provided the conditions in which writers could flourish. He was a sound judge of literature, and no mean performer: his thirteen books of autobiography are a great loss. He knew how to attract men of genius, get them started, and let them alone.

Apart from the emperor, it was an age of great patrons, which the shallow judgment of Martial took as a guarantee of great writers. Asinius Pollio (76 B.C.–5 A.D.), historian and astringent literary critic, bridged the gap between Catullus and Virgil. He encouraged Horace and Virgil in youth, and turned Virgil to pastoral poetry. He is said to have initiated the custom of publishing new works at a public recitation. Messalla (64 B.C.–8 A.D.), who had fought on the Republican side, wrote on history and stylistics, and gathered around him a group of elegiac poets. Above all, there was Maecenas, friend of Virgil, Horace, and Propertius; his name has become a synonym for lavish munificence, and he did for the literature of his day what Lord Burlington did for the art of eighteenth-century England. Literature was the characteristic art of Augustan Rome; "Learned and unlearned alike, on every side, we all write poems," said Horace. "Poems" is the key word: it was an age of poetry, not of prose. Livy does not really constitute an exception, for his work is a prose epic. "History is close to poetry" was the surprising judgment of one of the best of Roman critics. But it was this great literary public, extending beyond Rome to the chief cities of the provinces, that provided the Augustan writers with an audience, and by no means a docile one. The Golden Age of Roman literature is unmatched by any successor. For the arts the graph is rather different; however fine the architecture of Augustan Rome, greater heights were reached in the age of Trajan and Hadrian.

Virgil is the central figure of Augustan literature, and stands at the heart of the cultural tradition of the West. He was born in 70 B.C., the only son of a farmer near Mantua in Cisalpine Gaul. The land was still a province, a vigorous frontier region of healthy agriculture and growing cities. The young Virgil went to school first at Cremona, then at Milan. Later he was sent to Rome for a course in rhetoric, which he seems to have heartily disliked. It is not certain whether he served in the Civil War, but a moving passage on the Roman dead on the battlefield of Pharsalus, and his knowledge of the coasts of the Adriatic, have led Tenney Frank to suggest that he served with Caesar and Antony in 49 and 48 B.C. Certainly his descriptions of the horrors of war suggest firsthand experience. In 48 B.C. he became a student of the Epicurean school at Naples, hoping to find there a haven of refuge. Whether he found it in the Garden of Epicurus or not, such were Naples and Campania to be for him for the rest of his life. He had already made the acquaintance of Pollio, Messalla, and Maecenas, who were to be the literary patrons of the new age.

Apart from some youthful poems whose authorship is in doubt, his first published work was the *Eclogues*, which appeared in or before 37 B.C. These poems of an idyllic countryside, where the shepherds of Sicilian pastoral tradition sing and love in a landscape which is part Campania, part northern

Italy, and sometimes beyond the ken of geography, a war-weary generation took at once to its heart:

> That is the land of lost content,
>   I see it shining plain,
> The happy highways where I went,
>   And cannot come again.

But the hopes and fears of the present broke in even to Arcady. Two poems (I and IX) show the plight of the peasants of Mantua, evicted to settle the veterans of Octavian, and say that Virgil lost his own land in this upheaval, but recovered it from Octavian himself. The Fourth is the famous Messianic Eclogue—a prophecy of the Golden Age which would come on earth now that war had ceased. It was to be ushered in by the birth of a child. To the minds of the Middle Ages, this could only be a prophecy of the birth of Christ; hence the belief in "Virgil the prophet of the Gentiles," and also the medieval tradition of Virgil the magician. From 37 B.C. onward Virgil stood close to Maecenas and Octavian. He had a house in Rome, but spent most of his time on a country estate near Naples. He worked slowly and read deeply, soaking himself in the great authors of Greek and Latin literature, especially Homer, Ennius, and Lucretius. He studied philosophy, history, mythology, and the antiquities of Rome and Italy. He was deeply interested in animals, birds, flowers, and insects, and had a sharp eye for their characteristics.

When Octavian returned from Actium in 29 B.C., Virgil gave a public recitation of his second great work, the *Georgics*. A didactic poem, we are told—indeed, Virgil says so himself—Book I dealing with corn growing, Book II with vines and olives, Book III with cattle and horses, and Book IV with bees; and since Augustus was concerned to revive Italian agriculture, the poem fits in well with the official line. All this is true. But to regard the *Georgics* as a handbook for farmers, produced on a government commission, is to miss the point grotesquely. In the first place, such a handbook would have been superfluous; Varro had already written it. More to the point, the *Georgics*, like the *Aeneid*, move on three levels. The simplest is that of the didactic poem. There are, indeed, passages on testing soil for acidity, the points of a cow, the clinical symptoms of foot-and-mouth disease, and how to get a swarm of bees to settle. But beyond this level, Virgil cared deeply for the

farmers of Italy and the part they could play in the life of
the state. He had seen Italian agriculture at its healthiest
in Cisalpine Gaul and the Ager Campanus. So the *Georgics*
portray that life in all its variety: plowing and sowing, harvest
and vintage, holidays and country fairs, but also unremitting
toil, foot-rot and cattle plagues, failed crops and blighted
hopes—yet, all in all, the best life open to man. For Virgil
has a mystical belief in Italy—*Saturnia tellus*—as the most
favored land for agriculture, where food and crops, horses,
cattle, and men can all reach perfection. The landscape
of Italy has never been better described than in a famous
passage of the Second Georgic. Beyond this again, Virgil
was deeply concerned with the whole problem of man
and his relationship to the land. He knew that civilization is
only sustained on the basis of agriculture—a fact as true in
our day as in his. So, in the *Georgics*, we are given glimpses
of the agriculture and herds of the whole world of his time—
the rich lands of Asia, the forests of Media, the famous
wines of Greece, and also the nomad shepherds of Russia and
Africa. In a romantic passage of the Fourth Georgic, we
are taken into the subterranean world of the water nymphs
and see the source of all the rivers that sustain life on
earth. In short, the *Georgics* have a universal appeal in all
ages and countries for all who care for life on the land.

After the *Georgics*, the *Aeneid*. For years Virgil had
entertained the idea of an epic poem; he had once thought
of the wars of Augustus as a theme, as Milton once thought
of a poem about Arthur. Both made a second and a wiser
choice. Virgil worked for eleven years on the story of
Aeneas, and the poem was incomplete when he died in 19
B.C. It was Augustus himself who gave the order that the
poem should not be destroyed, as Virgil had wished on his
deathbed; it was published as it stood. His choice of theme
gave him a Homeric context, yet not in a field which Homer
had made his own. So Virgil describes the capture and destruction of Troy, and how Aeneas and his followers escape
and set out in their ships to find a new destiny in a western
land. After many false starts and hardships they reach
Italy, but a storm drives them on to the coast of Africa, to
the newly founded city of Carthage. For a moment, the
destiny of Rome and her great enemy seems about to join in
the love of Aeneas for Dido, queen of Carthage. But this
love comes to a tragic end. Aeneas sails and Dido dies by
her own hand, invoking a terrible avenger who arises centuries later in the person of Hannibal. Book VI is the core
of the poem. Aeneas consults the Sibyl of Cumae, finds the

Golden Bough, and with this talisman enters the underworld. Here, from his father, Anchises, he receives the final
revelation of his destiny—a superb prophecy of the future
history of Rome, and of the Roman mission to rule the world.
At long last, Aeneas has shaken off the Trojan past to face
the Roman future. Book VII brings the Trojans to the mouth
of the Tiber, and tells of the peoples of Italy and their heroic
legends, as they muster for war. In Book VIII, they reach the
site of Rome; Aeneas, first of all tourists at Rome, is shown
around the city by the Greek king Evander. He sees the
lowing cattle in the Roman Forum, the mysterious grove
where the Temple of Jupiter on the Capitol will arise, and is
led to the simple house of Evander on the Palatine Hill
where later the house of Augustus will stand. At the end of
the book, he receives the gift of a shield made by Vulcan
and engraved with another prophecy of Roman history, with
the Battle of Actium as its climax. So, "bearing on his shoul-
ders the fame and future of his descendants," he goes to
the wars against the Italians and their great hero Turnus
which form the theme of the last four books. When Turnus
falls at last, it is the good overcome by the better, as so
many noble barbarian peoples were destined to be overcome
by Rome.

Such, in outline, is the story of the *Aeneid* on its narrative level. But, again, there is so much more. It is also
the story of the men and the qualities needed to make
Rome great: leaders like Aeneas who would persevere
through all disasters and put aside all personal aims for
their duty; men who could leave a cherished love, if it
had to be—as Aeneas left Dido, and Antony did not leave
Cleopatra. And lastly, as a great poet must, Virgil passes
beyond Rome and the Roman Empire to deal with man and
his place in the universe. For this, and for his noble style,
Dante chose him as his guide in the *Divina Commedia*.
So was formed the great chain, Homer—Virgil—Dante,
the most majestic succession in the culture of Europe.

Horace (65–8 B.C.) was Virgil's friend, and also enjoyed
the patronage of Maecenas and the friendship of Augustus.
Younger than Virgil by five years, he came from the South,
from the colony of Venusia in Apulia. His father had once
been a slave, but had made enough money to buy his freedom and give his son the best education of the day. Though
he won the intimacy of the great, Horace never tried to con-
ceal those humble origins, nor his admiration and affection
for his father. From school at Rome he went to the university at Athens; there the Civil War caught him and swept

him into the republican armies to fight at Philippi—on the wrong side. There followed a period in an uncongenial and poorly paid civil service post, reflected in the bitterness of the *Epodes* and some of the early *Satires*. From this he was rescued by Virgil, who introduced him to Maecenas in 38 B.C. Henceforth he was free from economic worries, and able to follow his literary inclinations, in which meticulous technique was oddly combined with caprice in the choice of subject and genre.

He first made his mark with the *Satires* (35–30 B.C.) modeled on the *Satires* of Lucilius, but with much greater attention to finish, and with the invective and sarcasm of the older poet generally toned down to a good-natured humor. They also reflect the influence of popular philosophy, both Stoic and Epicurean. The setting is usually Rome, with some vivid pictures of the daily life of the capital in the years before Actium. But at heart Horace preferred country life, and its pull grew stronger with time. In 31 B.C. Maecenas gave him the farm in the Sabine country a few miles from Tivoli that became his dearest possession for the rest of his life. He was offered, but declined, the post of private secretary to Augustus, preferring to go off on another literary tack, that of lyric poetry.

In 23 B.C., after eight years' work, he gave the world what he regarded as his greatest poetic achievement, the three books of the *Odes,* containing eighty-eight lyric poems on a wide range of themes and in a variety of Greek lyric meters which Horace handled with consummate mastery. Lyric poetry is usually thought to go with youth—though Yeats wrote some of his best lyrics in old age—but the *Odes* of Horace are the work of his maturity. The first six poems of the Third Book stand together as a group in which Horace professes to act as an instructor for Roman youth in morality and patriotism, and are known as the Roman Odes. Apart from these, each ode is complete in itself and must be so appreciated. The *Odes* were not at first a success with the Roman public; and indeed the reader must be at pains to understand them, as Horace was to write them. But, of their kind, they are perfect. In the next century Petronius, in a famous phrase, spoke of Horace's "painstaking felicity" (*curiosa felicitas*); a modern critic has aptly compared his art to that of the mosaicist. Bit by bit the words are fitted in, carefully chosen for position, color, and effect. Like a Byzantine mosaic, an ode of Horace must be looked at from many angles. Once grasped, the impression does not quickly fade.

Men have carried with them all their lives odes of Horace which they learned at school.

Disappointed with the reception of the *Odes,* Horace returned to satire, or rather to a new and original development of it, in the *Epistles.* These are really sermons on conduct and morality in epistolary form, from a man who has come to terms with life and found happiness from knowing his limits and living within them. He views his own faults and those of others with a kindly tolerance which commends his advice. The *Epistles* show in the highest degree his quality of *urbanitas,* a combination of good sense, good humor, and good taste, which so endeared him to the great writers of the eighteenth century. Epistle VII of the first book, in which Horace, with great dignity and tact, issues to Maecenas a declaration of independence, is deservedly famous, and does credit to the poet and his patron. The second book of the Epistles is concerned with literary criticism. The *Ars Poetica* deals with the theory of tragedy, and was widely read in the seventeenth and eighteenth centuries, especially in France, and much misunderstood. In 17 B.C. Horace wrote the official *Carmen* for the Secular Games; a few years later, at Augustus' request, he published a fourth book of *Odes.* He died in 8 B.C., his works having become classics in his own lifetime.

The love elegy, a Roman literary invention, came to its peak at this time. Four names stand out above many of lesser fame —Gallus, Tibullus, Propertius, and Ovid. The Augustan peace had given men leisure to follow their own pursuits. For the young, in a gay and wealthy capital, this meant, above all, the pursuit of love. Rome, said Ovid, is the lover's paradise, the girls as plentiful as the stars in the sky. Gay, witty, clever, and charming, Roman as well as Greek, the girls of the Roman demimonde are the theme of Roman elegy. Propertius hoped to write a little book for a lonely girl to read while waiting for her lover—and when he comes she can throw it away. Whatever their debts to their Greek predecessors, Callimachus and Philetas, writers of Alexandria, it was the Roman poets who made elegiac poetry pre-eminently the poetry of love. The *Amores* of Gallus were published in 39 B.C.; of all the "lost" Latin poets, there is perhaps none we would rather recover. Tibullus (48?–19 B.C.) is a fine poet within his limits. His pictures of country life have the freshness of a spring morning, and his love poems have a charm and delicacy that no other Roman poet can match, though they lack the passion of Catullus. He belonged to the literary circle of Messalla, and poems by other members of that group have come down under his name. The best of these are six poems by Sulpicia, Messalla's ward; fine in themselves, they are of unique interest as the only poems by a woman to survive from that age.

Propertius (54?–16? B.C.) is one of the greatest of Roman poets, and a man of passionate and complex personality. Born in Umbria, perhaps at Assisi, his childhood was overshadowed by the Civil War, and his mother brought him to Rome to be educated. He must have had private means, for though he studied law in a desultory way, he soon gave himself up to the gay life of the capital. A love affair, as passionate as that of Catullus and Lesbia, made him turn poet, and his first book, *Cynthia,* was published about 28 B.C. His mistress' real name was Hostia, and she stands out vividly in his poems. Beautiful and capricious, she led him for five years through every phase of the romantic agony. When she left him his high poetic vein ran dry, though there are some fine poems on Roman legends in his later books. But it is the Cynthia poems one remembers—Cynthia on the beach at Baiae, surrounded by smart young men: a wild party with other women, interrupted by Cynthia, and the quarrel that follows; a night of love and the foreboding of death; above all, the superb poem in which Cynthia's ghost appears to remind him of their love and to exact his promise that they will be together in the grave.

Some obscurities of style and the chaotic state of the manuscripts have kept Propertius from the fame he deserves, though he is highly regarded today. By contrast, almost all ages except our own have placed Ovid among the very greatest of Roman poets. Few poets from Petrarch to Byron escaped his influence, and he has provided themes for countless painters of classical legends. An Elizabethan admirer of the young Shakespeare proclaimed that "the sweet witty soul of Ovid lives in mellifluous honey-tongued Shakespeare." He was born at Sulmo (Sulmona) in 43 B.C. of a well-to-do-family, who gave him a good education at Rome and Athens and did their utmost to dissuade him from becoming a poet, but in vain. Picasso, reproached for drawing worse than a child of twelve, replied "Ah, when *I* was twelve, I used to draw like Raphael." So, when Ovid was twelve, he wrote like Ovid—everything turned into verse of its own accord. His *Amores* (c. 14 B.C.) quickly became a favorite with the smart set, and his fame was increased by the *Heroides,* letters from the deserted heroines of legend to their lovers, together, in some cases, with the reply. Broken their hearts may be, but these ladies do not forget what they have learned from the Roman schools of rhetoric: the prevailing note is the gay flippancy of *Amphitryon '38*. Ovid's researches into love were going well, and later (about 1 B.C.), in the *Ars Amatoria,* he turned professor and wrote the standard textbook. A wonderful parody of didactic poetry, this witty and amoral poem describes (1) how to find a girl, (2) how to seduce a girl, and (3) how to keep a girl. This in two books, for men; a third handles the same problems for women, who are further supported by a book on cosmetics. It also provides a philosophic defense of love, the only true source of improvement in human life. A sequel, the *Remedia Amoris,* was a kind of postgraduate course on the lover's fourth problem—how to get rid of a girl. It prescribes forty-two ways of falling out of love, including new love affairs, farming, abstinence from such poets as Ovid, and foreign travel. Next, Ovid turned to mythology, and published a collection of stories on the theme of changes of shape, the *Metamorphoses.* Beginning with the change of Chaos into Cosmos, it was to end with the change of Julius Caesar into a god. In many ways this is Ovid's best work; it is certainly his most influential, for it became the great treasury from which the Middle Ages drew almost all they knew of classical legend.

But now a heavy change was to overtake Ovid himself. His poetry, to say the least of it, did nothing to advance Augustus' program of moral reform; when Ovid became implicated in a grave scandal (perhaps that of the younger Julia), it was altogether too much, and he was sentenced to banishment to the far confines of the Empire, to Tomis, the modern Constantsa, on the Black Sea. From exile he wrote the *Epistles from Pontus* and the *Tristia.* Often boring from their tone of unending complaint, they also give some fascinating pictures of life on the outposts of the Empire. It is as though Herrick had been banished, not to "this dull Devonshire," but to New Hampshire at the time of King Philip's War. But how gladly would we exchange the *Tristia* for the poems Ovid claims to have written in the Getic tongue! Augustus never relented, and he died in exile. His last work was the *Fasti,* posthumously published, dealing with the festivals of the Roman calendar and the legends associated with them —a work of permanent interest to the student of folklore and religion.

In grandeur of conception and in moral outlook no work of that age is more truly Augustan than the *Histories* of Livy. Like Virgil, he was a man of the North, born at Patavium (Padua) in 59 B.C., and he shows the same patriotism

for Rome and Italy, and the same reverence for their historic
past. About 29 B.C. he came to Rome, and began the great
task which was to occupy the next forty years of his life. In
no less than 142 books—three times the length of Gibbon—
he carried the history of Rome from its foundation to the
death of Drusus in 9 B.C. So vast a work—too big, as the poet
Martial complains, for one man's bookshelves—was certain
to attract summaries and extracts, with the unhappy result
that only thirty-five books survive. We have "epitomes" of
most of the rest, but they are no sort of substitute for Livy.
Livy's work has been called the prose counterpart of the
Aeneid, and it is indeed an epic history whose hero is Rome.
Like the *Aeneid*, it tells of the men and the qualities which
made Rome great. The "antique virtue" of the Roman character led to the conquest of Italy, and stood unshaken
through the disasters of the Punic Wars. But after the conquest of the Mediterranean world, luxury and corruption led
to a decline which continued to Livy's own time, when "we
can bear neither our diseases nor their cure." Yet cure was
still possible, if the moral virtues of the old Republic could
be restored; here the work of the historian accords with the
social reforms of Augustus.

Since the early nineteenth century, Livy has been exposed
to the critical standards of modern historical method, and he
does not emerge from the ordeal unscathed. No one could
now speak of him, as Dante did, as "Livy who does not err."
He errs in many ways, in the uncritical use of sources, in his
ignorance of military matters, his blindness to economics, his
failure to interpret the institutions of primitive society in
their own context. It would be vain to seek in him the qualities of the *Cambridge Ancient History*. Yet, in a sense, this
does not matter. Livy set out to give a great people an imag-
inative reconstruction of their past as an aid to an understanding of their imperial destiny, and in that he succeeded.
His belief that history is made by human beings, and his extraordinary powers of narrative, have produced a brilliant
pageant of Roman history which may be criticized in detail
yet which leaves an indelible impression as a whole. In dealing
with the first century of the Empire, we are always conscious
of the need to appraise the influence of Tacitus, but we are
hardly aware that our picture of much of the history of the
Republic is still substantially that of Livy.

There was a large output of technical and specialist works
in poetry and prose, not much of which survives. Grammar,
philology, medicine, botany, gardening, law, philosophy—
all figure in the list of subjects handled. Above all, for

quantity, was rhetoric; it had consolidated its hold on Roman education precisely at the time when, under the imperial system, a career like that of Cicero or Hortensius had become impossible. The writings of the elder Seneca (c. 55 B.C.–41 A.D.) give an insight into the Augustan schools of eloquence, and enable us to understand the harm which was done by this short-sighted addiction to an out-of-date vocational training. Professional rhetoricians also set up as historians and philosophers, which tended to lower the intellectual level of those subjects. Such were the works of Dionysius of Halicarnassus, who taught in Rome from 30 B.C. to 8 B.C., and wrote on oratory, literary criticism, and history. Half his *Roman Antiquities* survive; they went from the earliest times to the Punic Wars. This Greek literature of the Augustan age was considerable, although less distinguished than that of either the time of Polybius or the time of Trajan and Hadrian. No one would rank Diodorus Siculus among the major historians, but Strabo (64 B.C–21 A.D.), a Greek from Amasei on the Black Sea, was a geographer of quality, concerned to show the importance of his subject in public affairs, and to revise Hellenistic geography in the light of Roman conquests in the West. His seventeen books survey the world from Britain to India, from the Baltic to Ethiopia. He is sometimes superficial and credulous—though his skepticism about the famous voyage of Pytheas of Massilia to Britain and the North Sea displays the opposite fault—but his work is one of the main sources for the history of geographical thought in the ancient world.

In Latin, the long poem of Manilius has attracted scholars rather than readers. A kind of Stoic counterblast to Lucretius, it seeks to prove the divine ordering of the universe by arguments derived from astronomy and astrology. A poem entitled *Aetna* is closer to the spirit of Lucretius in assigning natural causes to volcanic phenomena and in its enthusiasm for the study of natural science. It has been attributed to Virgil, though this is not generally accepted; indeed, it may be later than the age of Augustus. But a typical product of that age, and a work of very high interest, is that of Vitruvius Pollio on architecture. The great building schemes of Augustus in Rome prompted its publication, and it deals very fully with Roman theory and practice in architecture, town planning, and civil engineering. There is an interesting section on the qualifications of an architect, which Vitruvius set at a high level. Only one building, the basilica at Fanum, is known to be his, but his book had its influence on Roman architecture during the first century A.D. As the only surviving work of antiquity on its subject, it became virtually required reading for the architects of the Renaissance in Italy. Through the work of Alberti and Palladio it exerted a far-reaching influence on the architecture of Europe.

The art and architecture of the age were a worthy match for its literature. Three chapters of the *Res Gestae* of Augustus summarize, in the laconic style of that monument, the chief buildings which Augustus himself constructed, those of Julius Caesar and others which he completed, and the vast program of restoration and repair which he carried out in the temples and other historic monuments of the city. All this activity was even more succinctly described in his claim that he had found Rome a city of brick and left it a city of marble; at last Rome looked the world capital it was. In Virgil's words, "Rome became the fairest thing in the world" (*facta est rerum pulcerrima Roma*), though this development was far from complete when he died. Today the building schemes of Augustus are best seen in the Campus Martius, whose possibilities as a monumental zone were first appreciated by Julius Caesar. A great artery, the Via Lata, connecting the Forum and Capitol with the Via Flaminia, led through the heart of this district. Now the Corso, it is still one of the principal streets of Rome. Near its northern end and closer to the river, Augustus constructed the huge mausoleum for the imperial family which still bears his name. Modeled on the burial mounds of Italo-Etruscan tradition, but on an enormous scale, it received the ashes of most of the leading members of the imperial family from Marcellus to Nerva. It stood in a park with trees, and on pillars outside the entrance a copy of the *Res Gestae* was engraved on bronze tablets. A few hundred yards closer to the center of the city stood the Altar of Peace, whose sculptures are the most perfect expression in art of the ideals of the Augustan age. To the south came a district associated with Agrippa rather than Augustus. One great portico contained the famous map of the world which he had compiled; another, built to commemorate the victory of Actium, had a fresco of the voyage of the Argonauts. Still more important was the architectural complex round the Pantheon. This included the first of the great imperial baths, the Thermae of Agrippa, a large hall, an ornamental lake, a canal, and the Pantheon itself, the whole being set in a splendid park. In its present form, a rotunda carrying the huge vault, and a portico of three rows of eight Corinthian columns, the Pantheon dates entirely from Hadrian's time, and there has been much discussion as to whether a rotunda formed part of Agrippa's plan. But the inscription on the portico still bears his name, and it must be remembered that Hadrian was conservative in his restorations. Hadrianic or Augustan, it is the greatest of all surviving Roman buildings, the only one which can be appreciated in aesthetic terms in the same way as a Gothic cathedral. The huge vault represents the vault of heaven, and the round "eye" (*oculus*), nine meters across at its apex, is open to the sky, which gives the only light. The seven niches, it has been thought, were in honor of the seven planetary divinities.

At the foot of the Capitol, by the Temple of Apollo, was a zone which Augustus seems to have dedicated to the arts. Here still stands part of the noble façade of the Theater of Marcellus, with its three rows of arcades, disengaged by Mussolini's archaeologists from the huddle of shops and houses which once encumbered it. Dedicated in 13 B.C., and seating perhaps twenty thousand, it is one of the finest buildings constructed for the pleasure of the Roman people.

In the old Forum Romanum, Augustus' work was mostly restoration and replanning, though he built one major building in the Temple of Divus Julius, placed significantly near the center of the Forum and close to the Temple of Vesta. He also completed the magnificent Basilica Julia at the southwest angle of the Forum and replanned the older Basilica Aemilia to match it. He finished the repairs to the senate house which Julius Caesar had begun, and renamed it the Curia Julia. The Curia we see is a restoration of the third century, but—like the British House of Commons after the Second World War—it probably preserves faithfully the original dimensions and plan.

But, however replanned, the ancient Forum Romanum was too congested for all the needs of the huge city, and it was necessary to build auxiliary fora to the north. Each was on the plan of a temple and surrounding enclosure. The Forum of Julius, planned by Caesar but completed by Augustus, contained the temple of Venus Genetrix, ancestress of the *gens Julia* and mother of Aeneas. The Forum of Augustus with its two hemicycles contained the temple of Mars the Avenger, in discharge of a vow made at the battle of Philippi. In the colonnades were statues and inscriptions of all the *triumphatores*, a kind of gallery or Hall of Fame perhaps suggested by the pageant of Roman heroes in the Sixth Book of the *Aeneid*.

Perhaps what he did on the Palatine was closest to Augustus' heart. Here stood the magnificent Temple of Apollo, the first great building in Rome entirely of Luna

marble, in honor of a vow made at Actium. Here were
placed the Sibylline books, transferred from the Temple of
Jupiter on the Capitol, and in the portico stood two famous
libraries founded by Augustus, one for Greek, the other for
Latin books. The temple was entirely destroyed by fire on
the night of the death of Julian the Apostate (March 18,
363 A.D.), and we know less about it than any other great
Roman building. Augustus also carefully restored the venerable sites on the Palatine, including (possibly) the House of
Romulus, and certainly the Lupercal, the grotto where the
wolf was said to have suckled Romulus and Remus. He
also restored the famous Temple of Magna Mater. But
there is one significant omission from Augustus' plans on the
Palatine. No great building was erected by him to house
the Roman *princeps*. The huge buildings which took their
name from the hill—and have given the term "palace" to
later ages—were the work of his successors, from Tiberius
to Domitian. Augustus himself lived in the modest house,
with its charming frescoes, still to be seen under the name of
the House of Livia.

Space will not allow mention of the many other public
works—aqueducts, market halls, warehouses, docks—built
by Augustus in Rome. Yet one thing should be said. Magnificent as they were, his schemes for urban development
were confined to public buildings and to extensions of the
civic center, leaving the old street plan untouched (save for
the Via Lata), and affording no improvements in private
housing. Examples of complete town planning are to be
seen, however, in several colonies of Augustan foundation,
and notably at Aosta.

In art, no less than in architecture, the patronage of
Augustus provided an effective stimulus. Sculpture was needed
for great monuments such as the Ara Pacis, whether in
Rome or the provinces. No doubt painting was used in the
same way, though it has not survived. Portraits of the *princeps* and members of the imperial family were in demand.
A style was evolved which combined the realism of the
Italian tradition with the idealism of Greek art. It is this
official or court style which historians have in mind when
they speak of Augustan art. Its masterpieces are such works
as the Prima Porta statue of Augustus, the Grand Cameo
of France, and the lovely portraits of the imperial ladies to
be seen in Rome, Paris, and Copenhagen. It is interesting to
note that we find no trace of this idealistic art in the many
funeral monuments of middle-class persons, which fully
maintain the Republican standards of ugliness.

Above all the other art of the age stand the sculptured panels of the Ara Pacis. This monument was set up to commemorate the return of Augustus to Rome in 13 B.C., and was dedicated in 9 B.C. The altar itself stood in a sacred precinct, and the chief sculptures were placed in two bands on the outside of the enclosing walls. Entrances broke the east and west walls, thus giving four slabs for individual themes, while there are two long unbroken reliefs on the north and south. The theme of the upper band of sculptures on these two long sides is the procession of the senate and people of Rome, with the magistrates and the imperial family, headed by the *princeps,* offering sacrifice for his safe return. They have been compared, or rather contrasted, with the Panathenaic procession on the Parthenon of Athens. The Periclean sculptures idealize the beauty of the youth of Athens and the dignity of the old men; there are no children. The Roman procession is one of real persons, not of types. We can identify the members of the imperial family: there is no doubt that the senators are portraits also. There are several children, depicted with tenderness and humor. The treatment of Augustus is to be noted. He is not put in a central position, the cynosure of all eyes, as is commonly done with the emperor in later imperial reliefs. But he comes at the head of the procession, followed by the Vestal virgins and the flamens: it is a visual expression of the concept of *princeps.*

The four short slabs are arranged in balancing pairs of mythological and symbolic scenes—on one side, the wolf and twins and the sacrifice of Aeneas, bringing together the Trojan and the Roman legend of the origins of Rome. On the other, a group of symbolic figures of great beauty surround a seated woman who is perhaps Tellus (the Earth goddess), but more probably Italia: this would be balanced by Roma. The floral frieze of all the lower panels is hardly less remarkable. Here great coils of acanthus are peopled by a profusion of birds, insects, and flowers, rendered with great naturalness. They have been well compared to that masterpiece of English medieval art, the leaves in the chapter house of Southwell Minster.

For the bimillenary of Augustus in 1938 the remaining fragments of the Ara Pacis were excavated, with great difficulty, from the mud beneath the Fiano Palace. The sculptured panels, which had been scattered through several galleries, were reassembled or copied, and the entire monument re-erected on a new site close to the Mausoleum of Augustus.

It is one of the triumphs of modern archaeology, and a permanent addition to the marvels of Rome.

In the absence of pictures, our knowledge of Augustan painting depends on a few frescoes. The most notable of these are the mythological scenes and architectural compositions from the House of Livia on the Palatine, the beautiful garden scenes from the Prima Porta Villa, and the frescoes from the villa at Boscoreale now to be seen in the Metropolitan Museum of Art in New York.

CHAPTER X

THE IMPERIAL PEACE: 14–192 A.D.

There is a fundamental difference between the history of the Republic and that of the Empire. With the disappearance of political parties and public discussion, political history narrows down to a few themes concerning the emperor and the court. The character of the emperor, his accession, his relations with the Senate, court intrigues, his death and the suspicions to which it gives rise—this is the kind of history represented at its best by Tacitus, at its worst by the writers of the *Historia Augusta*, with Suetonius and Dio Cassius in between. Essentially, these histories follow a senatorial tradition, hostile to the Empire in general, and to most emperors, except Nerva, Trajan, and the first two Antonines. Often they deal with lurid stories of sexual immorality, which read like case books of morbid psychology. Under the Empire the fierce light which shines upon a throne also penetrated to the bedroom, and the invention of scabrous stories was a minor industry. Most of this is easy to discount. But when we are dealing with the first century, it is never easy to escape the influence of Tacitus, who lights up the world of high politics with a powerful but narrow beam. We need to remind ourselves that there is another side to the history of the Empire, in which the Roman historians seldom took much interest. This has to do with the life of the provinces, and such great themes as the winning of new lands for agriculture, the Latinization of the West and the Danube provinces, the spread of Oriental influences in religion and thought, the enlistment of new classes in the administration of the Empire. For this picture of the social and cultural life of the Roman provinces, virtually unknown to Gibbon, we have to thank the progress of modern archaeology. It is as yet far from complete,

but gradually, at different rates for different parts of the
Empire, there is building up what may be called the local
history of the Roman world. It will be convenient to keep
these two aspects distinct, and to deal first with political
history from the accession of Tiberius to the death of Commodus, and then with the social and cultural history of the
Roman world of the first two centuries A.D.

When he succeeded Augustus in 14 A.D., Tiberius was
fifty-two, a soured and disillusioned man. Time and again
his solid services to the state had been passed over for a
rival. On the personal side, there was the double grief of
his divorce from Vipsania and his unhappy marriage to
Julia. His hesitation about accepting the succession, which
Tacitus put down to hypocrisy, and his plea for some remis-
sion of the burden in old age, may have been sincere. "Only
the mind of Augustus was equal to such a task"; that formidable example must have dismayed all the emperors of the
Julio-Claudian line. Tiberius' own inclinations, as well as
the influence of his mother Livia, led him to follow the
policy of Augustus whenever he could. Unfortunately, he
lacked entirely Augustus' gift for personal relations and his
skill in winning support.

With a *princeps* of his age, the question of the succession
loomed large. At first the position seemed secure. There
was Tiberius' own son Drusus; there was his nephew Germanicus, son of the older Drusus, who had his father's charm
and some of his gifts. Germanicus undertook the task of
restoring Roman prestige in Germany after the disaster of
Varus. He did well enough to be granted a triumph in
17 A.D., though the design of making Germany a province was
abandoned. Next he was given an important mission in the
East to settle relations with Parthia and Armenia. Tiberius
gave him *maius imperium* over all the eastern provinces, but
also sent Cnaeus Calpurnius Piso to the key post of governor
of Syria to hold a watching brief. The situation was im-
plicit with disaster, and the disaster occurred. Germanicus
behaved tactlessly in visiting Egypt, quarreled with Piso
and ordered him out of Syria, and died shortly after. Piso
was suspected of poisoning him, was tried in a sensational
trial at Rome, and committed suicide. This was taken as
proof of his guilt, and as implicating Tiberius in the death of
Germanicus to clear the way for Drusus.

Bitter hatreds now ruled the imperial court. Agrippina,
widow of Germanicus, and her children were estranged from
Tiberius. Drusus did not last long. A new and sinister influence made itself felt in the person of Lucius Aelius Seja-

nus, a knight of Etruscan family, the first man to rise to greatness as commander of the Praetorian Guard. He persuaded Tiberius to build a permanent barracks in Rome, and thus became master of the only troops in the capital. Moreover, he won Tiberius' confidence and made himself indispensable. In 23 A.D. Drusus died; the manner of his death came out later. Sejanus was now supreme, and Agrippina and her children in mortal danger. In 26 Tiberius retired to his villa at Capreae (Capri). To this step he was persuaded by Sejanus, who further won his gratitude by saving his life at the (prearranged?) collapse of the roof of a grotto where they were dining. This grotto, at Sperlonga, has recently been excavated with its statues—a striking confirmation of Tacitus. Absence increased Tiberius' unpopularity at Rome. In 29 Livia died, and Agrippina and her children were banished. Sejanus seemed to have all the trumps, and began to plan the removal of the last obstacle in his path—the emperor himself. But at last Tiberius was informed of his treachery. On October 18, 31 A.D., a special session of the Senate was held, and a "long and wordy letter from Capri" was read aloud. It began with a vague promise of further honors for Sejanus: it ended by denouncing him as a traitor. He was taken to prison and strangled, and his body was torn to pieces by the mob. Not even Wolsey met with so drastic a reverse of fortune. The disloyalty of Sejanus finally broke Tiberius' spirit —especially when it came out that Sejanus had poisoned Drusus, after first seducing his wife. The last years of Tiberius' reign passed in seclusion at Capri. The Roman people rejoiced at his death (37 A.D.), and the Senate refused divine honors.

The gloom of these last years would in any event have left an unfavorable impression of Tiberius, but this is heightened to an extraordinary extent by the account of Tacitus, a masterpiece of malice and innuendo. What influenced Tacitus was that he saw in the reign of Tiberius the beginning of the Terror which was to reach such heights under Domitian, with its twin horrors of a vague but far-reaching law of treason (*maiestas*) and the rise of a class of professional informers (*delatores*) to take advantage of it. Scholars who have carefully analyzed *maiestas* under Tiberius have been able to point out that Tacitus exaggerated, that the worst cases were due to the influence of Sejanus, and that Tiberius tried to exert restraint. It has also been shown that his civil administration was excellent—even Tacitus admits this for the first half of his reign—and that he showed care for the provinces and prudence in expenditure. Nothing can make him an at-

tractive figure, but it seems fair to regard him as a consci-
entious ruler.

No amount of whitewash can do much for the Emperor
Gaius (37–41 A.D.). Brought up as a child in army camps, he
acquired the nickname of Caligula (Little Boots) and the
dangerous popularity of the soldiers' darling. Tiberius did
nothing for his education, and he learned unwholesome lessons from Herod Agrippa and other young Oriental princes
with whom he was allowed to associate. One thing he had
grasped thoroughly—the world was his to do as he liked
with. This was, as a rule, to explore its possibilities for lust
and sadism; if only humanity, he once exclaimed, had but
one neck, so that it could be severed in a single blow! That
he was mentally deranged is certain, though we lack the evidence for a clinical picture. His political actions are portrayed as those of a madman—the mock triumph over the
Germans, with its hired "captives" in blond wigs: the abor-
tive expedition against Britain, with the soldiers ordered to
gather seashells: the fatuous insistence, which was driving
the Jews to despair, that a colossal statue of himself should
be set up in Jerusalem. Picard has given some explanation of
the first two, which remove them from the sphere of lunacy
to that of sympathetic magic. But it is certain that under
Caligula the Empire was being transformed into the worst
kind of Oriental despotism. It was a relief to the world when
he was assassinated by soldiers in 41 A.D.

The Principate of Claudius (41–54 A.D.) saw a return to
the tradition of Augustus. The younger brother of Germanicus, handicapped by physical defects, neglected by his eld-
ers, Claudius proved himself the best emperor between Augustus and Vespasian. He was thrust by the Praetorian
Guard on a reluctant Senate, who never forgave him; here
is the origin of the hostile literary tradition. Inscriptions,
documents, and the known facts of his reign show him in
another light.

Devoted to the military traditions of the Claudian house,
he resumed the policy of reasoned expansion which Augustus had abandoned in his last years. The success of the un-
dertaking was assisted by a wise choice of commanders.
Aulus Plautius, Suetonius Paulinus, the future emperor Vespasian, were all first-rate generals whom he placed in major
commands. In the East, Thrace was turned into a province:
combined operations gained control of the north shores of
the Black Sea: a client-king was on the Bosporan throne. A
stable solution of the Parthia-Armenia problem eluded him,
as it did every emperor up to Trajan, but he strengthened

the line of the Euphrates, and made Judaea a province on the death of Herod Agrippa I (44 A.D.). In Africa, Mauretania was annexed after a spectacular campaign in the Atlas Mountains, and turned into two provinces.

But the thing in which Claudius took most pride, and which captured the imagination of the age, was the invasion of Britain. Caesar, as Tacitus says, had shown the way, but for a hundred years no one had followed it. Meanwhile, contacts with the Roman world had raised material standards in Britain. In the southeast a powerful kingdom had grown up, with its capital at Colchester (Camulodunum). Under Cunobelinus (the Cymbeline of Shakespeare) a prudent policy toward Rome was followed, but he died about 40 A.D., and his sons Togodumnus and Caratacus were hostile. A powerful anti-Roman state in Britain would encourage Celtic nationalism in Gaul. Claudius decided to strike. In 43 A.D. Aulus Plautius landed a force of four legions and auxiliaries—about 40,000 men—at Richborough. The Britons were defeated after a two-day battle on the Medway, and the Romans advanced to the Thames to await the emperor. Claudius in person led them to Colchester, where he received the submission of eleven (?) British kings. Thence he returned to Rome to celebrate a magnificent triumph (44 A.D.). Aulus Plautius then mounted a three-pronged offensive to the west and north, and a Roman province took shape with a frontier along the lines of the Severn and Trent. It was buttressed by client-kingdoms—the Regni in Sussex, the Iceni in Norfolk, and the Brigantes beyond the Humber. There was resistance in Wales, where Caratacus, elected as war leader by the Welsh tribes, held out for eight years. His surrender in 51 A.D. was marked by a grand military review in Rome, notable for the proud bearing of the British prince and the clemency of Claudius. Within a few years of the conquest the mineral resources of Britain—especially the lead of the Mendips—were being worked, and an urban civilization along Roman lines was getting under way. Camulodunum was chosen as a capital, and a temple of Claudius built there. "Captured Britain is washed by a Roman ocean," wrote a contemporary poet; official propaganda always stresses the conquest of Ocean no less than the conquest of Britain. Now that the remote and mysterious island was reached, there was an exhilarating sense of barriers down.

Claudius undertook ambitious public works in many parts of the Empire. In Rome, the water supply was reorganized and two large aqueducts were added. The harbor facilities of Ostia were greatly improved, and a new basin was constructed three miles north at Portus. To reclaim land for agriculture in central Italy, a force of thirty thousand men was employed for eleven years on the vast project of draining the Fucine Lake. This was only partially successful: the project was taken up many times in the Middle Ages and later, but was not completed until 1875. Many new trunk roads were built. One of these ran for 350 Roman miles from the head of the Adriatic, over the Brenner Pass, to the banks of the Danube near Augsburg. A building inscription survives to testify to Claudius' pride in completing work begun by his father, Drusus. In Gaul, roads were built to the Atlantic coast at Brest, Cherbourg, and Boulogne—this last being chosen for development as the chief North Sea port.

Liberality in extending Roman citizenship provoked the comment that Claudius wanted to see all Gauls, Greeks, Spaniards, and Britons wearing the toga. But a study of his policy shows that he laid down strict conditions to be met— for communities, an adequate degree of Romanization; for individuals, a thorough command of Latin and service to Rome in the armed forces or in the grain trade. His speech on the admission of Gallic chiefs to the Senate is famous, and has survived in an inscription from Lyons, as well as in the version of Tacitus. The foundation of colonies such as Colchester in Britain and Cologne in Germany fostered the Romanization of the western provinces.

Perhaps no other of his works was so enduring—for good or evil—as his development of an imperial bureaucracy, which had begun under Tiberius. Three great bureaus were at work under Claudius for correspondence, accounts, and justice; there was also a fourth whose scope is uncertain, but which has been thought, from the name (*a studiis*), to be a research department. These were in charge of freedmen whose names—Narcissus, Pallas, Callistus, and Polybius— show their Greek origin. The bureaus worked well, and their heads became rich and powerful, to the disgust of the Roman aristocracy. Here is another source of the anti-Claudian tradition, which shows him as under the thumb of freedmen and women. It is certain that Messalina, the first of his consorts, was ambitious and profligate, though the more lurid stories of her nymphomania seem to be the invention of Claudius' enemies, later crystallized by Juvenal. But she plotted against him with her lover Silius, and was put to death in 48 A.D. She was succeeded by Agrippina, formidable daughter of a formidable mother. Not content with honors as empress which went beyond anything conceded to Livia, Agrippina murdered Claudius (54 A.D.) to secure the succession of her son Nero, through whom she hoped to rule.

The principate of Nero began with a period of good government under the influence of Burrus, prefect of the Praetorian Guard, and Seneca, Nero's tutor. It is significant that two provincials—one from Gaul, the other from Spain—should wield such power. But the young man who had become master of the world at sixteen soon found more congenial instructors than a Stoic philosopher, and his reign developed into the nightmare of conspiracy, debauchery, and murder for which it has become proverbial.

The effects of this were confined to Rome or to Nero's entourage. The imperial machinery functioned smoothly enough over most of the Empire, and prosperity was the rule in the provinces. Disorders were dealt with firmly. In Britain there was the grim rebellion led by Boudicca in 60 A.D., provoked by the rapacity of the Roman tax collectors. London, Colchester, and St. Albans were captured and the inhabitants massacred: for a time it looked as though the province was lost. After the rebels were defeated there was an inquiry, the governor Suetonius Paulinus was recalled to Rome, and a milder policy followed which proved successful. In Judaea there was a rising in 66, and at the time of Nero's death Vespasian was engaged in reducing the province district by district in the face of fanatical resistance. On the Parthian frontier there were ten years of varied fighting, in which Corbulo first licked into shape a slack Roman army and then led it to brilliant successes in Armenia, while another Roman force, led by Paetus, suffered a disaster that was in its way a minor Carrhae. Finally a settlement was reached which put a Parthian nominee on the Armenian throne but brought him to Rome to be crowned (66). This arrangement gave peace for half a century.

But in Rome there developed an atmosphere of horror which resembles that of Greek tragedy, and which provides the background for the melodramas of Seneca. The murder of Britannicus, Claudius' son by Messalina, was to be expected, but it was soon followed by that of Agrippina, who died cursing the womb that had borne Nero. After the death of Burrus in 62, Nero came under the influence of the new prefect, the notorious Tigellinus, and threw off all restraint. The conspiracy of Caius Piso (66), in which a number of aristocrats were concerned, led to many deaths, including those of Seneca and the poet Lucan. A kind of philosophic opposition had grown up around a few men of Stoic outlook and republican sentiment, successors to Cato. The deaths of Thrasea Paetus and Barea Soranus put an end to its lead-

ers. None of Nero's crimes shocked the Roman people so
much as the murder of his first wife, Octavia, to gratify her
rival Poppaea Sabina. When at last Nero ordered leading
generals like Corbulo to commit suicide, he had alienated all
classes, the armies became mutinous, the Senate declared
him a public enemy, and he died by his own hand (68).

So perished the last of the Julio-Claudians, and, in his own
belief, one of the world's great artists. Nero's artistic and
athletic ambitions provide some relief to the lurid story of
his crimes. He was consumed with the ambition to excel as
a singer, harpist, and charioteer. And excel he did. In his
famous tour of Greece he swept the board at every event in
every festival, and returned home with no fewer than 1,808
crowns—surely a record?—to a Rome curiously unimpressed
by the prowess of its emperor.

But the most famous event of his reign was the Great
Fire of Rome and its sequel. On the night of July 18, 64 A.D.,
Rome was visited by the kind of calamity for which town
planners pray. A fire started in the wooden seating of the
Circus Maximus, raged for a week, and devastated ten of the
fourteen regions of the city. Nero's measures of relief were
prompt, and he seized the opportunity to rebuild the city with
great zeal. So much so, that hostile propaganda put it around
that he had deliberately caused the fire. A scapegoat was
needed. The Jewish community in Rome might have served,
but they were protected by Poppaea. But there was a small
sect of Jewish heretics, already suspected of infamous crimes
because their services were in secret. They were called Christians "after one Christus, who had been put to death in the
reign of Tiberius by Pontius Pilate." Such, in Tacitus' version, was the origin of the Neronian persecution, from which
derives the belief in Nero as the Antichrist.

An acute crisis followed the death of Nero. There was no
heir of the Julio-Claudian line; the field was wide open for
claimants to the Principate, but the claim could only be asserted by force. So ensued the dramatic and terrible events
of 69 A.D., the Year of the Four Emperors. It was nearly a
hundred years since Actium. Once again Roman armies were
engaged in a complex series of civil wars, in which appeared
only too clearly the rivalries of the army groups and the
ruthlessness with which the troops of all sides treated the
civilian population. Galba was the candidate of the Praetorian Guard, supported by the Spanish army. He assumed the
title of Caesar in Spain, "revealing," says Tacitus, "a secret of
Empire—that a *princeps* could be made elsewhere than in
Rome." Otho replaced him because the Praetorian Guard

switched its allegiance; to quote Tacitus again, "Two soldiers undertook to transfer the empire of the Roman people, and transfer it they did." Vitellius was the candidate of the Rhine army. But the last word was to lie with the Eastern legions. Vespasian was proclaimed emperor at Alexandria on July 1; later he received the support of the Syrian legions, then those of the Danube. His forces captured Rome after fierce street fighting on December 20, and Vitellius was murdered. The events of this year are brilliantly described in the *Histories* of Tacitus, which give unforgettable portraits of the chief actors: Galba, "whom all agreed fit to be Emperor, if he had never ruled"; the brave death of the effeminate Otho; the stupid Vitellius, at a moment of supreme crisis "idling in his gardens, like a sluggish animal which will not move so long as you feed it, caring nothing for past, present, or future." Equally brilliant is the description of the two battles of Bedriacum, the brutal sack of Cremona, and the fight for the Capitol in Rome between Vitellius and the troops of Vespasian.

Vespasian was one of a new class of men brought forward by a career of public service. His family came from Reate in the Sabine country, and was of no more than local standing until the time of his father, a tax collector in Asia under Augustus. Vespasian was commander of the Second Legion in the Claudian invasion of Britain, consul in 51, and governor of Africa in 63. In 66 his public career nearly came to an untimely end because of his lack of tact in going to sleep during one of Nero's recitals in Greece. But the outbreak of the Jewish rebellion gave him another major command, from which he was swept up in the events of 69. The imperial purple did nothing to change his Sabine accent, simple living, earthy humor, and close-fistedness about money.

This last quality was timely. Nero's extravagance and the civil wars had almost bankrupted the state. Vespasian's reign was marked throughout by financial retrenchment and reform. As censor in 73, he overhauled the whole system of taxation. New burdens were placed on individuals and communities, and the provincial tributes were increased. A simple regime was observed by the imperial court, and strict honesty exacted from finance officers. These reforms were so successful that they not only made the state solvent, but also enabled the emperor to carry out large building projects in Rome.

In Gaul and Judaea Vespasian inherited a legacy of trouble. The events that led to Nero's death had been sparked off by a rebellion in Gaul under Vindex that had elements of a national rising. This was crushed, but soon a more formidable affair developed under Civilis. Commanding an auxiliary regiment of his countrymen, he was resolved to liberate Batavia from Roman influence. He was joined by tribes of free Germans from across the Rhine; later, Gallic auxiliaries under Classicus, a chief of the Treveri, also rebelled and set up an "Empire of the Gauls" which won the allegiance of the Roman troops at Vetera. Wild rumors were about in Gaul that the destruction of the Capitol in 69 meant the end of Roman rule and the passing of the Empire of the world to the Celtic peoples. A prophetess called Veleda also inspired the Germans. But when Vespasian was able to send a strong force the rebellion collapsed, and Civilis was driven back into the marshes. To avoid a similar danger in the future auxiliary regiments were henceforth officered by Italians, and posted outside their own country.

In Judea, Titus, Vespasian's son, pressed on with the war. After a terrible siege of 139 days Jerusalem was captured. The Temple was destroyed, its treasures carried off for the great triumphs of Titus and Vespasian, and its tributes appropriated for Jupiter Capitolinus. But Jewish resistance continued, and the fortress of Masada on the Dead Sea held out for two years. Traces of the siege works are still to be seen. All these events are vividly described in the *Jewish War* of Josephus, who was pro-Roman and who witnessed the capture of Jerusalem at Titus' side, but who cared deeply for Jewish culture and religion.

The end of this rebellion meant the re-establishment of peace in the Empire. The gates of the temple of Janus were closed, and a great Temple of Peace was built as an addition to the imperial *fora*. Vespasian, the founder of the second dynasty, was careful to model himself throughout on Augustus, the founder of the first. The arts were patronized, and chairs of Greek and Latin rhetoric established in Rome. The chief feature of his civil administration was the position of Titus, his elder son, who was made virtually coregent and the appointed successor, while his younger son Domitian was to carry on the Flavian line to a third reign. This caused a resurgence of Stoic opposition, and Helvidius Priscus, son-in-law of Nero's victim Thrasea Paetus, was put to death in 75. Apart from this, Vespasian treated the Senate with respect, though he did not give them much rope. After his death he was deified at their order—the second emperor after Augustus to whom that tribute had been paid.

The second Flavian emperor, Titus, eclipsed his father's

popularity in his short reign (79–81 A.D.), and was known as "the darling of the human race." Whether he would have retained his popularity had he lived longer may be doubted; Nero, and even Caligula, made good beginnings. But at least for two years Rome had a genial and open-handed emperor, kind to all men except informers and spies. Short as it was, his reign was marked by disasters and natural calamities—a severe outbreak of plague, a great fire in Rome, and the famous eruption of Vesuvius which destroyed Pompeii and Herculaneum.

The third Flavian, Domitian (81–96 A.D.), according to the poet Martial, made it seem that it would have been almost worthwhile not to have had the other two. The blast of hostile opposition to Domitian rises to gale force in Tacitus and Juvenal. On his death his statues were pulled down, his name was erased from inscriptions, and his memory was condemned. But it is clear that this hostility was limited to the Roman aristocracy, since it belongs to the last years of his reign (93–96), when he became an autocratic and capricious tyrant. Then there was indeed a reign of terror, informers flourished as never before, and those who stood in Domitian's way were liquidated. But for most of his reign he showed himself an able administrator, rather on the lines of Tiberius. Indeed, in many ways he was like those hard-working bureaucrats of modern times of whom it is said that they are dedicated, though to what—apart from their own power—is often uncertain. Certainly Domitian's view of his own power was extreme. By nature an autocrat, he liked to be addressed as "Our Lord and God," and he ruled with the absolutism of a Russian czar. The Senate was enfeebled, and it was reduced to impotence when he assumed censorial powers for life, which enabled him to admit or expel senators.

His foreign policy was marked by important moves on the frontiers. In Britain he was served by an able governor in Gnaeus Julius Agricola, the father-in-law of Tacitus. Agricola rounded off the conquest of North Wales and northern England, campaigned for five years in Scotland, and won a great victory over the Highland tribes. But he was recalled by Domitian, and his plans for the annexation of Caledonia were called off—no doubt wisely in view of what had been learned of the difficulties. In southwestern Germany Domitian completed a move, begun under Vespasian, to occupy the angle between the Rhine and the upper Danube. This was protected by the *Limes Germanicus,* an imposing

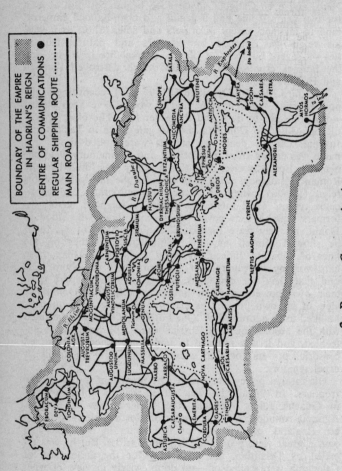

BOUNDARY OF THE EMPIRE
IN HADRIAN'S REIGN
CENTRE OF COMMUNICATIONS ●
REGULAR SHIPPING ROUTE ·········
MAIN ROAD ━━━━

2. Roman Communications

defensive line. But it was on the lower Danube that he faced his most testing problem. From then onward, this was to be the most dangerous of all the frontiers of the Empire.

The threat came from the kingdom of Dacia, roughly the modern Rumania, between the Danube and the Carpathians with the highlands of Transylvania at its heart. It was a land rich in minerals—silver, iron, and gold—with some good farming land in the valleys. Enormous hill forts, which are still to be excavated, commanded the strategic routes. In Caesar's time a strong ruler, Burebista, had built up a power so formidable that Caesar was planning to deal with it at the time of his death. But after the death of Burebista himself the Dacian menace receded for a century, to be renewed by an even more ambitious king, Decebalus. He created the strongest power in central Europe, made allies of his neighbors along the Danube, and entered into diplomatic relations with Parthia. In 85 a Dacian army invaded the province of Moesia, and Rome was faced with a major war. There was a disastrous defeat in 86, with the loss of the commander, Fuscus; next year came a Roman victory at Tapae, when Decebalus was nearly killed. But rebellion on the upper Danube and among the Rhine armies prevented Domitian from achieving a solution to the Dacian problem. Peace was made on terms which the Roman historians regard as dishonorable, and which certainly included the payment of a subsidy. Time would show that Decebalus had not abandoned his grand designs.

Meanwhile, the rebellion of Lucius Antonius Saturninus (88 A.D.) had drastically changed Domitian's reign for the worse. Here began the persecution of the aristocracy which has left such a grim reflection in Tacitus and Juvenal. Rome was a mixture of terror and adulation, in which the only opposition came from the Stoics, descendants of the Stoic martyrs under Nero, and their philosophic advisers. We hear of two expulsions of philosophers (including Epictetus and Dio Chrysostom), and of the deaths of several Stoic aristocrats. Tacitus disapproves of their useless obstinacy, as compared with the realism of such men as Agricola, who showed by a career of public service that there can be good men under a bad emperor. Whatever one may think of the intransigence of the Stoics, they did uphold human dignity in the face of tyranny. Nor were their beliefs without influence, for after Domitian had been assassinated in a palace conspiracy (96), it was clear that the Principate could not continue on dynastic lines.

A fresh start was therefore made by choosing an elderly

senator, Nerva, (96–98 A.D.), partly for his good qualities,
but even more for the lack of certain disadvantages. That he
was an old man was all to the good. "One does not become
dictator," we are told by Charles de Gaulle, "at the age of
sixty-three." Nerva was sixty-six. He was a civilian and the
Senate's man. But at least there would not be rivalry between
army groups, which had led to the events of 69. His would
be a stopgap reign, but perhaps long enough for spirits to
revive after the Terror, and for a more lasting solution to
be found. Tacitus says of Nerva that he blended two
things previously incompatible, the Principate and liberty.
By liberty is meant that of the Senate. Nerva showed them
great deference, and put first the interests of Rome and
Italy. But his was a weak administration, and serious trouble
was avoided only by the adoption as his successor of the
commander of the armies of Upper Germany, Marcus Ulpius
Trajanus.

The choice and the man were significant. All but a few
fanatics accepted the need for a principate; the grand problem of politics was to ensure that the best man would become *princeps*. It had long been pointed out, especially by
Stoic thinkers, that this might be done by the method of
adoption. And that method did, in fact, provide Rome with
its longest period of good government (98–180 A.D.) during
the reigns of Trajan, Hadrian, Antoninus Pius, and Marcus
Aurelius. Trajan was a Spaniard, of a "new" family, the first
emperor of provincial origin. His contemporaries and his
successors regarded him as one of the very best Roman
emperors, and set him by the side of Augustus. We are
handicapped by the poor literary evidence for his reign—if
only there were a single literary expression of the ideas of
that age fit to compare with its great artistic masterpiece,
Trajan's Column!—but it is hardly likely that we should
disagree with that estimate. For the reign of Trajan was
marked by a liberal program of social welfare in Italy, excellent administration in the provinces, and the maximum extension of Roman power after his conquests in Dacia and
Parthia. Moreover, the building of Trajan's Forum set the
seal upon urban magnificence in Rome.

The *alimenta*—maintenance grants for poor children in
Italy—were the most enlightened measure of social welfare
in the Roman world. Begun by private enterprise, the system
was taken up by the state under Nerva and extended by
Trajan. It was financed by state loans to farmers of up to
1/12 (or 1/20?) of the value of their land. They paid interest to their local communities at the low rate (for those

days) of 5 per cent; the local communities distributed this income in grants to the parents of poor children. An inscription from Veleia, near Parma, dated to 103 A.D. shows the detailed working of the scheme. A capital sum of rather more than 1,000,000 sesterces had been advanced to local farmers, yielding 52,200 sesterces per annum in interest. From this 245 boys received 16 sesterces per month, 34 girls 12 sesterces per month. Two illegitimate children also got benefit (one wonders why!), the boy at 12 and the girl at 10 sesterces. More than 40 Italian towns are known from inscriptions to have shared in the scheme, which was later extended to the provinces. It must have helped agriculture as well as child welfare, and the partnership of central and local authorities is a notable feature. No wonder that the reliefs on the arch of Trajan at Beneventum show the *alimenta* as one of the glories of his reign.

His supervision of public expenditure in all parts of the Empire was constant, perhaps excessive. More than seventy cities in the senatorial provinces had to account to his special commissioners (*curatores*). Sometimes whole provinces came in for such attention, as when Pliny was appointed governor of Bithynia. The famous correspondence between Pliny and Trajan cannot be taken as the norm of relations between an emperor and a provincial governor. Bithynia was a special area, Pliny a very cautious man. Even so, the degree of central control is surprising. Buildings, fire brigades, private societies, religious cults, municipal finance, legal decisions, all provided problems on which Pliny asked the emperor's advice. Their correspondence also provides some of the earliest evidence for the attitude of the imperial government to Christianity (see pages 232–37).

Yet Trajan's reputation has always been that of a soldier-emperor, distinguished above all for his wars in Dacia and Parthia. The Dacian Wars (101–106 A.D.) perhaps show the Roman army at its very peak, certainly under its greatest commander. It is lamentable that we cannot set Trajan's *Commentary* beside the relief on his column in Rome to do full justice to their achievement. From the column, it is true, we get a wonderful picture of the Roman army in the field, with full details of its tactics and equipment, and with emphasis on its dependence on the *imperator*. We see, too, the fierce resistance of the Dacians, their armor and weapons and tremendous fortresses, and their great king Decebalus, a worthy antagonist of Trajan himself. But all attempts of modern scholars have failed to construct from the reliefs on the column a continuous narrative history of the campaigns.

Enough, then, to say that by 106 Decebalus was dead and Dacia in Roman hands. The land was annexed as a province, and many of its inhabitants were driven out to provide new lands for settlers, as happened so often to the Indians during American westward expansion. It is this colonization of Dacia, from many parts of the Empire, which has left the permanent stamp of Latin civilization on Rumania. The treasury of the Dacian king provided the Roman *fiscus* with huge reinforcements of gold and silver.

The reasons for Trajan's Parthian wars (113–116) are not wholly clear, but they probably arise out of breaches of the Neronian agreement on Armenia. In three campaigns Trajan annexed Armenia and Mesopotamia as provinces, captured the Parthian capital of Ctesiphon, and descended to the head of the Persian Gulf, near the modern Abadan. There he watched a ship sailing for India, his mind full of thoughts of Alexander. It was the flood tide of Roman success against Parthia, but the ebb was swift. In 117 there was a rebellion in the conquered Parthian provinces, and a terrible Jewish rising affecting Egypt, Cyrene, and Cyprus. Many other problems had arisen in the absence of the emperor. Trajan turned home, but died in Cilicia. The Senate had already given its verdict on his principate, according him the title of *optimus,* a use of the superlative hitherto reserved for Jupiter himself.

The system of adoption provided a worthy successor to this great emperor in his ward and fellow-townsman, Publius Aelius Hadrianus. Hadrian (117–138) was a many-sided man of extraordinary energy, mental and physical, and a consuming curiosity to know the world. When he was with the army, he shared the rations of the common soldier, went on exercises and route marches, and refused to use a vehicle. He climbed Etna at the age of fifty and personally surveyed the line of the Roman Wall in Britain. A lifelong devotee of Greek culture, he was initiated into the Mysteries at Eleusis, and added a new quarter to the city of Athens. At Delphi he asked the oracle about the birth and origins of Homer, and got the surprising answer that he was the son of Telemachus. A patron of the arts, he was himself a bold and inventive architect, and few men in history are associated with such a list of buildings as the Olympieion at Athens, the temple at Cyzicus, that of Venus at Rome, the villa or rather summer palace at Tivoli, and the Mausoleum of Hadrian.

At the outset of his reign Hadrian had to face a major decision about the conquests of Trajan. He chose to abandon the policy of expansion and to renounce everything east of the Euphrates. It is said that he also thought of giving up Dacia but desisted because colonization was going well. It was probably this reversal of Trajan's policy which caused the conspiracy of the Four Consulars (117), all of them members of Trajan's general staff. Consolidation marked the policy of Hadrian in every sphere. Taxes were revised, arrears canceled, and a new fifteen-year cycle planned, though it is uncertain how far it came into force. An enlarged imperial civil service, staffed by Roman *equites,* took over all tax collection, and its direct descendant is to be seen in the inflated bureaucracy of the later Empire.

Hadrian's care of the army was incessant. Discipline was tightened, new tactics were introduced, and all units were kept at a high level of training. Fragments survive of his address to the troops after maneuvers at the African base of Lambaesis—an occasion which must have been repeated on every frontier. The frontiers themselves were strengthened and new defense lines chosen where necessary. The most notable example is in Britain, where in building the wall from the Tyne to the Solway (73 miles) as the northern frontier of the province, Hadrian undertook the greatest piece of military engineering in antiquity. Equally massive—and in the end more lasting—were the revision and codification of the law by jurists of that age, notably the *edictum perpetuum* of Salvius Julianus, which legal historians regard as one of the major works of Roman jurisprudence.

To all this must be added the countless local reforms arising from Hadrian's provincial journeys, which fill the decade 120–130. First came a tour of Gaul, Britain, Spain, and Mauretania (120–123); then Asia, Greece, Pontus, Sicily (123–127); in 128 Africa; and finally, another eastern tour including Syria, Arabia, and Egypt. No other *princeps* ever saw so much of the Empire at first hand. Of the reforms, two examples may be cited. In Britain, the little city of Viroconium (Wroxeter) had embarked on a scheme of town planning in the first flush of Romanization under Agricola. But funds, or enthusiasm, had run out; forty years later the city center had unfinished public buildings. It was no sight for an imperial visitor. Under the stimulus of Hadrian's visit to Britain, the Forum was completed on an ampler scale, and dedicated to him. The building inscription may be seen in Shrewsbury Museum. In Africa, there were serious problems concerning the tenants (*coloni*) on imperial estates, which had grown to an enormous size since confiscations under Nero. Hadrian confirmed their rights and protected them against abuse, and actually encouraged squatters to take up waste land. For the cities of the Empire, Dio Cassius' comment is succinct: "No Emperor visited so many as he did, and he brought help to all. To some, aqueducts, to others, harbors, to others, public buildings, property, and privileges." A series of coins, some of the finest ever issued by the Roman mint, commemorates his provincial journeys and displays the personality of each province.

Hadrian was childless, and his successor was bound to be by adoption. From all we know of him, it is as well that his first choice, Lucius Commodus, died before Hadrian himself. His second fell on the man who, as Antoninus Pius (138–161), was to be the most universally loved of Roman rulers. Antoninus was fifty-one when he was adopted by Hadrian. His reign was the zenith of that long imperial peace during which Gibbon thought the conditions of the human race most happy and prosperous. The Roman world was ruled by an upright gentleman, devoted to his subjects, austere in his tastes, and taking his pleasure in family life on his country estates. There could be no more blameless ruler. No great events marked his reign; there were no provincial journeys. Relations with the Senate were harmonious, and the law was steadily revised and made more humane. The tenor of his reign is summed up in the watchword which he gave to the guard as he lay dying—"equanimity." The contrast between the equanimity of his times and the unforeseen disasters that broke upon the Empire in the reign of Marcus Aurelius is so stark that historians take refuge in metaphor. They describe the age of Antoninus as a golden day in late summer, or a calm at sea, from which winds will arise to set the ship of state on a new course. This does not help. Unexpected disasters may be due to lack of foresight, equanimity a state of mind no ruler can afford. Modern scholars tend to regard the reign of Antoninus as the wasted years of the Roman Empire, when the army was allowed to slip away from the high standards of Hadrian, the provinces to become slack in the absence of the emperor, and the initiative to pass to the barbarians on the frontiers. Only in Britain was there a forward movement. Antoninus built a new wall, farther north, from the Forth to the Clyde. It gave a shorter line of defense (44 miles) than that of Hadrian, but was much easier to turn. Otherwise, there was calm within the Empire. But, outside it, in the barbarian world that stretched from the forests of Germany and Poland to the steppes of Russia and Mongolia, there was a seething, restless movement of peoples and tribes, unknown to the Romans until its last waves broke on the defenses of the Rhine and the Danube. The world was to pay a heavy price for the happy days Antoninus spent over the grape harvests at Signia.

But at least Antoninus did not fail to train his successor. No ruler ever came to the throne better prepared by education than Marcus Aurelius, and in happier times his reign (161–180) would have been a fair test of the blessings that Plato supposed to flow when philosophers are kings. For he was deeply imbued with that later brand of Stoicism, virtually confined to ethics, which is expounded in the *Handbook* of Epictetus. From it he learned ideals of service to others, self-communion, cheerfulness in distress, and a lofty view of the activities of mankind. "One man prides himself on hunting hares, another on hunting Sarmatians." His own *Meditations* were not composed in the study, but in his tent on active service—"This among the Quadi on the Danube." But his philosophy did not teach him to judge men. Early in his reign he got the Senate to agree to a novel proposal that his adoptive brother Lucius Verus should be co-emperor. It was a bad choice, for Lucius was unequal to the task, as he soon showed when he was sent out to repel an invasion of Syria by the Parthian king Vologeses. While Lucius enjoyed the pleasures of Antioch, his able marshals were—once more—licking the Roman army in Syria into shape. Then they pushed back the Parthians, and captured Ctesiphon as Trajan had done. The ablest of them was Avidius Cassius, a Syrian by origin, who won a great reputation throughout the East. It was an impressive reassertion of Roman power. But the armies of Avidius Cassius had overcome one foe to unleash another more terrible— the plague. They brought back with them one of the great epidemics of history, like the Black Death, which ravaged the Roman world, and may have been a potent factor, some suppose, in the decline of the Empire.

Next came disaster in the North. A great coalition of barbarian peoples attacked along the whole line of the Danube, overran Dacia and the Danubian provinces, and reached the head of the Adriatic at Aquileia (166). Not since the Cimbri, or the Pannonian revolt under Augustus, had there been such a crisis. It called for the presence of the emperor, and led to thirteen years of hard fighting, the so-called Marcomannic War, of which we know few details. But it does seem that in those years Marcus formed a grand design to avert such dangers for ever. This was to revive Augustus' plan of pushing the frontier north through Bohemia to the Elbe, and extending it to link with the northern frontier of Dacia along the line of the Carpathians. By 175 the design was taking shape, but a rebellion in the East proclaimed Avidius Cassius emperor. Marcus hurried from the Danube to Syria to find Cassius dead and the rebellion in collapse, but meanwhile his work in the North was undone. Grimly, he set about doing it again. There is an infinite pathos about the equestrian statue of Marcus Aurelius on the Capitol "returning the salute of legions which have been dust for two thousand years." The legions and their commander had almost completed their task; Marcomannia and Jazygia were on the point of becoming Roman provinces. The best lands of central Europe would have passed under Roman rule, to form a huge glacis against the barbarian assaults of the next two centuries. But suddenly Marcus was attacked by fever in the camp at Vindobona (Vienna), and died at his post, as a Roman emperor should. It only needed a resolute successor to drive home the last bolt. But that Marcus, by his own choice, had made impossible.

Marcus was the first emperor of the second century to have sons of his own, and the temptation to break with the system of adoption was one which he could not resist. Undeterred by the failure of his experiment of joint rule with Lucius Verus, he entered into another with his son Commodus, whom he made Augustus in 177. Commodus must be the outstanding example in history of the tendency of good men to have vicious sons. His reign (180–192) was in every way a disaster for the Empire. It began by his abandoning the conquests of Marcus—as his father had feared he would do—to leave himself free for dissipation in Rome. He fell under the influence of a succession of worthless favorites, the most influential of whom became prefects of the Praetorian Guard, and conducted a shameless traffic in the sale of public offices. A reign of terror developed, like the worst days of Caligula or Nero. With the Roman mob, Commodus enjoyed a certain popularity, as one who shared their debased tastes. He was not assassinated until 192, a year whose beginning he had signalized by appearing in public on the same day as consul and as gladiator. The evil that he did lived after him, for there was no heir. It was the same situation as in 69, and there was another disastrous series of civil wars. But this time there was to be no Vespasian to bring back good rule to the world.

CHAPTER XI

THE ROMAN PEACE: 14–192 A.D.

"Immensa Romanae pacis maiestas"—the boundless majesty of the Roman peace. Pliny's splendid phrase no one trying to describe the Roman world of early Empire can—or should—avoid. Boundaries, of course, there were to the world under the sway of the Roman peace. It extended from Scotland to the Sudan, from Portugal to the Euphrates; its longest axis east-west was about 2,800, north-south about 1,600 miles. It covered an area of Europe, Asia, and Africa that has never again been under a single rule. Only an estimate of its population can be made, but a figure of seventy millions is widely accepted. Many languages were spoken, although not nearly so many as today. We may instance Celtic in Britain, Gaul, some of the Danube lands, and Galatia, Germanic along the Rhine and upper Danube, Punic and Egyptian in Africa, and Aramaic in Syria. But two languages enjoyed a primacy, Latin in the West and Greek in the East. Knowledge of these two would take you anywhere, and such knowledge was the heritage of every educated person. A single currency, a single law, prevailed throughout. There were no frontiers or major customs barriers within the Empire. Travel, though slow and uncomfortable by modern standards, was a good deal faster by land than anything before the railway age. Indeed, over certain parts of the Empire Roman standards have not been restored. Sea travel was more uncertain; European nations reached and passed the Roman level three centuries earlier than by land. There was religious toleration. Only three religious cults ever met persecution at the hands of the imperial government—Druidism, Judaism, and Christianity. There was no color bar, and while there was dislike and friction between certain peoples, there was no racial dis-

179

crimination in the modern sense. In short, it is fair to claim that the Empire in these centuries was the nearest approach to a world state yet seen, and this is one of its greatest claims to the attention of the modern world.

Before looking at the provinces, we should note certain things about the Empire as a whole. First, the fundamental division between East and West. The eastern half of the Empire was a region of great historic cultures—Greek, Semitic, Oriental—and a long urban tradition, a world to which the Romans came as conquerors and administrators, not as the bringers of a higher civilization. The West was another story. There, Celtic, Germanic, Iberian, and other native tribal societies became civilized under Roman influence and assimilated to the general cultural pattern of the Greco-Roman world. The eastern frontiers of Illyricum and of Africa were the boundary between these two worlds. It was a division which hardened with time. The foundation of an eastern capital at Constantinople in the early fourth century accentuated it, and it became permanent after the death of Theodosius in 395.

East or West, the vehicle of civilization was the city. The Empire, it has been said, was a federation of cities under a central government. It is not the whole truth, but it will serve. The cities of the East had a long tradition of self-government with which Rome did not as a rule interfere, except to show dislike of extreme forms of democracy. In the West, she encouraged the growth of new cities on the lines of the municipalities of Italy. An elected town council of local notables would be in charge of local affairs. Physically, these new cities of the western provinces had a regular street plan, drainage, a good water supply, and dignified public buildings. Amenities such as theaters, baths, hotels, libraries, and colonnades were standard. The better houses had central heating, wall paintings, and mosaics. Town walls and monumental gateways complete the picture.

But despite the cultural importance of the city, the basic economic activity was agriculture. Romanization was most successful where a Latin-speaking peasantry cultivated the soil, and this would be in lands where a Mediterranean type of agriculture was possible. Hence the civilization of the Empire was, basically, that of the Mediterranean littoral and its hinterland. It did not take root in the forests of central Europe, nor on the shores of the Atlantic. There was a certain latent opposition between the economic primacy of the country and the cultural supremacy of the town, which developed into open conflict in the later Empire.

I now turn to a brief survey of the parts of the Empire: first the provinces, beginning with the western, then the eastern provinces; and finally Rome and Italy. If the western provinces are given what may seem more than their proper share of space, it is because there was performed the great task of Rome—the development of a Latin civilization.

Spain, the oldest province in western Europe, made great contributions to the economic and cultural life of the Empire. From it came Trajan and Hadrian, and a notable line of Latin authors, including the two Senecas, Lucan, Columella, Quintilian, and Martial. The dominance of Latin is shown by the fact that Basque is the only survivor of the native languages of the peninsula; all the rest (Spanish, Portuguese, Catalan) are Latin derivatives. A rich dividend was reaped for the bitter wars of conquest and for the Latin colonization under the Republic. But Romanization was not uniform throughout the peninsula. It was most intensive in the coastal regions of the East and the South, the modern Catalonia, Valencia, and Andalusia, where there was a brilliant urban civilization. Vespasian, a great benefactor of Spain, gave Latin rights to some two hundred cities. The charter of Malaca (Malaga), granted by Domitian, is the chief source for what is known of their administration. The cities of Baetica— Corduba, (Cordova), Italica, Hispalis (Seville), made the whole valley of the Guadalquivir "another Italy." Gades was the chief port of western Spain, full of rich merchants and captains, trading with the whole Mediterranean. Tarraco (Tarragona) was the capital of the largest of the three Spanish provinces, and the meeting place of the provincial council. A carefully planned road system served the whole peninsula, and many historic Spanish cities—Saragossa, Toledo, Salamanca, Mérida—stand on Roman foundations. There was little urban development in the North and West, and in Lusitania the tribesmen continued to live in the great hill forts (*citanias*). But Olisipo (Lisbon) became a port trading with Italy, and there was considerable Romanization in the lower Tagus valley.

Economically, development was impressive. Spanish wine was exported to Britain, Gaul, and the Rhineland as well as Rome; Spanish olive oil was second only to Italian; production of grain was important. Esparto grass was grown for ropes, flax for linen. The splendid fishing grounds of the Atlantic coast led to a fish-curing industry, and to the export of a fish sauce (*garum*) to all parts of the world. Tunny and mackerel, not the sardine, were the fish most used. But minerals remained the major economic asset of Spain.

The silver of the Sierra Morena and the copper of Rio Tinto continued to be heavily worked, as under the Republic; the Empire also opened up the iron, gold, silver, and tin of the Pyrenees and Cantabria. Spanish armorers became famous for their steel—compare the Toledo blades of later times. Two well-known inscriptions from Vipasca in southern Portugal show the working of copper and silver mines in Hadrian's time. The mines were state-owned but leased out to private operators, the imperial treasury taking a half share of the output. The labor force, as in most Spanish mines, was slave or convict. The regulations prescribe in detail the terms on which concessions were offered to mine operators, auctioneers, the lessee of the baths, the shoemaker, the fuller, and the barber. Attention is called to the tax exemption enjoyed by the schoolmaster. There was some improvement in mining technology at this time, such as the sinking of shafts and the use of water for washing and draining. Pliny gives a long account of Spanish mining, especially for gold. The gold mines of the northwest are estimated to have produced more than $80,000,000 per year in gross return.

Roman Africa was a Mediterranean land. Cut off from continental Africa first by the Atlas and Aures mountains, then by the Sahara Desert, it faced the Mediterranean along a thousand miles of coast, and reached close to Sicily on the east and Spain on the west. It was organized into four provinces: Africa proper (part of Libya and Tunisia), Numidia or New Africa, the former kingdom of Juba II (roughly Algeria) and the two Mauretanian provinces (Morocco) set up by Claudius. Here—and especially in Africa proper—was the scene of one of the greatest triumphs of Latin civilization. Opinions differ as to the scale of Italian colonization in Africa, but there can be no doubt that it was extensive. Kahrstedt gives a figure of 200,000 for Italian settlers, and claims that 40 per cent of all Latin speakers in the world lived in North Africa. Rome won this world for Western civilization; the Arab invasions made it part of Islam: now France and Islam struggle for its future. It was a land of many peoples at varying levels of culture. The oldest elements were the Berbers, grouped into many large tribes, some nomadic. They form the main strain in the population today, and their language survives. The Punic peoples were the product of the colonizing work of Carthage in Africa. Most of them lived in the coastal cities, but some were farmers who had penetrated inland. Punic was widely spoken, and was still the vernacular in the big cities in

Augustine's time. Latin was the official language. There were small settlements of Greeks and Jews in the larger towns.

Urban life in Africa grew from two sources, Latin and Punic. More than three hundred cities of a Latin type are known in the four provinces. Some of them were of Punic origin, but had become assimilated to Latin neighbors, and ended by acquiring Latin rights. It is possible to give a general picture of Romanization in the countryside. The land to be settled would first have to be protected against the nomads, who were sometimes confined to reservations. Then would come the question of water supply. French experts are full of praise for Roman hydraulic engineering in Africa, with its reservoirs, aqueducts, cisterns, and canals. An inscription from Lamasba in southern Algeria gives the irrigation schedule for a number of small farms. The skill derived from the old farmers of Latium was being put to use in a new land. As agriculture grew prosperous, the market towns would grow and equip themselves with amenities, thus attracting new inhabitants. So the area of settlement advanced southward under the Empire until, in the best parts, a thickly settled belt of towns and farms reached more than two hundred miles from the coast. The Roman *limes* in Africa was the southern edge of the farming land. Tunisia and Tripoli were the most heavily settled lands. Numidia did not contain many cities; Mauretania, like Britain, came late to Romanization and never felt its full impact.

From Carthaginian times, the staple of African agriculture had been grain. Under the Empire, the grain lands were extended to parts of Algeria and Mauretania. A famous passage of Josephus states that the African crop for the *annona* of Rome was twice that of Egypt, which would make it some forty million *modii* a year. We do not know how far fertility was maintained against erosion. About the olive in Africa we are better informed, for the olive presses are left, and distribution can be plotted. In both Tunisia and Algeria it became a major crop, for it can be grown in areas of low rainfall where cereals would not do. Roman "dry farming" of olives in Africa has been much copied by French colonists. Figs were a regular crop; wine production never approached the levels of today. Among other African products we may note the yellow marbles of Simitthus in Numidia (the *giallo antico* of so many Roman buildings), ebony and citrus woods from the Atlas, and wild animals for the arena. Camel trains plied on regular routes across the Sahara, bringing ivory to

Sabrata and other ports. This traffic was managed by nomad tribesmen, and was never on the scale of the caravans that crossed the Syrian Desert to central Asia.

Great estates had been a feature of African farming since Punic times, and some huge senatorial fortunes were founded on them under the Republic. The ultimate beneficiary of all this was the emperor. Under Nero, the six greatest estates in Africa were confiscated. By the time of Hadrian the emperor owned much of the agricultural land of the province, and his tenants were an important part of the population. Vespasian established a special office in Carthage for the administration of the imperial estates. They were managed by procurators in charge of a staff of freedmen and slaves. The tenants enjoyed security and low rents, though they were exposed to abuses at the hands of the imperial officials. There was a tendency for their occupation to become hereditary, and historians point to the imperial colonate as the precursor of the serfdom of the Middle Ages. Few Roman inscriptions are better known—or more disputed!—than a series which deal with affairs on some of Hadrian's estates in the Bagradas valley.

Only a few of the famous cities of Africa can find mention here. Carthage was the queen, the capital of the province of Africa, a major port, and the chief cultural center, famous for the magnificence of her public buildings and the mansions and parks of the rich. Her population must have reached 250,000, and she called Rome "the Sister City." Carthage far outstripped her old rival Utica, which was slow to recover from having backed the republican cause in the Civil War. Other important cities of Africa proper were Hippo (Bône) and Hadrumetum (Sousse), a prosperous port and one of the chief Punic centers in Africa. The cities of Tripoli flourished on shipping and on the camel traffic with the Fezzan. At Germa, capital of the Garamantes, in the Fezzan, is the most southerly Roman monument in Africa, perhaps the mausoleum of a merchant engaged in this traffic. Italian archaeologists have found Roman articles of export in the Fezzan which are now on display in the Museo Coloniale in Rome. Many Allied soldiers who fought in Africa will remember the remains of Leptis Magna, which are the most impressive in all of North Africa. Cirta, to which Caesar had added a colony of veterans, was the capital of Numidia. Marble and copper were won in the district, the product of which went through the ports of Rusicada (Philippeville) and Chullu (Collo). Lambaesis (Lambessa) on the slopes of the Aures mountains was the great military base; today the camp of the Third Legion is the best preserved in the Roman world. Twenty miles west is the famous site of Thamugadi (Timgad). Founded by Trajan, and built as a showpiece for the new territory of southern Algeria, its huge Capitolium is a showpiece still. The chief city of eastern Mauretania was Caesarea, a port with a population of a hundred thousand, embellished by King Juba II, philhellene, connoisseur, historian, botanist, and the husband of Cleopatra's daughter. The western province was ruled from Tingis (Tangier), which looked across the straits to Spain rather than to its eastern neighbor.

A distinctive brand of Latin culture evolved in these cities of North Africa, with traces of Punic influence, but owing much less to Greece than did the cultures of contemporary Rome or Italy. The Latin classics, from Plautus to Virgil, were widely read, but contemporary authors were disliked. In the second century Africa contributed Fronto and Apuleius to Latin literature. In the late Empire it was to produce many of the great figures of Latin Christianity.

No one who has seen the Roman cities of Provence needs a reminder of the brilliant and varied urban civilization of the old province of Narbonensis, the most fully Romanized part of Gaul. The capital, Narbo, used its lagoons to develop a trade with Africa, Syria, Spain, Italy, and Sicily, and was noted for the wealth of its merchant princes. Still more important was Arelate (Arles), where goods brought down the Rhone by barge were transferred to ocean-going ships. Its forum, capitol, theater, baths, colonnades, amphitheaters, aqueducts, cemetery, water mill, and bridge of boats, present a picture of urban splendor scarcely matched in the West outside Rome. It outstripped the old Greek city of Massilia, which remained famous for its schools of philosophy and medicine. Nemausus (Nîmes) was noted for the shrine of Apollo and for its city walls, six kilometers in length. Forum Iulii (Fréjus) was a naval base, "the Toulon of Gaul," Aquae Sextiae (Aix) a spa, Genava (Geneva) a summer resort. Along the Rhone were important cities at river crossings, Vienna (Vienne), Valentia (Valence), Avenio (Avignon). Some of the small cities such as Vasio and Glanum have left rich remains. The whole province stood at a level of development that could stand comparison with Italy itself.

Nor was urban development confined to Narbonensis. Lugdunum (Lyons), capital of the huge province of Lugdunensis, had a cosmopolitan population, a garrison, and an imperial mint. Gold- and silversmiths, wine exporters, and shipping on the Saône and Rhone attest its economic impor-

tance. Politically, it was the meeting place of the sixty tribes
of the Three Gauls, which met in council at the altars of
Rome and Augustus by the confluence of the two rivers. In
the north the greatest city was Augusta Treverorum (Trèves),
where the Claudian colony had grown into a flourishing city
by the middle of the first century. It is notable for its rectangular street plan and for the size of its public buildings,
most of which belong to the late Empire, when it was an imperial capital. There was a remarkable temple quarter, with
over seventy shrines, large and small, dedicated to Roman,
Celtic, and Oriental divinities. In Aquitania, Burdigala
(Bordeaux) was the port for the wealthy valley of the
Garonne. Inscriptions show residents from the eastern
provinces, and a wine trade with Britain and, it would seem,
with Ireland. But outside Narbonensis the canton—the old
tribal area—was more important than the city. Several of the
cities of northern France have grown from cantonal capitals
and still preserve the tribal name. Such are Rheims, Sens,
Arras, Soissons, and Paris itself. The *civitas* of northern Gaul
was thus a blend of Celtic and Roman institutions, unlike
the full Romanization of Provence. The same may be said of
the villas, or country houses, of which more than three thousand are known. The Celtic aristocrat had lived on the land
with his dependents. The villa brought Roman amenities to
this traditional way of life. Two regions in particular are
notable for the size and luxury of their villas. One is the
Moselle valley, with such sites as Nennig and Welschbillig,
where the estate covered more than 120 square miles and
may have been an imperial property. The other is the Haute
Garonne, in the southwest, where the villa of Chiragan near
Toulouse is perhaps the finest ever found in the provinces.
Here a simple dwelling of the first century A.D. with a central
house and workers' cottages grew in the next century to a
luxurious château with more than forty tenants' houses
grouped in an area of some sixteen acres. In the third century this estate was in decline, and it does not seem to have
survived the Vandal invasion of 408.

It is a far cry from this sophistication to the less Romanized parts of Gaul. In the north the roads to the Channel
ports are through lonely forests; lonelier still were the heaths
and woods of Brittany, a land little touched by Roman civilization.

Agriculture and industry were stimulated by the needs of
the cities of Gaul and of the armies on the Rhine. Grain
was grown for home consumption and for export; both
Arelate and Narbo shipped grain to Ostia. From Augustus'

time the vine spread northward across Gaul, until by the second century the foundation of the noble viticulture of France had been established along the Moselle, Rhone, Rhine, and Garonne. Gallic cheeses and hams were famous. Geese reared on the Channel coasts were driven as far as Rome. Industrially, an important woolen trade grew up in the North. The iron of Lorraine and the building stones of the Pyrenees were exploited. But pottery—the famous Gallic *terra sigillata*—stands first among Gallic industries. The factories of La Graufesenque, shipping from Narbo, had won a world market by 50 A.D. Later (75–150) supremacy passed to Lezoux, which cornered the British and Danube trade, and finally to Rheinzabern, supplying the northern armies. An intensive study of potters' marks has given the archaeologist an indispensable aid for dating.

Gaul was noted for its transport system. The road network, radiating from Lyons, was mostly the work of Claudius. But nature itself provided a wonderful system of navigable rivers of which the Romans took full advantage. We have mentioned the shipping on the Rhine, Rhone, Saône, and Moselle. On these, and also on the Loire, Seine, Durance, and Garonne, were guilds of shippers and haulers, making arteries of commerce like the Mississippi before the railroads.

This Gallo-Roman civilization was at its most prosperous about 150 A.D. Latin was everywhere the language of education in a province noted for its schools. Gallic survived into the second century, and has left a few inscriptions. But, apart from Breton—a Celtic tongue reintroduced from Britain in the Dark Ages—Basque, and the German of Alsace, all the languages of France derive from Latin. In religion, Roman and Celtic cults existed side by side, or blended happily. Sculpture represents such Celtic divinities as the horse-goddess Epona, the antler-horned Cernunnos, Sucellos with his mallet, and the mountain god Esus, identified by the Romans with Mercury. The population of Roman Gaul was undoubtedly high, even if one does not accept the 15 or even 20 million put forward by some French archaeologists. Certainly it is fair to see in this large population and high civilization contributing factors to the primacy which France so long enjoyed in Europe.

In Britain the pattern of settlement followed the dualism of the personality of the island. The highland zone of the north and west—Scotland, northern England except the Vale of York, Wales except the sea plain by the Severn, the southwestern peninsula beyond Exeter—is a land of mountains and moors, high rainfall, and poor soils. The lowland zone south and east of this is a land of plains and gentle

hills, rich soils, and moderate (comparatively!) rainfall. In the
lowland zone developed the civilian province; Rome treated
the highland zone, as much of it as she cared to hold, as a
military area. Romanization in lowland Britain was on much
the same level as in northern Gaul. Here, too, the canton was
the unit of local self-government. Some fifteen Romano-
British *civitates* are known; from their capitals have grown,
among others, Leicester, Chichester, Dorchester, Canterbury,
Winchester, and St. Albans. Some Roman centers were
abandoned in later times; thus Shrewsbury has superseded
Viroconium, and Reading has replaced Calleva. There were
four *coloniae*, Lindum (Lincoln), Glevum (Gloucester) Ebor-
acum (York), and Camulodunum (Colchester). This last
Claudius intended as the capital of the province, but it was
superseded by Londinium (London). London became the
largest city in Britain (population c. 25,000), the center of the
road system, and the chief port for trade with the Continent.
Corinium (Cirencester), Viroconium (Wroxeter), and Veru-
lamium (St. Albans) may have been about 10,000; the other
towns range from 2,000 to 5,000. Urban life in Britain began
slowly and reached no great heights. None the less, public
buildings were fairly lavish, and there were comfortable town
houses. Baths, hotels, and amphitheaters are standard; three
theaters are known; there may have been others. The spa at
Bath (Aquae Sulis) is remarkable for its huge bath buildings
and the temple of the goddess of the hot springs.

Like his cousins across the Channel, the wealthy British
landowner appreciated Roman amenities. The six hundred or
so villas of Roman Britain are mostly concentrated in favored
areas, such as the Cotswolds, Somerset, northern Kent, western Sussex, Hampshire, and the Isle of Wight. None rival
Chiragan or Nennig, but the owner of Chedworth or Wood-
chester must have lived in a comfort not reached again in
Britain until the reign of Elizabeth. Over much of the province, however, the native system of farming, with its isolated
farmsteads, continued, as indeed it does today in Wales and
the Pennines.

Britain lies beyond the limits of Mediterranean agriculture
and could have had no attraction for settlers, apart from the
veterans with their free land grants. But British agriculture,
in native hands, provided for the basic needs of the province, with an occasional surplus of grain for export. It also
had to meet the needs of the Roman garrison for grain; for
this a part of the Fenland was drained and cultivated under
imperial management. British cloth was exported, and is mentioned in the tariff of Cyrene in Africa. British oysters had

been prized by gourmets before the conquest. Pearls, hunting dogs, hides, cattle, and sealskins also found a market on the Continent, and enabled Britain to import wine, pottery, luxury clothing and furniture, and professional services.

But minerals came first, as with Spain, though on a smaller scale. Lead was worked intensively soon after the conquest in the Mendips, and later in Flintshire, Shropshire, Plynlimmon, and the Pennines. Copper was worked in Anglesey, North Wales, and Shropshire, iron in many places, notably the Weald and the Forest of Dean. British gold has made no millionaires, but the Romans mined it at Dolaucothy in South Wales. Cornish tin was worked very little at first—perhaps to avoid competing with Spain—but became important in the late Empire. Outcrop coal was mined in several places, but coal never became as important as in modern times. All the major building stones of Britain were used by the Romans, who also exploited the salt of Droitwich and Cheshire.

Although Agricola used to praise the promise of the British, the province never did make a serious contribution to the culture of the Roman world. The only known Romano-British writer is Pelagius, the contemporary and opponent of Augustine. Latin was certainly the language of literacy. There is not a single inscription in Celtic. Yet the linguistic history of Britain is vastly different from that of Gaul. Celtic languages (Welsh and Cornish) have survived in those parts of the island that escaped being overrun by Teutonic-speaking barbarians in the Dark Ages, and it is believed that, for most of the population of Roman Britain, Celtic was the language of everyday speech.

The military areas of Britain provide a study which has attracted some of the greatest modern archaeologists. Four strategic points held down Wales—on the east the legionary bases of Chester and Caerleon, on the west the forts of Caernarvon and Carmarthen, linked by a series of forts and strategic roads. The Welsh solution proved inapplicable to Caledonia (Scotland), where Agricola's explorations by land and sea convinced the central government of the hopelessness of conquest. A fine passage of Tacitus shows the Roman reaction to the fiord scenery of the western Highlands. "Nowhere does the sea bear a wider dominion. . . . He winds about and inserts himself into the land as though in his own realms." Anyone who has waited for a Highland ferry will agree. A northern frontier had to be found. We have alluded to Hadrian's solution, the great barrier of the Wall, from the Tyne to the Solway, with its 16 forts, 80 milecastles, and 160

signal towers, the whole supported by a legionary base at
York and forts in the Pennines. A score of years later the
Wall of Antoninus enabled the garrison of Hadrian's Wall to
be reduced, and brought southern Scotland under control.
Even this proved not to be the final solution, and a withdrawal to Hadrian's Wall became necessary about 200 A.D.
Perhaps the most surprising feature of the whole system is
the manpower locked up in Britain, for the Roman garrison
of forty to fifty thousand men was between an eighth and a
tenth of the armed forces of the Empire. Why, in so remote a province, and was it worthwhile? It is true, of
course, that Britain herself provided some eighteen thousand
battleworthy troops. Even so, there seems a problem here to
which we do not know an answer.

The provinces of Upper and Lower Germany, created by
Domitian, were, economically and strategically, an extension
of Gaul. Under the influence of their armies, and of the veterans settled near their old garrisons, the Rhineland became
Romanized. The now familiar pattern of the growth of historic cities from Roman military centers is well seen at
Cologne, Mainz, and Strasbourg. Glass was worked at Cologne, iron near Aachen, pottery at Mainz. There were notable
schools of stonemasons at Neumegen and Arlon in the Moselle
valley, whose funerary monuments depict the life of the rich
merchants of that district. The *Agri Decumates* ("Tithelands")
of southwestern Germany were so called from the Gallic settlers introduced in the late first century. Behind Domitian's
fortifications it was a land of forests and small farms—
especially in the Neckar valley—and few towns, although
Wiesbaden, Rottweil, and Baden-Baden stand on Roman
foundations.

We have seen how strategic considerations led Rome to the
control of the Alpine and Danube lands from the time of
Augustus. No secure civilization could develop in Cisalpine
Gaul without control of the passes from Germany into
Italy. Moreover, a land route was needed to link East and
West, the armies of the Rhine and the Danube with those
of Syria, and was found in the artery running from Aquileia
to Byzantium, via the Sava valley, Naissus, and Adrianople.
So by Hadrian's time the whole vast area from Switzerland
to the Black Sea with its population of Celts, Germans,
Illyrians, Thracians, and many other peoples had been
brought into the provincial system, which extended north of
the Danube after Trajan's conquest of Dacia. But these
Danube provinces must not be thought of only as a military
zone. They developed a varied economic life and, in places,

an urban civilization. Only Austria can show a record to compare with Rome in these lands. The Rumanian scholar Parvan
has shown how the prelude to all this rapid Romanization was
the penetration by Italian merchants, businessmen, and engi-
neers of the Danube lands while they were still in barbarian
control. Here, as often in the Roman Empire, the flag followed
trade.

The Alpine province of Rhaetia (larger than the modern
Switzerland) did not develop much, for the Romans could not
ski or cure tuberculosis, and made their own cream cheese.
But the capital, Augusta Vindelicorum, preserves in Augsburg
its founder's name, and Innsbruck and Regensburg stand on
Roman sites.

In the rich iron ores of Styria, the old Celtic kingdom of
Noricum had a commodity that has been in demand for
millennia. Long on friendly terms with Rome, it was made a
province by Augustus, and developed a Latin-Celtic culture
very like that of Gaul, with which it was in close touch.
Some fascinating traces of this survive in the art of its old
capital, Noreia.

In Pannonia, the next province to the east, Romanization of
the Sava and Drava valleys was so successful that they have
been called an eastward extension of Italy. Nauportus, Siscia
(Sisak), Sirmium, and Singidunum (Belgrade) became important cities. A Roman fleet patrolled the Sava and Danube and
commercial traffic went down to the Black Sea. On the Adriatic coast Pola, Tergeste (Trieste), and Salonae could compare with the cities of Italy. Near Pola is the famous villa of
Brioni Grande, one of the most sumptuous in the Empire. Inland, the limestone plateau of Dalmatia was a backward
region. But the manpower of all Pannonia and Dalmatia—
loosely termed Illyricum—was invaluable for the armies of
the Empire. Illyrian emperors and soldiers were to bring the
Roman world through the disasters of the third century.
Farther north, along the line of the Danube, was the world
of army camps and frontier campaigns. Carnuntum, of which
there are extensive remains, headquarters of the XIV legion,
was the chief Roman base. Vindobona was also a legionary
base and the harbor of the Danube fleet. From it has grown
the city of Vienna; its rival Budapest grew from Aquincum.

Moesia, the most easterly of the Danube provinces, was extended to the Black Sea by Claudius. Its capital was Naissus, the modern Nish. Trajan founded other cities, and a
stream of colonization helped to Romanize the lower Danube.
The settlement of a hundred thousand barbarians from across
the Danube on the south bank by Plautius Silvanus (c. 62-63)

3. *The Roman Empire at Its Greatest Extent*

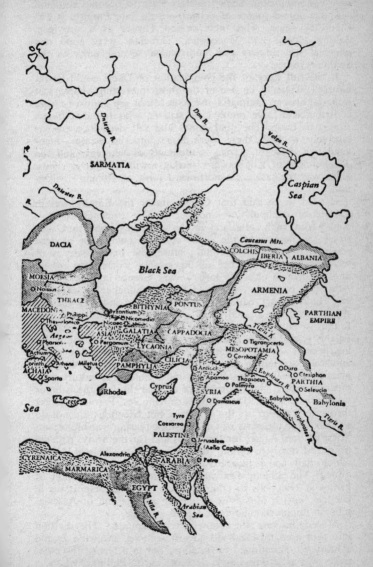

A.D. was significant. Such transfers were to become common —and a potent source of danger—in the late Empire. It was Claudius, again, who incorporated Thrace as a province, linking Moesia and Macedonia. Thracians were good raw material for soldiers and contributed several units to the auxiliary forces.

If the full story of the colonization of Dacia could be recovered, it would be one of the most interesting chapters of imperial history. Dalmatia and Asia Minor are known to have contributed a large number of settlers, who found a *lingua franca* in Latin. The gold mines and salt deposits were extensively worked, there were large imperial estates, managed like those of Africa, settlements of veterans, and the development of villages into market towns with civic rights. Here was the last great northward push of Roman civilization.

It used to be said that Greece under the Empire was in a state of depopulation and decay. The evidence for this comes from such authors as Strabo and Dio Chrysostom, who stress the decline of the small country towns. But modern research presents a different picture, the main features of which are the emergence of big estates, worked by *coloni*, and the growth of a few large towns. Greece in general, and Athens in particular, benefited by the philhellenism of Nero and Hadrian. Art, education, and the tourist industry enabled Athens to make a good living out of her glorious past. She found a patron in the multimillionaire Herodes Atticus (d. 177), and under Hadrian enjoyed one of her great building periods. Sparta, uncharacteristically, went in for peace and trade, exploiting the quarries of Taygetus. Corinth was a market between East and West and a noted—or notorious— pleasure resort. Nero's project of a canal through the isthmus was never completed. Of Augustus' colonies, Patrae (Patras) throve as a packet station for Italy, but Nicopolis did not do so well. In many parts of Greece stock rearing was important. Thessaly bred horses for the circus and for the army. Arcadia produced sturdy asses and mules. Some of the federal leagues which had come into existence in Hellenistic times continued. The athletic festivals went on with the addition of games at Nicopolis to commemorate Actium. Delphi was in decline, but the Mysteries at Eleusis and the cult of Aesculapius at Epidaurus maintained their prestige.

Macedonia was still a largely tribal country. The division into four areas of local self-government, set up in the second century B.C., continued to function. But in a few of the cities there was a strong Latin element, as in Philippi, where a colony of Antony's veterans was established, Beroea, an important trading center, and Thessalonica, which displaced the old capital of Pella to become, what it has remained, the greatest city of northern Greece.

Asia Minor comprises the land mass between the Black Sea and the Levantine coasts of the Mediterranean. It is large and varied enough to be almost a subcontinent. Rome brought it under single control, which it has known at very few periods of history. Rome entered this region as the successor to the Hellenistic monarchies, in whose times there had always been a strong contrast between the brilliant cities of the coastal fringes on the north and west and the backward life of the Anatolian plateau. We have seen how the cities were harried by Roman *publicani* in the Republic; their recovery was cut off by the contributions forced from them for the armies of Brutus and Mark Antony. But the Empire brought peace. The economic recovery that set in under Augustus carried the prosperity of Asia, by the early second century, to heights unprecedented—indeed, unrepeated, for never again has it reached the Roman level.

A fine network of roads opened up the interior and led to the growth of cities in Phrygia and Pisidia. But it was still the cities of the coast that were the most prosperous. At least six topped the figure of 100,000, and from the Flavian period they entered into a competition in public magnificence, and of rivalry for such titles as Metropolis of Asia. A speech of Aelius Aristides on the amenities of Smyrna would do credit to any modern publicity bureau. Smyrna's rise dated from her support of Rome against Mithridates, and she became a great port and a center of science and medicine. Ephesus was the largest city of the Greek world after Alexandria and Antioch. The priests of the Temple of Diana had charge not only of the most famous of Asian cults but also of one of the largest banks in the Roman world. In the northwest Alexandria Troas became important. Cyzicus on the Propontis was out of favor in the early Empire, but found a good patron in Hadrian. In Bithynia, Nicaea and Nicomedia developed a twin cities rivalry which ended in favor of the latter in the third century, when it became an imperial capital. On the south coast only Tarsus in Cilicia, with its linen industry, grew to any size. St. Paul's description of it as "no mean city" is well known, and a reminder of how much incidental information we get from the Acts of the Apostles about the cities of Asia in the first century. All these Asian cities were much subject to earthquakes, and we hear repeatedly of gifts from the emperor to repair dam-

age. Galatia remained a Celtic outpost. Missionaries from
Gaul came to preach in Celtic in the second century, and
the language lasted until at least the fourth.

The industries of Asia were the most highly developed in
the world. Textiles were first, based on the fleece of famous
breeds of sheep and goats reared on its excellent pastures.
There were many specialties, from heavy felts to the luxury
clothing of Miletus and Cos. Laodicea produced a notable
raven-black wool. The leather industry of Asia was also
prosperous, and she produced pottery for the whole Eastern
market. A wide range of herbs were grown for drugs and
perfumes. The Cos lettuce will serve to remind us of the skill
of Asian market gardeners with vegetables. Pontus and
Cilicia supplied ship timbers. The carrying trade with the
West, cornered by Italians under the Republic, was now back
in Asian hands; only the shippers of Gades continued to show
the flag on these important routes. There were many precious
marbles, particularly the purple stone of Proconnesus, exported from Cyzicus as far as Gaul. Iron continued to be
worked in Pontus. The Black Sea and the Bosporus are one
of the world's best fishing grounds, yielding caviar, tunny,
soles, sardines, lobsters, crabs, and oysters. There were many
big private landowners, and also imperial estates, with
agricultural land, mines, and quarries in many parts of Asia
Minor. There were also large temple estates, many of them of
immemorial antiquity. The section on Asia in Tenney Frank's
Economic Survey of Ancient Rome, should be consulted
for a full documentation of its varied and highly developed
economy.

The same prosperity is found in the Roman Near East—
except Palestine. The Roman provinces of Syria, Palestine, and
Arabia, together with the western provinces of the Parthian
Empire, Mesopotamia and Babylonia, made up a world whose
cultural and economic unity transcends local differences, and
which profoundly affected the civilization of the Roman
World. It produced many of the chief Greek writers, philosophers, and sophists of the early Empire, and some of its cities
were centers of Jewish and Syrian learning. It developed new
forms in architecture which influenced those of late Roman
and Byzantine times, and are known to us from Heliopolis,
Palmyra, Petra, and Ctesiphon. Out of it came the great
world religions, Mithraism, the cult of the sun god, and
Christianity.

The population of Syria and Palestine may have been
as high as ten million. Apart from the old Phoenician cities of
the coast, it was a land of a few big Hellenistic cities set in

an Aramaic-speaking countryside. Greek was the language of culture, Latin that of administration. Antioch on the Orontes, capital of Syria, was the third city of the Roman world, with perhaps 600,000 inhabitants. The entire district around the city, with its estates and country houses, formed a truly metropolitan region. Not even Corinth or Canopus in Egypt eclipsed the pleasure gardens of its suburb of Daphne. Berytus (Beirut) was a port and cultural center, with a famous school of Roman law. The old Phoenician ports flourished, and Syrian traders went as far as Britain. Tyre proclaimed to the smell her industry of the purple dye. Sidon throve on the new invention of glass blowing. We can trace the history of a single firm, that of Ennion of Sidon. His glassware is found in Egypt, Russia, and Italy; later he opened a branch near Rome, and finally moved his whole business there. In the palmy days of Herod, Jerusalem had a population of about a hundred thousand, but she was impoverished, with the whole of Palestine, by the wars under Vespasian and Hadrian.

But it was above all the caravan traffic that enriched Syria and the whole area. The most important routes led from the Mediterranean coast to Persia, Afghanistan, India, and China; on the north, from Antioch through Aleppo and Thapsacus to Seleucia on the Tigris, and farther south, from Damascus through Palmyra to Dura on the Euphrates. Other routes led via Petra to Arabia and the Gulf of Akaba, and from Africa to Armenia and the Black Sea. Traffic along these routes was highly organized. They were policed and patrolled, water was stored at regular intervals, and there were hotels and resting places. Caravans traveled in convoys under the care of experienced camel masters. Along this route came the silks of China, the cinnamon, pepper, and spices of India, the incense of Arabia. The trade made the fortunes of individuals and of the famous caravan cities. Damascus, in its rich oasis, with its date palms and balsam, is the best-known today. In the first two centuries A.D., Palmyra was the greatest. The whole of its oasis was cultivated, and such was its wealth that in the third century it became the metropolis of a detached portion of the Empire. Among its inscriptions is one which gives the customs tariffs of Hadrian's time. Its necropolis is one of the archaeological wonders of the Near East. Even more astonishing are the rock tombs of its rival Petra, which so delighted the world when they were discovered in the nineteenth century. East of the desert—and usually beyond the imperial frontiers—were Seleucia (near Baghdad) and Dura. Seleucia, formerly the Eastern capital of

Hellenistic Syria and as big as Antioch, remained a center of Greek culture in Mesopotamia. Its destruction by Avidius Cassius in 164 was sheer folly, for it destroyed Hellenism in western Parthia, and strengthened a resurgent Oriental nationalism, hostile to Rome. Of all the caravan cities we know most about Dura, thanks to the excavations carried out by Yale University. They have disclosed how Greek, Parthian, Roman, and Jewish elements were blended in the life of a community whose prosperity depended on peace between the two empires and which was finally destroyed by the Parthians in 257. Before that it had been in Roman hands for nearly a century, and the excavation of the Roman fort brought to light a fascinating set of military documents. The religious art of the temples and synagogue of Dura is also most interesting, and has been treated in a masterly series of studies by Michael Rostovtzeff.

For Roman Egypt there is no lack of evidence, but it is hard to reduce it to coherence. The enormous number of papyri—mostly from Oxyrhynchus and the Fayum—give an unselective mass of information about social and economic life south of the Delta. They are full of complaints—high taxes, unjust officials, inflated prices, forced labor, famine, and flights from the land. Yet the two or three towns which have been excavated show prosperity maintained until the third century. It has been pointed out that some at least of the gloom of the papyri must be discounted. It is the abnormal that is reported, the complaint that is filed. None the less, there is no doubt that the Egyptian peasant found the Roman Empire a harsh taskmaster. We have described how Augustus took over from the Ptolemies an Egypt scientifically organized and taxed as a royal estate. This organization had grown lax under the last weak Macedonian rulers; Roman efficiency tightened it up. Fertile the alluvium of the Nile might be, but it was easier to squeeze the last penny of tax and ounce of effort out of the peasant rather than the last unit of production from the land.

But other classes of the population were favored by Roman rule. Many veterans were settled on the land, and developed into a village aristocracy, as Greek mercenaries had done before them. There was an influx of traders and businessmen to the towns, and opportunities were opened up by the abandonment of some of the imperial monopolies, though those on linen and—probably—papyrus were maintained. Mines and quarries were owned by the emperor but usually leased to private contractors. The Roman quarries of Egypt are well known, especially the Mons Claudianus, whose gray granite was extensively worked for seventy years. Traffic along the Nile and the canals was well organized, for waterways carried most of the country's commerce.

The world market of Alexandria made it the greatest entrepôt. The sea routes to India brought the produce of the East to the ports of the Gulf of Suez, and thence by canal to Alexandria; from there they were re-exported (made up or raw) to the West. Another route brought the produce of Ethiopia and southern Egypt down the Nile. The workshops of Alexandria had a large output of metalware, luxury goods, perfumes, and glass. Huge freighters of three to four thousand tons—the largest ships built in the ancient world—took Egyptian grain to Ostia for the *annona*. The city had a population of perhaps three-quarters of a million, second only to that of Rome. That of Egypt was some seven million. Alexandria continued to be a great cultural center. The Museum, patronized by several Roman emperors, did good work in medicine, philology, and philosophy. In science its best days were over, though it did produce the astronomer and geographer Ptolemy (fl. 150 A.D.). The Hellenized Jewish savants of Alexandria played an important part in Jewish and Christian thought. The city was also notorious for its urban mob, given to riots, pogroms, and insolence to distinguished visitors.

Outside Alexandria, the only new city in Egypt was Antinoopolis, founded by Hadrian in memory of his favorite, Antinous, and peopled mainly by Greeks. Some of the old Egyptian administrative centers grew, and went in for public buildings of a Greek type. But the general picture of Roman Egypt—apart from Alexandria—is not rosy. The land and its people were geared to the demands of the state, enforced by a large and tyrannical bureaucracy. In short, the conditions of life in the late Empire were anticipated by two centuries in Egypt.

Crete and Cyrenaica were organized as one province, but they had little in common. Crete was a backwater. The old city of Gortyn was its capital, but there was little development of any kind, though the most ancient shrines of the Greek world attracted tourists. Cyrenaica had a flourishing agriculture and was a kind of miniature Africa. The region suffered badly in the Jewish rebellion under Trajan.

Sicily under the Empire shows many parallels with Greece. There was the same growth of large estates—here called *massae*—farmed by tenants. Some of these supported sumptuous country houses, of which a famous archaeological discovery of recent years, the villa at Piazza Armerina with its

wonderful mosaics, will give a good picture, though it belongs to the late Empire. A few large towns flourished—
Catania and Syracuse in the east, Panormus (modern Palermo) and Lilybaeum (modern Marsala) in the west—but the
decline of the small market towns does not seem so marked
as in Greece. Sicily, too, had a thriving tourist traffic, attracted not only by its antiquities, but by the mild climate
and sunshine, and by its great natural marvel, the volcano
of Etna. Here organization seems to have been thorough.
Professional guides took the tourist to the summit, where
he could stay the night under shelter and watch the sunrise.
There were also hotels at the many hot springs on the
mountain's slopes. In the west the great draw was the temple
of Venus at Eryx, restored by more than one emperor, and
its famous festivals. Sicilian exports included grain to Ostia,
wines, which had a growing reputation, and the sulphur of
Agrigentum, today one of the island's chief assets.

We have left to the last the heartland of this world empire.
The population of Italy, some fifteen million in the time of
Augustus, is thought to have reached twenty million by
Trajan's time. Its economy calls for a more detailed regional
survey than space allows. The decay of southern Italy continued, and Etruria seems to have been in decline, but these
are black spots in an otherwise prosperous picture. Campania continued to balance agriculture, industry, and tourism
in healthy proportions. Capua, not Naples, was the big city in
these parts; Puteoli, until the competition of Ostia proved too
strong, was the chief port of Italy. The great eruption of
Vesuvius in 79 has preserved in lava two Campanian towns,
the smart resort of Herculaneum and the port and market
town of Pompeii. Thanks to nearly two hundred years of excavation, we know more about their life than about any other
towns of the ancient world. Holiday resorts—Baiae, Stabiae,
Sorrentum—and luxury villas lined the entire coast of the
Bay of Naples, the Riviera or Florida of the Roman world.
There was another such district in Latium, in the Alban Hills
and around Tivoli; the villa of Domitian at Albano and
that of Hadrian at Tivoli were on a truly princely scale.
The galleys of Caligula, dredged up with their contents
from the bed of Lake Nemi, show imperial magnificence
applied to the service of an ancient cult. Farther east, Latium
was a land of small farms and modest but historic market
towns. This was the high noon of prosperity for the Po valley.
Patavium (Padua) with its woolen industry, had more than
five hundred wealthy men among its citizens; in all of Italy,
only Rome had more. Aquileia was the mart for the trade

with the Danube lands, northern Europe, and the Baltic. To it came amber, fur, hides, and steel, and it exported Italian wine, pottery, metal goods, and clothing. Its prosperity won it the title of *"Roma Secunda."* Ravenna, headquarters of the Adriatic fleet, was built on piles like Venice. Mediolanum (Milan) was an industrial center, the capital of a rich agricultural district, and the chief road junction in northern Italy. Both Milan and Ravenna became important capitals in the late Empire. These were only the chief places of a land which, then as now, teemed with a busy, self-confident urban life. Some idea of it may be had from the archaeological remains of Aquileia and Susa, and the ampitheaters of Verona and Pola.

All economic histories stress the loss of Italian export markets during the first century. Wine, olive oil, pottery, woolen goods and metalware all ran into competition from the Western provinces during this period. The ousting of Arretine pottery by that of southern Gaul is the best-known example. Here, and perhaps in other cases, it may be that Italian manufacturers deliberately set up branches in the provinces to cut transport costs—as today British motor manufacturers set up in Australia. Furthermore, the growth of population in Italy itself must have been some compensation. But in the long run the economic consequences were to be serious.

Rome, capital of the world, was an extraordinary combination of metropolitan splendor and filthy slum. The satires of Juvenal, and perhaps modern Naples, may give some idea of the latter. No city of the modern world can approach Rome's magnificence. We have seen what Augustus did for the city. From his death to that of Hadrian much of the building in Rome was directed to two ends, the amusements of the Roman people, and the proper housing of the emperor and the court. The greatest of all projects for an imperial palace, the Golden House of Nero, was never completed. It was meant to establish the emperor in a sumptuous villa, set in a superbly landscaped park in the heart of Rome. Incomplete as it was, the Golden House was a landmark in the history of Roman architecture. Domitian and his master architect Rabirius completed a process which virtually turned the entire Palatine into an imperial residence. For the builders of the great amphitheaters, stadia, and baths, the handling of huge crowds was the basic problem. The Colosseum gave 50,000 people their regular ration of sadism; 300,000 could attend the chariot racing in the Circus Maximus; 30,000 spectators could watch the events in the Stadium of Domi-

tian, whose arcades that emperor had thoughtfully furnished
with brothels. This is the stadium whose dimensions are today
preserved by the lovely Piazza Navona. The great *thermae*
provided not merely baths, but also restaurants, bars, lecture rooms, concert halls, art galleries, shops, and courts for
ball games, and were a kind of huge *Kursaal* in which thousands of people could find amusement for an entire day.
Vespasian and Nerva built new fora in Rome, but theirs, and
all earlier work, was eclipsed by the magnificent Forum of
Trajan, designed by Apollodorus of Damascus, and built
from the spoils of the Dacian wars. The piazza with its hemicycles, the noble Basilica Ulpia (reproduced by St. Paul's-
without-the-Wall), the Greek and Latin libraries, and the Column itself with its reliefs, all form a complex of architectural
splendor which was agreed to be without a rival in the world.
Hadrian wisely expressed his own architectural ambitions in
individual great buildings, notably his mausoleum, now the
Castle of St. Angelo, set by the river over against that of
Augustus.

Amusements the Roman *plebs* could find more easily than
work, for Rome was a parasite on the economy of the world.
The catering, building, and distributive trades would flourish
in a city of more than a million people, but Rome had few
manufacturers, and exported little but administrators and
civil servants. Her cosmopolitan population was drawn from
all quarters of the world, but especially from Asia and Syria.
Juvenal's picture of a population of immigrants is borne out
by the funeral inscriptions, in which only about a quarter of
the names are Italian.

To supply this huge population there grew up a great port
at Ostia and heavy barge traffic on the Tiber. No archaeological site in Italy is more interesting than Ostia. Here we get—
what is not to be had in Rome—an idea of the large apart-
ment houses with their neighborhood bars and cafés, the
scenes of a noisy, vivid, gregarious life like that of Trastevere
today. Then there are the specialized buildings of the port, the
docks and warehouses and barracks of police. There are splendid public buildings, the Capitolium on its lofty podium, baths
with fine marine mosaics, and a group including the theaters,
the Temple of Ceres, and the great piazza surrounded by
the offices of shipping firms dealing with Africa, Spain, Gaul,
and Egypt. Silting at the mouth of the Tiber was a constant
problem, and first Claudius and then Trajan built new harbors and roadsteads. By Hadrian's time Ostia and its sub-
urbs must have had a hundred thousand people.

Trade between the Empire and the outside world is a fas-

cinating study, to which the best guide is a recent book by
Sir Mortimer Wheeler, *Rome Beyond the Imperial Frontier*.
By far the most important commerce was with India. We
have already mentioned the overland routes from the desert
cities of Syria through Parthia to Afghanistan, India, and the
Far East, and also the sea routes from the Red Sea ports.
The latter gained enormously in importance when a certain
Hippalus discovered how to use the monsoon winds for a
direct sea passage to and from the east coast of India. His
date is uncertain, but it does not seem later than Augustus.
We know a good deal about this trade, thanks to the *Periplus
Maris Erythraei*, a mariner's guide to the Indian Ocean, written in the first century A.D. and giving details of ports, sailing
conditions, and cargoes between the Gulf of Suez, East Africa, and India. The East Africa traffic went as far as Zanzi-
bar or Dar es Salaam, taking pottery and tools, and bringing
back ivory, ginger, cinnamon, and rhinoceros horn. An Arab
port called Muza, near the Strait of Bab el Mandeb, played
an important part in this trade, and was the Aden of its day.
More evidence of this trade may be expected with the development of archaeology in Africa. In India the *Periplus*
mentions two major terminals, Barygaza (Broach) on the Gulf
of Cambay, for the northern sea route, and for the southern,
Muziris (Cranganore) on the Malabar coast. But it also names
many other trading stations (*emporia*), and one of these has
been excavated by Wheeler and French archaeologists at
Arikamedu near Pondicherry. Here the western imports were
wine, tableware, lamps, and glass. Wheeler compares these
trading stations with the "factories" of European nations in
India in the seventeenth century. In the North, archaeology
has found evidence of the overland traffic at two sites in particular, Taxila near Peshawar in Pakistan, and Begram in
Afghanistan near Kabul. Both were on the great route from
Bactra (Balkh) across the Hindu Kush to the Indus Valley.
Here the chief western goods are *objets d'art* of high quality,
which fit into the pattern of the western-influenced Buddhist
art of northern India about 150 A.D.

Roman trade with northern Europe is attested by hun-
dreds of finds in Germany, Poland, Denmark, southern
Sweden, and even Norway. A major route led from Aquileia
to Carnuntum on the Danube and thence by the river routes
to the Baltic coasts, some of which had been used by the amber traffic since the early Bronze Age. By these means Italian
wines, pottery, metalware, glass, and luxury goods reached
the wealthy chieftains of the North. The man buried at Hoby
in southern Denmark may serve as an example: he took to

the grave several nonclassical objects, two joints of pork
and a splendid table service of Augustan date. Still more remarkable is the great hoard of Mediterranean silverware
found at Hildesheim near Hanover, but it is uncertain
whether this represents trade or loot. When the products of
Gaul and the Rhineland began to win a market in the North,
they were sent eastward across the Rhine from Vetera and
Moguntiacum. In the late Empire there is evidence of traffic
from the Black Sea to the Baltic along the Dniester and the
Vistula, in which it is thought the Goths may have been
middlemen. To round off this survey, mention should be
made of the trade with Caledonia, for which crossing places
and custom posts were provided on Hadrian's Wall, and that
with Ireland from ports in Britain and in Gaul.

The endless diversity of the Empire—that, surely, is the
impression left by such a survey as this. But what of its
unity? How far was there a feeling of common loyalty,
whether springing from self-interest or personal conviction,
or officially fostered by such devices as emperor worship and
the cult of Rome? In the armed forces, there can be no doubt
of the vigor of the policy of Romanization among the auxiliary units. The *Feriale Duranum,* a third-century military
calendar from Dura, is instructive on this point. The unit
was one of troops from Palmyra serving at this eastern outpost, yet not a single festival in the year concerns any but a
Roman cult or an imperial anniversary. Whatever his nationality or posting, whether on the Euphrates or the Rhine,
among the snows of Armenia, or on the high moors of North-
umberland with the curlews calling through the rain, the
auxiliary was made to feel that he was a Roman soldier, and
Roman citizenship, for himself, one wife, and their descendants, was his reward on discharge. Officials of higher rank,
military or civilian, would naturally take an ecumenical view.
From the numerous inscriptions which record their careers
I select two examples. Plautius Silvanus, mentioned earlier
(pp. 163, 191), was buried in his family mausoleum at Tivoli.
His inscription says that he first served in Germany under Tiberius and was later on Claudius' staff in the invasion of Britain. Consul in 47, he then became governor of the senatorial
province of Asia. Next he was made governor of Moesia,
the most eventful stage of his career. He settled large numbers of tribesmen on the Roman bank of the river, suppressed a rising among the Sarmatians, took part in war and
diplomacy along the entire lower Danube and the Black Sea
as far as the Crimea, and sent a large supply of grain—the
first from his province—to Rome. Under Nero he was out of

favor, but Vespasian first made him governor of Hispania Tarraconensis, then city prefect, and finally gave him a second consulship in 74. In the next century one M. Claudius Fronto held a special command in Dacia and Upper Moesia, and served with distinction under Verus in the Parthian War. He became recruiting officer in Italy, then led a mixed force to Armenia and Osroene. He commanded, successively, the First and the Eleventh Legion. His last service was in the Marcomannic War, where "after several successful battles against the Germans and Jazyges, he fell fighting bravely to the last for his country. For this, by decree of the Senate and at the instance of the emperor Marcus Aurelius, his statue, in uniform, was set up at public expense in the Forum of Trajan."

Two famous tributes in literature to the blessings of the *Pax Romana* are the speech which Tacitus gives to Petilius Cerealis after the Gallic revolt of 70, and the speech *To Rome*, delivered in the city by the Greek sophist Aelius Aristides in 150. Both stress peace, prosperity, the generous extension of privileges and of Roman citizenship, and equal justice for all before the law and the emperor. But we must not forget that there was another voice—the voice of those who hated Rome. Tacitus lets us hear it in the speech of the Caledonian chief Calgacus before confronting Agricola: "The Romans make a desert, and call it peace." In Dio Cassius, Boudicca utters very similar sentiments. Anti-Roman sentiment is heard in the writing called "The Acts of the Pagan Martyrs" from Alexandria. Naturally, in view of the history of the Jews, it is common in Jewish literature of the first and second centuries—above all, in Revelations. "And they cast dust upon their heads, and cried, weeping and wailing, saying, alas, alas that great city, wherein were made rich all that had ships in the sea by reason of her costliness! For in one hour is she made desolate. Rejoice over her, thou heaven, and ye holy apostles, and prophets; for God hath avenged you on her."

CHAPTER XII

DECLINE AND FALL: 193–476 A.D.

Despite the longings of the author of Revelations, the Empire did not come to a precipitate end. Almost three centuries separate the death of Commodus from the last Roman emperor of the West. But final disintegration might well have come in the middle of the third century, when the Rhine and Danube frontiers had been breached, separate empires set up in Gaul and in the East, and economic collapse and social anarchy raged in what was still left to Rome. That disaster was avoided was due, first to the exertions of the three Illyrian emperors, Claudius Gothicus, Aurelian, and Probus, and then, in the respite gained, to the reforms of Diocletian and their revision and consolidation in the long reign of Constantine (312–337). But these reforms were so harsh and radical that they transformed the whole life of the state. The difference between the Republic and the early Empire is not so great as that between the time of, say, Marcus Aurelius and the late Empire. This fact, and the adoption of Christianity by Constantine, cause many historians to see in his reign the beginning of the Middle Ages and the end of classical antiquity. From 350 onward the last phases of dissolution in the Western Empire set in with the renewal of large-scale barbarian attacks. For a short time under Valentinian and Theodosius the Great they are withstood, but with the death of the latter in 395 came the final division of the Empire into an eastern and a western part. From then until 476 the story in the West is one of utter feebleness and incessant crises, although Rome performed one last political service to mankind in the defeat of Attila and the Huns (451). By the middle of the fifth century Gaul was in the hands of Franks and Burgundians, Spain of Visigoths and Suebi, Africa of Vandals. Britain was cut off from the Empire, and parts of it were overrun by Angles, Saxons, and Picts. Rome itself was captured and sacked by Alaric the Goth in 410, and by the Vandal Gaiseric in 455. When in 476 the German Odoacer deposed the last puppet emperor of the West, Romulus Augustulus, and declared himself Master of Soldiers in Italy, the end had really come.

No detailed treatment of the period can be attempted here. Even if space allowed, the result would be confusing, for so much of it could only be a recital of the accession and death of a string of short-lived emperors. It will be enough to give some account of the chief events and trends in a period which begins with the first fadings of the imperial splendors and ends on the brink of the Dark Ages.

The long civil wars after the death of Commodus were destructive in themselves and in their consequences. Their ultimate winner, Septimius Severus, was of African birth, and had been governor of Pannonia. He never forgot that he owed his victory to the army, and that to retain its loyalty was the supreme objective. He was most vindictive to the adherents of his rivals Niger and Albinus, and built up a huge private fortune by the confiscation of their estates. The same was done by the praetorian prefect Plautianus, so long as he remained in favor. After a period of conciliation, Severus turned hostile to the Senate. Openly modeling himself on Sulla and Marius, he put twenty-nine senators to death and confiscated their estates. His military reforms were chiefly undertaken to improve the condition and prospects of the common soldier. The old Praetorian Guard was dissolved and a new one set up open to any suitable legionary soldier. From this staff college the higher commands were filled. Besides increased pay, he further pampered the army by frequent donations—"bribes" would be a better word. To meet increased expenses, it was more and more necessary to resort to "requisitions"—compulsory labor or services, which became one of the great curses of the late Empire. But at least in his reign the frontiers were restored and there was freedom from invasion. His important victories over the Parthians and Arabs are commemorated by the Arch of Severus in the Roman Forum.

In Britain he was faced with a serious situation. The withdrawal of the British legions by Albinus in 196 in his bid for the throne gave the Caledonians a chance which they did not let slip. The northern frontiers were overwhelmed, Hadrian's Wall was razed to the foundations, and the province was overrun as far as York and Chester. Two governors of Britain pushed the barbarians back, but Severus decided on a great offensive. In two campaigns he penetrated farther into Scotland than any previous Roman army—probably reaching the Moray Firth. But Roman losses were heavy, and the strain too much for the aging emperor. In 211 Severus died at York. His Scottish conquests were abandoned, and Hadrian's Wall became the northern frontier, so thoroughly reconstructed that as late as the nineteenth century some archaeologists attributed it to Severus rather than Hadrian. On his deathbed, Severus left his political testimony to his sons in words that may be paraphrased, "Stick together, pay the soldiers, and to hell with the rest."

The first was soon disregarded, for Caracalla murdered his brother Geta and thousands of his followers, and erased his name from all inscriptions. But to the second Caracalla stuck fast. "No one," he used to say, "should have money except myself, so that I could give it all to my soldiers." By enrolling soldiers as spies and secret police he did much to advance this aim, even, it would seem, to the frequent elimination of himself as middleman. His reign also saw a drastic adulteration of the currency (215), at once symptom and cause of the Empire's decline. The famous Edict of 212, which conferred Roman citizenship on virtually all inhabitants of the Empire, is probably to be explained as a measure to increase the numbers of those liable to taxation. Modern scholars are inclined to regard it as a landmark in Roman constitutional history, and to commend its liberal spirit. At the time it seems to have aroused little comment, and that skeptical. What seems clear is that Roman citizenship became universal when it was no longer a privilege but a burden. That Caracalla could entertain grandiose projects is seen in his scheme for a Roman-Parthian empire, with himself in the role of the new Alexander. He read up the life of Alexander, trained and equipped a Macedonian phalanx for the sake of realism, and then launched an invasion of Parthia, with something less than the *élan* of his great model (215). Nothing decisive had been achieved when he was murdered in 217.

This bizarre episode is overshadowed by the extraordinary nature of the reign of Bassianus, who succeeded him after the brief rule of Macrinus. This boy of fourteen, high priest of the sun god Elagabal at Emesa, and usually known as Elagabalus (or Heliogabalus) was placed on the throne by the support of the Eastern legions, purchased by liberal use of the Temple treasure. For the three years of his rule Rome was given over to a kind of perverts' carnival, sanctioned by religion, the startling details of which may be read in the *Historia Augusta*. In 222 Elagabalus and his mother were murdered by the Praetorian Guard. He was succeeded by his cousin Alexander Severus, a high-minded and virtuous young man, much under the influence of his mother Julia Mammaea. Rightly or wrongly, his reign is represented as an age of tranquillity, economic recovery, and collaboration with the Senate. But in 235 war broke out on the German frontier, and the troops, disgusted with the emperor's lethargy—or with the favor shown to the Oriental legions—murdered him. In his place they put one of themselves, the soldier Maximinus Thrax, the first Roman emperor to have risen from the ranks.

With this reign began an appalling time of troubles for the Roman world. There were twelve emperors, and almost incessant civil war, between 235 and 260. Taxes, confiscations, requisitions, sapped the strength of the cities and reduced the well-to-do to impoverishment and despair. There was a dreadful visitation of the plague, which raged unchecked for fifteen years. Earthquakes devastated many of the cities of Asia. Commerce dwindled, and land went out of cultivation. Persia, under the new Sassanid dynasty, became a formidable foe, and the Emperor Valerian was taken prisoner by Sapor in 259. Meanwhile, a sinister enemy had appeared on the Danube—the Goths. This formidable people came from southern Sweden—where Gotland preserves their name—and spread down the Vistula to the Black Sea. During the years of Roman weakness they began raids on the Danube lands, Greece, and Asia, very like those of the Vikings on western Europe centuries later. In 250 the Emperor Decius fell fighting against them. In 257 a plundering expedition by land and sea captured Chalcedon, Nicaea, and Nicomedia. In 258, another Germanic people, the Alamanni, invaded Italy itself, and were only checked at Milan. Small wonder that, with the central government so enfeebled, some parts of the Empire broke away to look after themselves. In the West, Postumus set up an empire of the Gauls, recognized by the troops in Spain and Britain. In Syria there was a short-lived Empire of the East, followed by a more successful venture under Odenath, King of Palmyra. He drove Sapor out of the Roman provinces, and was himself recognized by the Roman emperor Gallienus.

Under Gallienus (260–268) there was some improvement. A mobile reserve was created, and the Goths were heavily defeated at Naissus (267). The time was not ripe for winning back the lost parts of the Empire, but a start had been made. It was followed up brilliantly by the work of the three Illyrian emperors, Claudius Gothicus (268–270), Aurelian (270–275), and Probus (276–282). The coinage bore the proud legend "The Valor of the Illyrians" (*virtus Illyri-corum*), and that valor shone bright in troops and emperor during these years. In his short reign Claudius smashed the great army of the Goths in two battles, cleared the Black Sea of their ships, and settled those who surrendered as *coloni* in the Danube lands. Aurelian pushed Germanic invaders out of Italy and across the Danube, and fortified Rome with the huge wall, twelve miles long, which bears his name. It is today one of the most striking things in Rome, and a witness to the times in which it was made. Then he went east to attack the Palmyrene Empire, now under the brilliant and gifted Queen Zenobia and her son Waballath. In two arduous campaigns the Palmyrene power was broken, the city captured, and Zenobia taken to Rome as a prisoner, to support the discomforts of house arrest in Hadrian's Villa at Tivoli. In 274 the Gallic emperor Tetricus was defeated, and the unity of the Empire was restored. To cement it Aurelian instituted a new state cult, that of the Unconquered Sun, Lord of the Roman Empire. This had an important bearing on the nature of the monarchy, if Aurelian pro-claimed—as it seems he did—that the purple was the gift of God, not of the Senate, nor of the army. The Roman em-peror, then, was no longer the first magistrate of Rome, but the Elect of God; the monarchy was a despotism like that of Persia. So, though Aurelian's coins proclaim him *Restitutor Orbis* (Restorer of the World), it was not the world of Augustus or Hadrian that he restored. That had passed away forever in the anarchy of the third century. Nor was the Empire geographically the same world. For Aurelian had abandoned Dacia—last in, first out of the Roman provinces in Europe—and it was taken over by the Goths. But his work and that of his successor Probus, who followed it up and consolidated it, ensured that the Empire should have a new lease of life. What that life would be was determined by the reforms of Diocletian and Constantine.

The parallels between Augustus and Diocletian have often been remarked. Both came to power in a world exhausted by wars, disposed to accept radical measures for the sake of peace. Both had long reigns, Augustus of forty-five, Diocle-tian, before he retired, of twenty years. But the problems that confronted Diocletian were far more desperate, and the mar-gins of recovery much slighter. Where Augustus was the phy-sician whose treatment restores and improves health, Diocle-tian was the surgeon who carries out a major operation to permit a few more years of life at a lower level. His first task was to put a stop to military coups and the endless struggle for the throne. Hence the famous Tetrarchy or Board of Four Emperors, who should divide the Empire between them. Two of these would be Augusti, senior emperors, each of whom should choose a Caesar as his junior. As an Augustus died or retired (and it looks as though their term was to be twenty years) he would be succeeded by a Caesar already experienced in administration. To prevent coups by ambitious provincial governors, the provinces were divided into smaller units—nearly a hundred of them—and regrouped into twelve dioceses, six in the East and six in the West. In each province there was a complete separation of civil and military authority. A thorough overhaul of the military system, begun by Diocletian, was completed by Constantine, and it will be best to describe it in its final form.

Two glaring lessons stood out from the military disasters of the third century. The first was that the Augustan system of armies stationed on the frontiers was no longer viable. It provided no central reserves, and a threat at one point could be met only by weakening another. Now that war on several major fronts at once was a grim reality, to continue with it was to invite disaster, as Gallienus had seen. The second was the military fact, underlined in the Persian and Gothic wars, that supremacy had passed to the cavalry— the infantry no longer ruled the battlefield. The best cavalry and infantry units were therefore organized in a new field force, itself divided into *palatini,* or Guards regiments, and *comitatenses.* Both were recruited mainly from Germans and Illyrians, and in both the cavalry was the senior arm. The frontier troops—*limitanei*—now became a local militia, recruited from the province in which they served, and of little military value beyond that of a trip-wire.

It will be obvious that all these reforms swelled the payroll of the state. There were now four courts, and four imperial capitals, at Nicomedia, Treves, Sirmium, and Milan or Rome. The armed forces and the bureaucracy were greatly increased. How could all this be paid for, when the state was impoverished and production declining? Only by a rigorous system of taxation, which no one could escape, and by requisitioning goods and services to add to the money got by taxes. Inevitably, then, the reforms of Diocletian took the Empire far on the road to the totalitarian state. The guilds or corporations (*collegia*) supplying essential services—bakers, millers, shipowners, and the like—were forced to perform free services for the state. They could not avoid this unremunerative task by retiring, for they were bound to their profession, and their sons after them. Soldiers' sons likewise

had to follow their fathers' trade, and to keep up agricultural
production the *coloni* on the great estates were bound to the
land. Town councilors were made to act as unpaid tax collectors for the state, and to make up themselves any short-
comings in the assessment of their community. Their status,
that of the *curialis*, became unpopular—and hereditary. So
there grew up a system of castes, like those of the old Oriental monarchies or the Middle Ages, but a far cry from the old
freedom of a Roman citizen. But even Diocletian learned
that there were limits to what the state could enforce. His
famous Edict of Prices (301)—significantly prefaced by a
denunciation of the inroads made by profiteers on the
soldiers' pay—attempted to enforce ceilings for prices and
wages throughout the Empire, but proved unworkable and
had to be withdrawn. At least it has provided us with the
most informative economic document from antiquity. And
Diocletian, for all the chains he riveted on men's necks, was
neither a tyrant nor personally ambitious. After his twenty
years as Augustus he duly retired to his palace at Spalato
(Split), perhaps the grandest of all surviving Roman buildings, and his colleague Maximian was persuaded to retire as
well. Their retirement is the most noteworthy because the
reforms of Diocletian had invested the position of emperor
with a new grandeur, regularizing the trend toward an Oriental type of monarchy which had set in since Aurelian or even
Gallienus. The Roman emperor now wore the diadem, and
was surrounded by an elaborate ceremonial derived from the
Persian court. Deification after death was no longer enough;
Diocletian claimed to be descended from Jupiter, Maximian
from Hercules, Constantius Chlorus, father of Constantine,
from Apollo. Everything was done to set the emperor apart,
above the rest of mankind.

For so long as Diocletian was there to captain the team,
the Tetrarchy worked well. The frontiers were held and disorders in several parts of the Empire suppressed more effectively than might have been done by a single ruler. The
most notable of these was the British Empire set up by
Carausius, commander of the Channel fleet in 289, and
finally suppressed by Constantius Chlorus in 296, to the joy
of the provincials. A gold medallion commemorates the relief
of London, and hails Constantius as *Redditor Lucis Aeternae*,
the restorer of the eternal light of Roman civilization. But
after Diocletian's retirement the machinery did not work, and
it is hard to see why it was ever thought that it could. Far
from eliminating rivalry, it organized and perpetuated it. In
the confused years after 305 there were at times six Augusti

—for no one would hold the second-grade post of Caesar—
then four again. Next Constantine eliminated Maxentius, his
rival in the West, at the battle of the Mulvian Bridge (312),
and Licinius got rid of his in the East. The uneasy partnership of Constantine and Licinius lasted until 323, when
after a series of enormous battles Constantine won the final
round and possessed himself of the prize—sole rule of the
world.

By far the most important political question of Constantine's reign was that of relations with the Christian Church,
and the decisions he took were momentous in their consequences for the Roman Empire and for the whole world.
Despite popular belief, persecution of Christianity by the
Roman government was neither frequent nor extensive. But
Chrisitanity was not a permitted cult (*religio licita*); and its
adherents were notorious in their refusal to offer sacrifices to
the state cults on behalf of the emperor. It was therefore
always exposed to suspicion, and to attack in times of crisis
when a scapegoat would be useful. We have seen what
happened to the Christian community in Rome at the time
of the Fire under Nero. Trajan was asked by Pliny for guidance on the treatment of Christians in Bithynia. His reply
was that there should be no inquisition, nor any notice taken
of anonymous denunciation, but those who had been reported in due form, investigated, and found guilty, must be
punished if they still refused to worship the Roman gods.
These were spacious days, and a similar tolerance was not
shown in the disasters of the third century. There was a sharp
persecution under Decius in 251, and two others under
Valerian in 257 and 260. But these, and the sporadic martyr-
dom of individuals, did nothing to weaken the Christian faith.
On the contrary, the blood of martyrs was, indeed, the seed
of the Church. By 300 there were Christian churches in
every province, and the Church was the strongest organization in the Empire, with perhaps 10 per cent of the population as its adherents. The last and greatest persecutions, under
Diocletian, though largely through the influence of Galerius,
were the final attempt to stamp out Christianity. Neither
Constantine nor his father sympathized with the persecutors,
and after the battle of the Mulvian Bridge the prospects of
the Church altered dramatically for the better. The persecutions were stopped by order of Constantine. In 313 the
Edict of Milan proclaimed freedom of worship for all, and
turned the churches into legal corporations. From then to
the end of his reign Constantine showed partiality toward
Christianity in every way. He promoted legislation in its

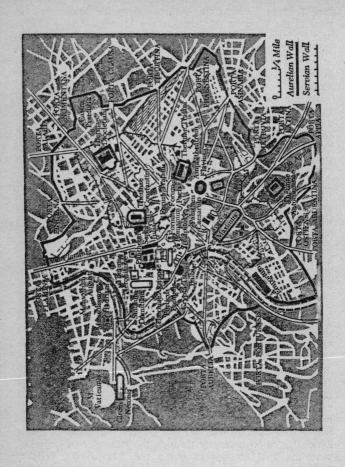

*4. Rome in Late Imperial Times Superimposed
on Modern Rome*

favor; took part in ceremonies and presided at the Council of Nicaea in 325; built the basilicas of St. John Lateran and St. Peter's in Rome, besides other great churches; founded Constantinople as the first Christian capital; and was baptized on his deathbed.

There has been endless discussion as to whether his support of Christianity was due to personal conviction or political opportunism. At least we know what Constantine himself said to Eusebius, Bishop of Caesarea. On his daring march to Italy to challenge the much greater forces of Maxentius, Constantine had a vision of the Cross in the sky, with the words *In hoc signo vincas* ("Conquer by this sign"). Later that night Christ appeared to him in his dreams, and confirmed that victory would be his. It was under the famous *Labarum,* the standard bearing the Cross of Christ, that his troops won their victories against Maxentius and later went into battle against Licinius. After his final triumph he claimed, "I am the agent whose services God deemed suitable to the accomplishment of His will." Constantine, then, looked to Christ as the giver of victory, and was never failed. From Christianity he expected a basis for unity, not only within the Empire, but, it would seem, with those beyond its borders. Here he met with disappointment, for Christianity in his time was torn by serious heresies. Hence his anxiety to secure the suppression of the Donatist and Arian heresies, although it was not until fifty years later, under Theodosius, that the imperial power enjoined orthodoxy as the duty of all. Such a pronouncement could not have been made in the time of Constantine, when the pagan cults were still strong, especially in Rome. He had to maintain a studied ambiguity in religious policy, for much the same reasons as did Elizabeth I of England. And the dark shadows cast on Elizabeth's reign by the execution of Mary Queen of Scots are matched by those of two even more cryptic events under Constantine —the execution, first, of his son Crispus and, second, of the empress Fausta.

The foundation of Constantinople met the urgent need for a capital for the eastern part of the Empire. Nicomedia had for some time played that part, but in the long run a new foundation would have advantages over any existing great city. There was some talk of the old project of refounding Troy; Naissus, Constantine's birthplace, was also canvassed. But the superb natural advantages of the site of Constantinople carried the day. Here the great land route from the Danube to Asia crosses the seaway from the Black Sea to the Mediterranean. If this were not enough, the land-locked Golden Horn provides one of the finest natural harbors in the world. All this is described in a splendid passage of Gibbon, which should be read by every student of Roman history and of English prose. The site had long been occupied by the flourishing Greek colony of Byzantium, but this was eclipsed by the new imperial foundation, from the very first one of the great cities of the world. Construction began in 325, and the city was formally inaugurated on May 11, 330. Dedicated to the Holy Trinity and the Virgin Mary, it was a Christian foundation. But its institutions were Roman—down to the grain dole for the urban poor—and its libraries and museums made it a stronghold of Hellenism. Its cosmopolitan population contained a large number of Latin speakers, from the Danube lands as well as Italy, and although Constantinople soon superseded New Rome as the name of the city, the inhabitants called themselves Romans (*Romaioi*) to the very end.

So Constantinople began its noble mission as a bulwark of Christianity and classical civilization, which it sustained through many vicissitudes until the tragic day of May 29, 1453, the date of its capture by the Turks.

Two further services of Constantine to the state call for mention. One—if it be his and not Diocletian's—was the setting up of a new Privy Council, the *consistorium*, of which the heads of all the major departments were members. The old *consilium* had consisted, for the most part, of the emperor's nominees. The other was his reform of the coinage—the third since Aurelian—by the introduction of a trustworthy gold piece, the *solidus*. This proved reliable in a world of inflation and mounting economic crises. Apart from this, neither Diocletian nor Constantine was able to do much to help economic problems. Taxation grew ever more oppressive, the bureaucracy larger, more corrupt, and more inefficient. There is a depressing contrast between the humanity of some of the later legislation, as in the Code of Theodosius, under the influence of Christianity, and the increasing savagery of punishment for attempts to cheat the Treasury of its voracious demands. But despite their failure in economics, the reforms of Diocletian and Constantine had strengthened the state, and even led to a modest revival of prosperity, which lasted until about 350.

But events soon took a dramatic turn for the worse. First came a self-inflicted disaster, the struggle between Constantius II and Magnentius, usurper of the West. The terrible battle of Mursa in 351 saw the finest armies of the Empire engage in mutual slaughter. A second disaster was also self-inflicted, in a way, for it arose from the incessant tendency to heresy that afflicted the Church throughout the fourth century. The Council of Nicaea, called by Constantine to establish unity in the Church, did not put an end to the powerful heresy of Arianism. Constantine himself inclined to that belief in his later days, and Constantius gave it more positive support. For the Empire, rivalry between Orthodoxy and Arianism (which denied that the Son was of the same nature as the Father) was to have the same grim consequences of strife and disunity as that between Catholicism and Protestantism for Europe in the Thirty Years' War. Many of the barbarians outside the Empire had been converted to Arianism, among them the Goths and the Franks. Disillusionment with Christianity accounts for the short-lived pagan reaction promoted by Julian the Apostate (361–363). It is natural that Christian tradition paints Julian in the colors of the great Adversary. He was, rather, a hero of the Byronic kind—young, ardent, revolutionary, and destined to an early death in a lost cause, for the new paganism did not gain many adherents. His attempts to rule as a new Marcus Aurelius was a hopeless anachronism. Politically, he rendered the Empire a great service by clearing Gaul of an invasion of Franks and Alamanni. But his expedition against Persia was ill-organized and ill-led. It cost Julian his life, and the Empire the last army it could muster for action in the East. About the reign of Julian and his next-but-one successor Valentinian (364-375) we are well informed, thanks to Ammianus Marcellinus, the only great historian after Tacitus.

Valentinian avoided religious issues, being fully occupied by new and more menacing barbarian invasions. The great attack on Britain in 367 shows the scale on which they were now made. A simultaneous assault—concerted by an intelligence of a high order—was made on the province by Irish, Picts, and Saxons. The defenses were overwhelmed, the *limitanei* cooperated with the invaders, and Nectaridus, Count of the Saxon Shore, and Fullofaudes, Duke of Britain and Commander of the field army, were killed at their posts. Agricola would have found their barbarian names as surprising as their essentially defensive duties. But the position was restored by Theodosius, father of the future emperor of the same name, and there were again garrisons on Hadrian's Wall, although only of the new type of farmer-soldier.

In 375, the year that Valentinian died, new adversaries appeared at the Danube frontiers of the Empire. The Huns, a nomadic warrior people, had long been known to the Chinese as the Hsiung-Nu. The Great Wall of China had been built

(c. 200 B.C.) to keep them out, and strong Chinese dynasties had maintained the frontiers. This turned the Huns westward to build up a great power in Turkestan, north of the Tien Shan mountains. The endless steppes drew them westward, past the Aral Sea and the Caspian, and in 375 they fell like a tidal wave on the Gothic kingdom between the Dniester and the Danube and shattered it. In 375 a part of the Gothic nation under arms appeared on the Danube and demanded admission to the Empire. This was granted, but soon the Goths were complaining of oppression and raiding into Macedonia. The Emperor Valens brought up the Field Army of the East to deal with them, and on August 9, 378, was defeated and killed by Gothic forces near Adrianople, "the irremediable disaster"—to quote Ammianus—"which cost the Roman state so dear."

What made Adrianople irremediable was that the Empire was no longer able to repair its losses from its own resources. The surviving emperor, Gratian, summoned Theodosius to repair what could be salvaged, but he was obliged to come to terms with the Goths, give them many responsible posts within the Empire, and hand over the defense of the Danube to Gothic forces (*foederati*) serving under their own commanders. What was meant by "Roman" armies at this period is vividly illustrated by the battle of Siscia (388). Against Maximus, who tried to win the Western Empire, Theodosius led an army of Goths, Alans, and Huns to victory over a Western army of Gauls, Britons, and Germans, themselves the last real representatives of the old Roman army. One of Theodosius' generals was the Frank Arbogastes, who later became *magister militum* (Master of the Soldiers) to the Western emperor Valentinian III. This office was to be the chief source of power in the last phase of the Western Empire. But when Arbogastes, with the support of the pagan party in Rome and Italy, set up a puppet emperor of his own in the West, Theodosius broke his power at the battle of the Frigidus near Aquileia (394). After this, pagan ceremonies were abandoned, and pagan temples in the West turned into museums. It was the end of paganism as a political force. Theodosius' championship of orthodoxy had also greatly weakened Arianism in the East, so that he well deserved the title of "the Great," bestowed on him, as on Constantine, by Christian tradition. His was an age of a flourishing Christian art and literature, and of the building of churches in Rome (St. Paul's-without-the-Walls) and in Milan. St. Ambrose, Bishop of Milan, foreshadowed the great ecclesiastics of the

Middle Ages when he made the emperor do penance for his share in an atrocity, the Massacre of Thessalonica.

But Theodosius was to be the last ruler of a united empire. At his death (395) it was partitioned between his sons, Honorius ruling in the West, Arcadius in the East. The two halves were never reunited, except briefly and partially by the conquests of Justinian in the sixth century. And now the last stage of dissolution had begun for the West. The emperors were all insignificant: Honorius bred poultry, Glycerius was promoted from the post of emperor to that of Bishop of Salonae. They counted for so little that two of them had long reigns, Honorius for twenty-nine and Valentinian III for thirty-one years. For safety the court was moved to Ravenna, a city of refuge among its marshes, and a port from which a hasty evacuation could be made if need be. Provincial administration was in the hands of the *consistorium*, which always had a weak hand of cards but was occasionally able to play off one set of barbarians against another. Real power lay with the *magistri militum*, all barbarians, ambitious and unreliable. Central and northern Europe were seething with the turmoil of the greatest folk migrations of history. The Goths were inside the frontiers, and it was uncertain where they would go. The Empire was like a great whale, slowed down and stopped by a school of killers, the barbarians, who were now closing in to tear it to pieces. The Goths ravaged Greece and then moved to Illyricum. When they attacked Italy, they were stopped by a great general, Stilicho, *magister militum* to Honorius. But on the last night of 406 the Rhine defenses collapsed before a horde of Vandals, Alans, and Suebi, who poured into Gaul and ranged beyond it into Spain. Britain was already severed from the Empire, probably for ever, although some historians think there was a brief restoration sometime between 410 and 446. When, in 408, Stilicho was murdered by the ill-advised order of Honorius, nothing stood between the Goths and Italy. The capture of Rome by Alaric in 410 sent a shudder through the world. "Of what use now," men asked, "are the tombs of the Apostles?" The question was the more pointed because, less than a generation earlier, the statue of Victory had been removed from the Senate house, despite the impassioned plea of the pagans and their appeal to tradition and to the fortune which Rome had so long enjoyed. The Christian answer was given by Augustine in the *City of God*, that tremendous demonstration that here we have no abiding city. But though there was no hope of recovery, it was not yet the end for

Rome. Alaric passed south and died in Calabria. The Goths
were encouraged to turn to Gaul and reconquer it for the
Empire. When Ataulf, King of the Goths, married Galla
Placidia, daughter of Theodosius, the Goths seemed established in the role of barbarian protectors. Boniface, Count
of Africa, and Aëtius, *magister militum* in Italy, divided
power in what was left of the Empire in the West. Unhap-
pily, they became rivals, and after the defeat of Boniface the
Vandals captured Africa and set up a powerful kingdom
ruled from Carthage. Then came the most dreaded of all
barbarian invasions, that of the Huns, under their King Attila, the Scourge of God. After ravaging in Illyricum, Attila
crossed the Rhine into Gaul in 451. Against him Aëtius
had mobilized a coalition of all the earlier invaders of Gaul,
Goths, Franks, Burgundians, Alans, Armoricans, and what
was left of the imperial army. This strange combination defeated the Huns at Châlons-sur-Marne, the first Battle of the
Marne to rank among the decisive battles of the world. When
Attila invaded Italy in the next year he was turned back by
an even stranger combination of factors—gold, prayers, the
awe aroused by the appearance of Pope Leo, the absence of
siege equipment, and the fickleness of the barbarian mind.
But before they went the Huns blotted out Aquileia; refugees from the city founded a village which was the origin of
Venice. In 453 Attila died and the moment of extreme peril
passed. Europe was not to be the most westerly province of a
Mongol empire. No man had deserved better of the West
than Aëtius, and he met his reward—assassination at the
hands of Valentinian III.

In the Eastern Empire, events after the death of Theodosius followed much the same pattern as in the West. Honorius had kept poultry; now Arcadius copied manuscripts.
There was the same power in the hands of barbarian Masters
of the Soldiers. But there had been a healthy massacre of
Goths in 400, there was peace with Persia, and the menace of
the Huns was contained, for a time, by the payment of tribute. Their departure for the West was a major stroke of fortune for Constantinople. Then in 457 the East produced—
what the West never did after Theodosius—a strong and
capable emperor in the person of Leo I. He built up the
power of the East to a point where he could undertake an invasion of Africa as a prelude to the reconquest of the West.
However, the Vandals withstood him, and the opportunity
passed. But its lessons were not lost on the barbarian generals who controlled the West. An effective emperor would
be the last thing they could afford. So, when Marjorian

looked the part for a while, he was deposed (461) and followed by a string of short-lived puppet emperors, under the control of Ricimer, Master of the Soldiers. Finally, in 476, Odoacer found a better solution. He deposed the boy-emperor, Romulus Augustulus, and induced the Senate to pass a resolution saying that they would be satisfied to have him as *magister militum* in Italy. The imperial regalia were returned to Constantinople. The Western Empire was at an end. *Romania* existed only in the world ruled from Constantinople, and in the minds of men.

Yet contemporaries did not think of 476 as a turning point. Indeed, in a way Odoacer's action preserved the unity of the Empire, since he held Italy of Zeno, Roman emperor at Constantinople. The unity of *Romania* might be a ghost, but it was very hard to lay. Justinian in the sixth century did re-establish Roman power for a time with the reconquest of Africa, Italy, Sicily, and a part of Spain. Then, after the fading of Byzantine power in the West, the crowning of Charlemagne as Roman Emperor in 800 was the origin of that curious phenomenon, the Holy Roman Empire of the Germanic peoples. "Neither holy, nor Roman, nor an empire"— but at least its title lasted until 1806, when it was renounced by Francis II for that of Emperor of Austria. More realistically, the prestige of the great Popes, a Gregory, a Hildebrand, an Innocent III, gave to the Middle Ages the impression of the continued authority of Rome. Then, in the twentieth century, there was the New Roman Empire of Mussolini.

But the historian must stand firm and not lend currency to illusions. If it be denied that the Western Empire fell in 476, he can summon an unusual witness. When Romulus and Remus in 753 b.c. sought for a sign from heaven as to which should be the founder of the new city, Romulus won by a score of twelve eagles to six. According to Roman occult lore, these twelve eagles portended an existence of 1200 years for Rome. And from 753 b.c. to 476 a.d. is, in fact, 1229 years. The margin of error is not great.

CHAPTER XIII

CLASSICAL CULTURE AND
CHRISTIANITY: 14–476 A.D.

It is by no means easy to give unity and coherence to the cultural history of the Empire. It is true that Greek literature, though it contains scarcely one name of the first rank, does maintain continuity from Augustus to the fourth century. With Latin the case is different. The Silver Age of Latin literature, which begins with the death of Augustus, does not extend beyond the death of Hadrian in 138. After this, in the age of the Antonines there are Apuleius and Fronto; then a long silence; finally, a late flowering in the fourth century with Ammianus Marcellinus, Claudian, and Ausonius. For this reason, schools and universities often end the study of Latin literature with Tacitus and Juvenal, the last of the truly "classical" Latin authors. But if we are to list those Latin writers whose work has most profoundly influenced mankind there is a third name to set beside Cicero and Virgil—that of Augustine. In him the classical and Christian traditions were blended at the highest level. Nor has any work in Latin been read so often and so continuously as the Vulgate, the Latin translation of the Bible by Jerome. These two mighty instances establish, of themselves, that the main theme of the cultural history of the Empire, from the second century onward, is that of the mutual reactions of Christianity and classical culture, alike in religion, philosophy, art, and literature.

But this great cultural conflict did not get under way before the Antonines. Latin literature from Augustus to Hadrian developed from that of the late Republic and the Augustan age, modified by the conditions of the early Empire. The most important of these were the influence of rhetoric, the overpowering reputation of certain authors of the Golden Age, and especially of Virgil, and the existence of an imperial government liable to take drastic action against authors of whom it disapproved. These factors combine to give a common stamp to all the literature of the period, recognized by the term "Silver Latin." Silver is a precious metal, second only to gold, and the Silver Age produced writers of high stature. Tacitus and Juvenal can stand comparison with any other writers of their kind in any age. Lucan, Petronius, Seneca, Martial, to name no others, command attention in their own right and for their influence on later literature.

If one is frequently conscious that the silver is not sterling but electroplate, it is due to the all-pervading influence of rhetoric on the literature of the age. We have seen how rhetoric had begun to dominate Roman education in the reign of Augustus, and how its mark is to be seen in the poetry of Ovid, and his constant striving after effect by epigram, antithesis, and verbal display. These were what commanded the alpha marks in the prize exercises of the rhetorical schools. Moreover, they were applied to themes which had as little to do with reality as the space fiction of modern times. "They are always dealing," complains Petronius, "with tyrants ordering sons to cut off their fathers' heads, or oracles demanding the sacrifice of three virgins. . . . Fed on this diet, what chance have the students of learning sense?" And sense, one is bound to admit, is not the characteristic note of a good deal of Silver Latin. Moreover, the tendencies fostered in the rhetorical schools were further developed by the public recitations. Here reputations were made and kept, and here again, all was for effect. The audience wanted to feel its flesh creep from the horrific and melodramatic, to carry away *sententiae,* memorable sayings, epigrams, startling juxtapositions of words. In this display of verbal tennis, it had applause only for the smash.

But if (as with baroque architecture) we accept the conventions, it is possible to derive much pleasure from the best of Silver Latin. And certain periods, such as Elizabethan and Jacobean England, have found it so congenial as to be a major source of inspiration. Such was the case with the tragedies of Seneca (c. 5 B.C.–65 A.D.), which have exercised a greater influence on the stage of England, France, and Italy than the infinitely finer works of Aeschylus and Sophocles. To read Seneca's *Thyestes* is to understand where *Titus Andronicus* comes from. The legend requires that Thyestes should eat his children's flesh, but Seneca describes how their flesh is cooked—and makes Thyestes belch. The Senecan world of ghosts and witches, of murder, treachery, and revenge, is at best precariously balanced on the edge of the ludicrous. Yet, after all, how many corpses are there in *Hamlet*? We have seen recently that even *Titus Andronicus* can be staged. A play-reading of a Senecan tragedy, in the age of Nero, could not have lacked effect. His philosophical writings are harder to take. The multimillionaire Stoic, who retained his wealth because great riches make as little difference to virtue as great poverty, the author of a treatise on mercy (*De Clementia*), whose harshness as a creditor may have precipitated the rebellion of Boudicca—such a teacher of morality cannot win a hearing by any virtues of style. But the *Apocolocyntosis*, a skit purporting to show how the Emperor Claudius was turned into a pumpkin instead of a god, can be enjoyed for its wit if not condoned for its taste, written as it was by Claudius' protégé for the amusement of his murderers. Yet even Seneca, when condemned to death for his part in the conspiracy of Piso, could make a good end— the supreme accomplishment of a Roman noble under Nero and Domitian.

Much more profit may be had from his nephew Lucan, who met the same fate at the age of twenty-six. His *Civil War* deals with one of the great issues of Roman history, the struggle between Caesar and the republicans, from the point of view of those who sympathized with the losers. He portrays well the stubborn virtue of Cato and the demoniac energy of Caesar, and while his treatment of the events of the war is melodramatic, it sometimes rises to tragedy. He withstood a tyrant before his death, and has inspired tyrannicide in others.

There is less to be said of the other epics of Silver Latin. Silius Italicus (26–101) chose a good theme in the Punic Wars, but thereafter did no more than write the longest poem in Latin. Valerius Flaccus (d. c. 90) wrote on the legend of the Argonauts. Some have put his handling of the Medea-Jason theme not only above that of his model Apollonius of Rhodes, but even above Virgil's treatment of Aeneas and Dido—strange eccentricity of taste! Statius (45–96), who wrote under Domitian, produced a *Thebaid* in twelve books and an *Achilleid* in two. He enjoyed popularity in his own time, and Dante placed him by the side of Virgil and Ovid. His epics have found few modern readers, but some of his shorter poems—the *Silvae*—must find a place in any anthology of Latin verse.

The *Satyricon* of Petronius is far the most attractive work of the age of Nero. What survives is only a part of a vast picaresque novel, dealing with the adventures of three dissolute young men in the taverns and stews of the ports of southern Italy. Its best-known episode is the *Cena Trimal-chionis,* a riotously comic account of the dinner party of a vulgar *nouveau riche.* The ridiculous creature is brilliantly exposed by simply being allowed to speak for himself. And he is only one of a great range of characters—all disreputable but none wholly unsympathetic—of whom Petronius has caught the authentic voice.

Martial (40–104) was, within his chosen limits, one of the most accomplished of Roman poets. He has wit, grace, and sensibility, and his twelve books of epigrams give many a vivid picture of life in Domitian's Rome. Only the absence of any moral standards or any sense of personal dignity keeps him out of the first rank.

Of the many Silver Latin poets whose works have not survived, there is perhaps most cause to regret the loss of Albinovanus Pedo. He lived under Tiberius, and wrote on the expedition of Germanicus into northern waters. Some twenty lines of the poem survive, and their exotic quality makes this fragment one of the most arresting things in Latin. It would be fascinating to have the poem to set beside those which record the reactions of European man to the new and unexplored continent of America.

We have already mentioned Pliny's *Correspondence with Trajan,* which forms one of his ten books of *Epistles.* Pliny (61–c. 114) had a successful public career, and owned large estates in northern Italy. His letters depict a provincial world of public spirit and rather dull moral worth which contrasts strikingly with the lurid life of the metropolis. Quintilian (c. 35–95), first holder of the Chair of Rhetoric at Rome, achieved that rarity, a really sensible book on education, though even he does not escape the occupational risk of being tedious in the twelve books of the *Institutio Oratoria.*

Tacitus and Juvenal are the last classical Latin authors of the first rank. Both show the characteristics of Silver Latin, but transcend its limitations as no other writers were able to do. Both wrote in the happier days of Trajan and Hadrian, but their minds were scarred indelibly by the tyranny of Domitian. Not much is known of Tacitus' life, except that he was of senatorial rank, that in his public career he was consul (97) and governor of Asia (112), and that he married the daughter of Agricola. His first historical work was a biography of his father-in-law. One of the best of ancient biographies, it is a tantalizing book for the student of Roman Britain, about which Tacitus says something but might have said so much more. But to Tacitus the province

was chiefly interesting as the background to Agricola's exploits. The anthropology and geography of the *Germania*
are much fuller and make it of permanent value as the first
historical document on Germany. It is also interesting as an
early instance of the theme of the Noble Savage. Unfortunately, on it was founded much of the nineteenth-century
nonsense about the origin of democracy in the forests of
Germany. These monographs were the prelude to his major
historical works, the *Histories*, dealing with the years 69–96,
and the later and greater *Annals*, from the death of Augustus to the death of Nero. On these he claims a place among
the great historians. Only Thucydides can match his dramatic powers, and his works have been a quarry for later
dramatists. Whatever may be thought of his critical ability,
his narrow range of interests, or his permanent bias against
the Empire and all its works, no one who has worked with
Tacitus can escape the compelling force of his personality
and outlook. On every topic one is concerned to know what
Tacitus will say, and how he will say it.

Juvenal (c. 50–127) was of humbler origin, a bourgeois
family from the country town of Aquinum. His hopes of a
public career were blasted at an early age, and for most of
his life he knew the humiliation of dependence on a wealthy
patron in Rome. Hadrian seems to have given him some relief in his old age, for there is a mellower tone about his
last writings. But it is the "blazing indignation" (*saeva in-
dignatio*) of his earlier works that set him by the side of
Swift and Voltaire. Satire iii, on the miseries of the poor in
Rome, and a scathing indictment of what Lewis Mumford
would call Megalopolis as the setting for human life, Satire
vi on the vices of women, Satire x on the vanity of human
wishes, are deservedly famous and have had many imitators.
But perhaps Juvenal's qualities are nowhere better seen than
in Satire iv, which describes a meeting of Domitian's Privy
Council. The occasion is ridiculous—to decide how to dis-
pose of a huge turbot—but the description of the hangers-on
of tyranny is perfect. One is an informer "who can slit
throats with a whisper," another a bland and genial old man,
whose longevity is ascribed to his never having swum against
the stream. Domitian is given only a line—a routine chair-
man's remark—but one is frighteningly conscious of his
malignity and power.

Tacitus and Juvenal were strong and original personalities
who had no successors. But historians owe a debt to Suetonius (c. 69–140), secretary of the imperial archives under

Hadrian, who had access to a good deal of what we should call classified material. His *Lives of the Twelve Caesars,* though as biography far inferior to Plutarch, often help when Tacitus fails.

It will be convenient to mention here the African writers, Fronto and Apuleius, though they do not belong to Silver Latin. Indeed Fronto, the most famous orator of his day, was the inventor of the New Style (*elocutio novella*) which was designed to supersede it, and was itself a curious blend of archaism and colloquialism. His correspondence with his pupil Marcus Aurelius was discovered in 1815. But the finest literary expression of the New Style is in the *Metamorphoses* or *Golden Ass* of Apuleius (b. 123). The only Latin novel to survive complete, it contains the only ancient folk-tale, that of Cupid and Psyche. Describing the adventures of one Lucius when he was turned into an ass, it is a kind of allegory of the mysteries of Isis. Style and content make it one of the most interesting books in Latin, and there is a fine modern translation.

The economic prosperity of the eastern provinces in the first century, and perhaps the philhellenism of such emperors as Nero and Hadrian, led to a revival of Greek literature. It is partly bound up with the Second Sophistic, the term used to describe the activities of a new kind of itinerant orator and lecturer. These men won wealth and fame by their public appearances in the great cities of the eastern world, and indeed of Italy and Gaul. Their learning might be superficial, but their rhetoric was genuinely impressive and their public personality carefully cultivated. They were a mixture of the university extension lecturer, the newspaper columnist, and the television personality of the modern world. Like these, they sometimes gave verbal firework displays, but sometimes handled serious issues. Many of the most famous are only names to us, but we can judge their work by the eighty surviving speeches of Dio Chrysostom (40–c. 112), and the fifty-five of Aelius Aristides (lectured in Rome 156). Dio's speech on kingship, delivered in the presence of Trajan, and Aristides' eulogy of Rome, are well known: otherwise these authors have been neglected, though they are a valuable source for the life of the Greek world in their day. The Sophists found the formless Koine—the Greek dialect which was the common language of the eastern provinces—unsuitable for their purpose, and this led to a revival of Attic for oratory and literature.

This neo-Attic is seen at its best in the works of Lucian of Samosata in Syria (born c. 120), one of the most suc-

cessful humorists of the ancient world. He had been a Sophist
at one stage of his life, but then took up philosophy, and wrote
the satiric *Dialogues* on which his fame depends. *The Dialogue of the Dead,* and the journey to the moon in his
True History show his method of attacking folly and vice
by making them ridiculous.

Plutarch of Chaeronea (c. 46–120) followed the opposite
method, of making virtue attractive. He was a voluminous
writer, but only one of his books has had great influence,
the noble *Parallel Lives of the Greeks and Romans.* As the
lives of "the greatest men of the most foremost nations of
the world," the *Lives* were the favorite historical reading of
Renaissance Europe. Princes found them useful as a guide
to conduct. They were fortunate in their translators, Amyot
in France, North in England. It was from North's Plutarch,
principally, that Shakespeare formed his idea of the Roman
world. Two historians of merit wrote on Rome, Appian in
the time of Antoninus, Dio Cassius in that of Alexander
Severus. Arrian (fl. c. 140), a Greek of Bithynia, but a
Roman provincial governor and a capable general, wrote
our most reliable history of Alexander the Great.

There was no scientific advance under the Empire, but
much industry went into works of synthesis and compila-
tion. Industry, indeed, is the chief virtue of the *Natural
History* of the Elder Pliny. It has been called "a compen-
dium of all the errors of the ancient world," which it perpetuated through its immense popularity in the Middle Ages.
A single major error marred the work of the great Alexan-
drian astronomer Ptolemy (c. 150), whose work, known to
the Middle Ages under its Arabic title of *Almagest,* perpetuated the geocentric theory until it was overthrown by
Copernicus. Ptolemy's geography—alike in its virtues and
its errors—influenced the great explorers of the Age of Discovery. To become a standard authority is, sooner or later,
to become an obstacle to knowledge, but Ptolemy must be
given credit for much valuable work. The same is true of
Celsus and Galen in medicine, and Dioscorides in botany.

Philosophy produced little new. The schools at Athens,
Alexandria, and the other centers of learning attracted pupils and expounded received doctrine. Cynics preached a
popular morality—"the philosophy of the poor"—in the
marketplaces and squares of the Greek cities. Cynicism was
a kind of left-wing Stoicism, which influenced many of the
Stoics of this period, especially Epictetus. In Rome, only
Stoicism counted for much in the early Empire. The inti-
mate connection between Stoicism and the senatorial opposi-

tion in the first century was adherence to the traditions of Brutus and Cato, but there was no necessary alignment of Stoicism with the opposition. After Domitian, it was on the side of the Establishment; it formulated ideas of kingship that inspired Trajan and Hadrian, and set a Stoic on the throne in Marcus Aurelius. The considerable Stoic literature is represented to us by the writings of Seneca and Musonius Rufus, the *Handbook* of Epictetus, and the *Meditations* of Marcus Aurelius. Epictetus is the most interesting of these. An ex-slave, he was expelled from Rome by Domitian, and set up a school in Nicopolis which attracted pupils from all classes. He taught a sturdy and bracing morality, equipping men to face any situation through trust in the providence of God. For the Stoics, the existence of God is known through reason, the essential part of man. The last great school of classical philosophy, Neoplatonism, was based on the mysticism inherent in Plato's thought. Its chief exponent was Plotinus (205–270), who taught in Rome under Gallienus. His *Enneads* is one of the classics of mysticism. He taught the transcendence of God, pure Mind cognizable by mind alone— "let us stretch forth our minds to Him in prayer, for this is the only way we can pray, alone to Him who is alone." Such a stretching can be done only by the spiritual athlete, whose supreme reward is the Beatific Vision, which Plotinus had three times in his life. Neoplatonism had many followers in the third and fourth centuries, and the art of the period often depicts "the Philosopher," his eyes turned upward in contemplation. The philosopher has become a *guru*.

That philosophy should end in religion was natural in an age when religion absorbed more and more of the minds and energies of men. An immense number of inscriptions, from every part of the Roman world, attest the thousands of cults that flourished in an easy and tolerant polytheism. The native gods of the Celtic, Germanic, and Spanish peoples were not submerged. Like their devotees, they became Romanized, more or less, and in their new guise often attracted Roman worshipers who equated them with gods already known. So arose Syncretism, the most characteristic religious phenomenon of the early Empire. Sometimes it might take the form of a divine marriage; the Celtic Rosmerta, goddess of trade, is paired off with her Roman equivalent Mercury. Sometimes the native god would take a Roman name, as did so many of his devotees. Thus Mars Belatucader, a fusion of Roman and Celtic war gods, was worshiped in a small defined area close to Hadrian's Wall. How far this fusion of cults could go is attested by another example from Britain. At Lydney a low hill above the Severn was crowned by the temple of a divinity whose Celtic name was Nodens. Philologically, the name is close to that of an Irish sea god: that would be natural, for the Severn bore which swept past Lydney could be the god in majesty. But the Romans equated him with the forest god Silvanus: naturally again, for in this aspect he would be the hunter god of the Forest of Dean. However, the excavation of buildings in the temple precincts by Sir Mortimer Wheeler shows the existence of a healing cult, with features such as "sleeping in the temple" like those of the cult of Aesculapius at Epidaurus. Nor is this all. The ground plan of the temple is very like that of an early Christian church, though the dating evidence points to the pagan revival under Julian. Such is the blend of Celtic, Roman, and Greek features in the cult of Nodens-Silvanus.

But cults of this kind were of no more than local significance and limited function, nor—so far as we know—could they offer the worshiper much in the way of devotional life. The really significant feature of the first two centuries was the spread of the great Oriental religions, with their universal appeal. We have already seen how the cults of Cybele, Bacchus, and Isis came to Rome in the late Republic, and how they sometimes met official hostility. Under the Empire that hostility was no more. Caligula encouraged the worship of the Egyptian divinities Isis and Serapis, and enrolled them in the calendar of state cults. Claudius did the same for Cybele, whose priests were no longer confined to the temple on the Palatine. Both cults were marked by elaborate and splendid ritual. There were daily services in the temples of Isis, and great festivals, with impressive ceremonial, at certain seasons of the year. Apuleius describes the *Navigium Isidis*—the Ship of Isis—on March 5, with masked revelers, magnificent processions, and the launching of the Sacred Ship. It is sometimes said that this is the origin of the Carnival in Mediterranean cities. In November was the celebration of the Finding of Osiris, with its sacred drama of death and resurrection. The Spring Festival of Attis, the greatest festival of the cult of Cybele, lasted for twelve days (March 12–25), ending with the wild rejoicing of the *Hilaria* (Feast of Joy). It was the life work of the great Belgian scholar, Franz Cumont, to show the importance of all these Oriental religions, the forerunners of Christianity. Here we can give only a rather fuller description of the most important, that of Mithras.

The cult of Mithras spread in the Roman world during the

second half of the first century A.D. It came from Persia, where it had been known from the earliest times, and was carried by Oriental slaves to the great ports of the Mediterranean, and by Roman soldiers to all the frontiers of the Empire, being especially strong among the garrisons of the Rhine and the Danube. It is strikingly absent from the Greek world. In his Persian form Mithras is the God of Light, the intermediary between the Supreme God of the Universe and humanity. A divine epic told of his life in this world. Shepherds saw his miraculous birth from the rock, and brought gifts. As a youth he engaged in a series of heroic exploits, culminating in the slaying of the divine bull, from whose blood spring all plants and animals beneficent to man. Translated to heaven, he cares for the souls of the faithful.

The Mithraic sacred writings are lost, but we know something of the ceremonies. There were seven grades of initiates, bearing the names of the Raven, the Hidden One, the Soldier, the Lion, the Persian, the Sun-Runner, and the Father. Elaborate ceremonies marked the initiation into each grade, and perhaps only the last four beheld the sacred mysteries. A Mithraic service, in an underground cave or temple, brilliantly lit, with the various grades in their masks and costumes, must have been an impressive occasion. There were sacraments of baptism, confirmation, and communion. The temples were the property of the congregations, which were small, probably not above a hundred. When numbers rose above this, a new conventicle was founded. Women were excluded from the cult. Mithraic temples were very like the Early Christian churches of the basilica type—small rectangular buildings of a nave with two aisles, a sanctuary, and an apse in which the sacred images were kept. Frequently they were underground, in memory of the period when the worship of Mithras was carried out in caves. There was an elaborate sacred art, the chief features of which were the representation of Mithras slaying the sacred bull, attended by his two divine companions, Cautes and Cautopates. Together they formed a trinity of gods. Perhaps the two assistants with their torches represent the sun at dawn and at evening, while Mithras himself is the sun in full vigor.

The great soldier-emperors of the third century naturally favored the god so popular among the Roman soldiers, and we have seen how the armies of Aurelian and Diocletian fought under the banner of the Invincible Sun God. This period was the high-water mark of the cult. But Christianity always regarded it with implacable hostility, probably be-

cause of certain obvious parallels between the two, of which
enemies of Christianity made damaging use. After the victory of Christianity in the fourth century, Mithraism was
driven underground; literally, in some cases, as with the
Mithraic temple beneath the church of San Clemente in
Rome. But some of its features were to re-emerge in the
heresy of the Manichees, and its successors in the Middle
Ages.

Our concern here with Christianity must be limited to its
effect on the history and culture of the Roman Empire. A
full-scale treatment of the life of Jesus, the spread of the
Gospel, the relations with Judaism, Christian doctrine, the
organization of the Church, the rise of heresies, and the
great theological controversies would be out of place.

To the historian of the Roman Empire, Christianity appears
as the last and greatest of the universal religions. Like its
predecessors, it offered through ritual and sacrament a personal spiritual experience, and proclaimed life after death
and redemption through a divine savior. Such ideas were
already familiar in the Greco-Roman world, and so far
Christianity did not come as something strange. But in two
respects it was indeed novel and startling. Life after death,
in the Christian concept, was not for initiates only but for
all mankind, for whom it had been won by a Divine Savior
who was also an historical figure. Jesus of Nazareth, born of
poor parents in the reign of Augustus, conducted a mission
for some three years in Galilee and Jerusalem. His whole
life was passed in Palestine, he taught in Aramaic, and his
work cannot be understood without the Jewish religious
background. His teaching was that of a "prophet" in the old
Hebrew tradition. It is fascinating to compare the Sermon
on the Mount with a dialogue of Socrates. The first is a revelation of truth by a man of superior spiritual insight . . .
"Verily, verily, I say unto you." Jesus won the assent of his
hearers through parables, using the events of common life
to illustrate his teaching. Socrates conducts a discussion with
one or more partners; as a man of superior intellectual power
he induces them to follow his argument to the conclusion
he desires. Jesus himself was respectful to the older Hebrew
teaching—"Think not I am come to destroy the law; I am
come not to destroy but to fulfill." And many of his countrymen were ready to see in him the Messiah who had been
so long awaited. But the ideas he proclaimed were little to
the liking of the official hierarchy in Jerusalem, and they secured his condemnation to be crucified as a common criminal under Tiberius (30? A.D.). Such are the purely historical
facts of the life of Jesus, but Christians claim that there

are others that transcend them. He was the Son of God, and, after the Crucifixion . . . "on the third day He rose from the dead."

The life and teaching of Jesus, the Resurrection and what it implies, constitute the Christian faith as taught by the Apostles. The teaching of the Gospel began in Jerusalem fifty days after the Resurrection. Thirty years of intense activity by the first Christian missionaries—chief among them the Apostles Peter and Paul—established Christian communities in the principal cities of Asia, Syria, Greece, and Macedonia, and also in Alexandria and Rome. They taught and wrote in the Koine. In the reign of Nero Christianity came into collision with the imperial authorities. Peter and Paul were martyred in Rome. Christianity itself became an unlawful religion (*religio non licita*), a status from which it did not emerge until the Edict of Milan in 313.

In this condition, Christianity always ran the risk of persecutions, the chief of which have been mentioned in an earlier chapter. But while it is natural that Christian tradition should especially recount the deaths of the martyrs, the historian is chiefly impressed by the spread of Christianity to every part of the Empire—and indeed beyond the Roman frontiers— by the organization of the clergy, and by the emergence of a strong "catholic" church. It is these last two features that chiefly distinguish the Church of the second and third centuries from primitive Christianity. The clerical orders of deacon, priest, and bishop are established and their functions defined. There are parallels to deacon and priest in the Jewish synagogue, and that may be their origin. But the bishop, ruling his diocese which (at least in the East) consists of a city and the surrounding territory, is clearly based on Roman civil administration. The next stage—a long one, and not complete until well on in the fourth century—was the grouping of dioceses, the emergence of archbishoprics, and the long struggle for primacy between the great metropolitan sees, which ended with the supremacy of Rome in the West and Constantinople in the East.

At an earlier stage, the emergence of churches with regional or local characteristics is a commentary on the cultural diversity of the Empire. Thus there was a Palestinian Christianity, which included the older Jewish Christianity descended from the mission of Jesus but a recessive influence after the Jewish wars, and the purely Gentile churches, such as that in Hadrian's new colony of Aelia Capitolina, built on the site of the ruined city of Jerusalem. There was a Syrian Christianity, teaching both in Syriac and in Greek, with Antioch as its headquarters. There was an Asian Christianity, headed by

the venerable Seven Churches. In Phrygia and Cappadocia
there was a distinctive form, marked by the asceticism and
fanaticism of the New Prophecy introduced by Montanus, a
former priest of Cybele. In Greece there were the historic
churches of Athens and Corinth. There was an Egyptian
Christianity, famous for the scholarship of Alexandria and
(in the fourth century) the origins of monasticism. Finally,
there was the Christianity of the West, with its two great
centers of Rome, City of the Apostles, and Africa. From
about 150 Latin became the language of the Western Church,
and Africa produced the first Christian literature in Latin.

The appeal of early Christianity had been mainly, though
not wholly, to the poor of the great cities. Simple, unedu-
cated people, the first Christians were uninterested in classical culture, which seemed to them unimportant because of
their belief in the imminence of the second coming of Christ.
But with the second century apocalyptic beliefs began to fade.
Converts were now of all social classes and occupations, including, it is said, members of the imperial household. Christianity began to feel the need to explain itself to a pagan
world with which it was clearly destined to coexist—especially to those educated in the classical tradition, for it was
above all as an educational tradition that it was confronted
by classical culture. Conversion was one of the chief ways in
which the Church added to its numbers, and conversion was
an individual thing. Whether by preaching or example, by
argument or mystical experience, it meant that a man educated in the classical tradition of rhetoric, literature, and philosophy had to be won and kept for the Christian faith. If
the pagan world was an enemy, it was an enemy that had to
be fought, in this respect, with its own weapons. Nor was the
only danger from pagan thought. Heresy within the Christian
community was more formidable when equipped with the
dialectic of the Greeks, as was the case with the great Gnos-
tics Marcion and Valentinus. Gnosticism has been called the
many-headed monster of the religious and philosophical
thought of the second and third centuries; all its many va-
rieties draw from Platonic or Stoic thought the idea of a link
between the divine Logos and the mind of the adept, who thus
has access to a secret wisdom (gnosis).

It was to meet this situation that the Christian writers of
the second century produced their works of "apology" and
scholarship. The apologies were written to put the case for
Christianity in terms that the educated pagan could understand. Justin and Aristides addressed themselves to the emperor; the Apology of Tertullian was intended for Roman provincial governors. In scholarship the lead was taken by the

Christian lay school at Alexandria, whose greatest names are Clement (b. c. 150) and Origen (185–255). Research was carried out on the text and interpretation of the Scriptures, and the school specialized in giving instruction to converts. The *Protreptikos* of Clement presents Christianity as the true philosophy, consummating and superseding all that had been done by the Greeks. In their methods of work, and in their outer way of life, men like Clement and Origen might be described as "Christian Sophists." Not Greek philosophy, but Roman law and rhetoric, inspired the African writers Tertullian (c. 160–225) and Cyprian (c. 200–258). Cyprian, Bishop of Carthage, was martyred; the great basilica which is his memorial is one of the most impressive Christian monuments in Africa. Tertullian's training at the bar comes out in everything he wrote. Even his *Apology* is based on the maxim that the best form of defense is attack, and his polemical works are informed by a bitter hatred and vindictiveness that have too often marred Christian controversy. A very different tone pervades the works of Lactantius (c. 250–317). Believing that the aridity and lack of style of Christian literature were a bar to educated pagans, he addressed this class in his *Divine Institutes,* written in Ciceronian Latin and steeped in Latin literature.

The fourth century saw a certain revival of pagan literature. We have already mentioned the historian Ammianus Marcellinus (b. 330). A Greek of Antioch, who learned Latin late in life, he set himself to continue the historical work of Tacitus, and met with an astonishing measure of success. The surviving books, which deal mainly with the reign of Valentinian, suggest that the lost books of Ammianus would be as well worth having as the lost books of Livy. Ausonius (d. 395), who taught at Toulouse and Bordeaux, was a voluminous, uneven poet. His *Commemoration of the Professors of Bordeaux,* interesting as it may be to educationists, describes surely one of the dullest senior common rooms ever known. But the *Order of Noble Cities* shows a feeling for places, and this quality, and an eye for natural beauty, make his *Mosella* a delightful poem—the first, it is often said, in the literature of France. Claudian (fl. 395–404) is a greater figure, although his official epitaph (now in the Naples Museum) pitches it rather high in bringing in Homer and Virgil. None the less, his *Rape of Proserpine* is one of the best mythological poems in Latin, and the *Consulship of Stilicho* deals with an important historical theme as Lucan might have done. Finally—for it probably belongs to this century —there is the *Pervigilium Veneris*—a poem unique in Latin

for its romantic beauty and haunting cadences. It deals
with the spring festival of Venus in Sicily; one can only
compare the *Primavera* of Botticelli and say no more.

In general, the best minds of the fourth century had been
won for Christianity. It is no part of the plan of this book
to discuss the great theological controversies which engaged
Athanasius, Arius, and their peers. But it is to be noted
that the minds which wrestled with the subtle doctrines of
the Incarnation and the Trinity had been trained in Greek
philosophy. So, too, had the great Cappadocians, Basil, Gregory of Nyssa, and Gregory of Nazianzen, who all studied
rhetoric and philosophy at Athens. Prudentius (b. 348), the
first considerable Christian poet, used Latin lyric meters and
a deep knowledge of Horace and Virgil for Christian themes.
The three great Latin Fathers, Jerome, Ambrose, and Augustine, dominate the thought of the West. Jerome (348–420)
was in touch with all the cultural trends, classical and pagan.
Born in Dalmatia, educated in Rome, he first followed the religious life at Treves. He pursued theological studies at Antioch, and then returned to Rome to receive from Pope Da-
masus the commission to revise the Latin text of the Gos-
pels. Then he went to Egypt to see monastic life; finally
(389) he founded the religious house at Jerusalem where he
completed his great work of scholarship. His Vulgate, the
translation of the Bible into Latin, has influenced not only
the Latin of the Church, but also the vernacular literature
of western Europe. Nor should it be forgotten that his *Chronicle* is one of the best sources for the dates and lives of classical authors. In Ambrose (337–397) we see a great Roman administrator in the service of the Church. He was governor of
Aemilia and Liguria when he was appointed bishop of Milan,
then one of the most important sees. He won distinction alike
as bishop, preacher, writer, and ecclesiastical statesman, and
he wrote four of the earliest and finest Christian hymns.

It is fitting that this brief survey should end with Augustine (354–430). Apart from his influence on Christian thought,
Augustine occupies, like Virgil, a position of cardinal importance in the whole cultural history of the West. Master of
all that was vital in the intellectual life of his time, he trans-
muted it through his own works into a synthesis of experience that set the pattern of a new age. He was educated in
the Latin culture of Africa (Greek he never knew well), and
flirted at one time with Manicheism. The *Hortensius* of Cicero attracted him to philosophy, and he became professor of
rhetoric, first in Rome and then in Milan. Then he came
under the influence of Ambrose and in 386 underwent the
conversion so movingly described in the *Confessions*. Stroll-

ing in a garden, perplexed in mind because his study of Greek philosophy seemed to have led him to a dead end, he heard a child's voice say *"Tolle lege, tolle lege"* (take up and read). He obeyed the omen, opened at random the Epistles of Paul, and came upon the text that won him to Christianity (Romans 13:13-14). Returning to Africa, he took orders, and in 395 became bishop of Hippo, the scene of his lifework. No Latin author was more prolific, none had greater influence. The *Confessions,* together with the later *Retractions,* are probably the finest intellectual and spiritual autobiography ever written. But by far his most massive work is the *City of God.* Begun in 413, three years after the capture of Rome by Alaric, it develops in twenty-two books a Christian philosophy of history. The object is to show how Christians should view the greatest secular event of the age —the collapse of Roman power in the West. In the course of a survey which attacks and overthrows all the ideas of classical historiography and the ethics on which they are based, Augustine sets in opposition the two great polities—the City of the World and the City of God. Earthly cities are numerous, and should not command our allegiance. They are all ephemeral, and their rise and fall—even that of the Roman Empire—has significance only as part of the divine plan. But man as man is a citizen of the City of God. In the fullness of time the kingdoms of this world will pass away, and after the second coming of Christ and the Last Judgment the Heavenly Kingdom will be established for ever. The lesson of history is to teach us to look to the world that is to come.

It must not be thought that contact with classical culture was approved by all Christians. Tertullian had asked, "What has Jerusalem to do with Athens?" and many were ready to answer, "Nothing." Early monasticism, in particular, renounced culture, with all other worldly goods, for a more perfect asceticism. Even Jerome and Augustine felt at times alarmed by the seductions of the older culture. "I am a Ciceronian, not a Christian!" Jerome exclaimed in self-reproach. In his book *On the Christian Education* Augustine deprecates in turn all the subjects of the pagan curriculum. The conflict of the two cultures was bound to lead to such periods of stress. But the great work of the Greek and Latin Fathers, as we have tried to treat it in this brief survey, was to produce a fusion of Christianity and classical culture which enabled Christianity to win general acceptance in the Roman world, to survive its fall, and to remain the strongest ingredient in the culture of the West.

EPILOGUE

What were the reasons for the collapse of Roman power in the West? The question cannot be avoided, though it is pre-eminently one of those historical problems which can be posed but not finally answered. There is a formidable literature on the subject, scholarly and otherwise. Gibbon had no doubt of the answer—"I have narrated the triumph of barbarism and religion." To these primary factors modern inquirers have added, among others, class warfare, the hostility of the army to the bourgeoisie, race suicide, soil exhaustion, climatic change, the mongrelization of Rome and Italy by Oriental immigration, malaria, plague, and sexual immorality. The great catastrophe has provided moralists with an endless supply of ammunition. We are often told that history teaches that the decline of the Roman Empire was due to—whatever the vice under attack. Unfortunately, the lessons of history are by no means so clear. The advance of historical knowledge has taken us far from the calm certainties of Gibbon, and few would now assent to his neat solution. But on certain propositions there is a large measure of agreement. First, no single cause could by itself have been sufficient. Second, any final solution must, before it can be accepted, explain why the Eastern Empire survived for a thousand years after the collapse in the West. Further than this, it is possible to point to a number of weaknesses in Roman society; their effects may be variously estimated, but in combination they must have been largely responsible for the collapse.

The German scholar Rehm has assessed the part this problem has played in the thought of the Western world, and has shown how men of different ages have propounded and answered it in terms of their own experience. Our own times understand technology, if nothing else, and there were certainly grave weaknesses in the technology of the Roman Empire. Judged by modern standards, there was little general advance in the five centuries after Rome had taken over the technology of the Hellenistic world. Large-scale exploitation, not advances in technique, were the strong point of the Romans. No doubt this stagnation can partly be set down to the influence of slavery. By providing a cheap and expendable supply of human labor, slavery discourages invention, which tends to replace human labor by the machine. In all periods of history slavery has affected enterprise and efficiency as deeply and insidiously as it has morals and humanity. And yet slavery cannot be the whole answer. The number of slaves in the Roman world declined after the great wars of conquest under the Republic. There were no more markets on the scale of Delos. The early Empire is marked by the increased use of free rather than slave labor. This, and the economic boom of the period, should have provided conditions to suit the inventor. But there was no large-scale advance—certainly nothing to equal even the earliest phases of the Industrial Revolution. It is not enough to ascribe this to the Roman bent for the practical and dislike of theory. Some of the inventions that would have been of most benefit to the Roman world were precisely those which might have been expected from men of practical skill. Why did none of the thousands of Roman teamsters invent a harness that would not half-strangle a draft animal by pulling on its windpipe? Why was there no improvement in the clumsy rigging of Roman ships? Above all, why did no employee of a Roman mint ever take the easy step from stamping to printing—a discovery which would have been of incalculable importance for the spread of knowledge? There is something here as hard to explain as the failure of Peruvian civilization to invent the wheel.

Partly, no doubt, this failure in technology is bound up with the failure in education. Despite the patronage of the emperors and the eagerness of the municipalities to found and maintain schools, education under the Empire was neither sufficiently wide nor sufficiently deep. It was certainly a grave weakness that natural science and practical subjects were neglected, but it is not enough to say, as do some critics, that the Romans were satisfied with a mere literary education. The real weakness was the undue attention paid to rhetoric, and this was due to a short-sighted preference for the form of vocational training which seemed to offer the quickest way to success. Roman education produced lawyers, administrators, and teachers of rhetoric. In so doing it gave them considerable powers of expression, some feeling for literature, and the rudiments of an education in morals. But it failed to stimulate intellectual curiosity, and it added nothing to knowledge.

Less imponderable are certain political and military weaknesses. The failure to establish any lasting and generally accepted basis for the succession to the Principate stands out. Had the hereditary principle been accepted, it would no doubt have produced many weak or vicious emperors. But it would at least have been a principle that all could understand, and usurpers would have been seen for what they were. Had adoption been consistently followed, there would have been struggles for the succession, but more often through intrigues in the palace than in arms on the battlefield. But the Romans did not consistently follow either system, and so often got the worst of both worlds. Hereditary succession produced some bad emperors in the first century. A disputed succession, especially after the time of Commodus, led to many struggles which gravely weakened the state, and not only in loss of manpower and material resources. The army became corrupted by the discovery that it was more profitable to plunder the civilized world than to defend it against the barbarians. Little more than a century separates the army of Maximinus Thrax from that of Trajan, but they were poles apart in discipline, morale, and fighting spirit.

In any case the system of defense against the barbarian world established by Augustus would only work so long as Rome retained a clear military advantage over her enemies. Things do not stand still on a frontier. The barbarians would become Romanized, at least in the sense that they understood Roman methods of warfare; Arminius and Alaric both served in the Roman army. And the Roman army itself, as we have seen, became increasingly barbarian in its personnel—even, in the fourth century, in the higher command. Under such circumstances Roman superiority could only have been maintained by greatly superior technical resources such as the use of firearms. It is true that various ballistic devices in the third and fourth centuries gave it superiority of a kind, but not sufficiently effective to give a decisive margin over the enemy. By the middle of the fourth century an army of Goths, Vandals, or Huns could take the field against the Roman army on at least equal terms. Even at that stage the Empire must have had far superior resources of manpower, but these could not be mobilized

and brought into action without increasing the already stag-
gering burden of taxation.

Crippling taxation was only one of the burdens which the
late Empire imposed on its citizens. From the time of Diocletian on it had degenerated into a totalitarian state, control-
ling and directing all activities in its own interests. The agents
of the state were everywhere; its regulations covered every
side of life. Frozen into their hereditary occupations, struggling under the twin burdens of taxes and inflation, further
harassed by incessant demands for loans, gifts, and labor,
exposed to the greed of an army of corrupt officials, the citizens of the late Empire had neither the means nor the motive
to better their lot. Walbank is right to emphasize that the
emperors of the third and fourth century had no choice but
to act as they did if the state was to survive. Their reforms
did indeed make survival possible, for a time, but at the
terrible price of the destruction of all enterprise and public
spirit. The citizen was reduced to a helpless individual, to
whom the state and its agents were no longer a *res publica*,
but They. And the barbarians must often have seemed pref-
erable to Them. The excessive demands of the state were,
without doubt, the chief cause of the final downfall of the
West.

Since these conditions also existed in the East, the question arises as to why there was no such collapse there. It has
already been shown that the main force of the barbarian
invasions fell on the West, which had to face the worst assaults of the Goths and the Huns. There are no parallels
in the East to the Frankish kingdom in Gaul, and those of
the Vandals in Spain and Africa. Above all, as Baynes has
pointed out, the comparative immunity of Asia Minor meant
that the East had a reserve of manpower and material resources such as Italy could not afford to the West. From this
springboard Justinian, in the early sixth century, launched
the great offensives which offered a brief hope of the restoration of the Empire.

We have set out what are now thought to be the chief
reasons for the collapse of Roman power in the West. No
doubt, as knowledge advances, it will be possible to trace their
effects in greater detail, to establish their relative importance,
and, perhaps, to add to their number. Certainly the inquiry is
one of perennial interest to those nations which are the heirs
of Roman civilization. But in making it, we should do well to
avoid any assumption of superiority on our own part. Great
Britain did not begin to provide education for all until 1870.
Slavery lasted in the United States until the Civil War. Our

society is having to pay a high price for survival; if, so far, that price has been met, there is no guarantee that the demands of the state on the individual may not become too heavy for him to bear. Above all, the tremendous advance in man's control over nature, achieved in the last three centuries, has not been matched by an equal control by man over himself. Thus, for all the immeasurable superiority of our science and technology over that of the Romans, we are caught in a dilemma they did not know. We have no assurance of a margin of superiority over the technology of our potential enemies, and in trying to attain it we run the real danger of the total destruction of civilization on this planet.

A knowledge of the past may serve to make us vigilant in the face of our own dangers. To many at the present time the threat of atomic warfare seems as real and as imminent as did the forthcoming end of the world to the early Christians. It may be some comfort to reflect that the second century was marked, not by the end of the world, but by the prosperity of the age of the Antonines. Our society, too, confronts the alternatives of cataclysm or prosperity. Roman history is a reminder that the latter has its own perils, not less real because they are concealed. There is a pertinent comment of Gregory the Great on the apparent prosperity of the Roman world in the second century—"There was long life and health, material prosperity, growth of population, and the tranquillity of daily peace, yet while the world was flourishing in itself, in their hearts it had withered away."

Appendix

Place Names and Their Latin Equivalents

Modern	Latin
Agrigento	Agrigentum
Alise-Ste.-Reine	Alesia
Arezzo	Arretium
Arles	Arelate
Augsburg	Augusta Vindelicorum
Bologna	Bononia
Bône	Hippo
Bordeaux	Burdigala
Budapest	Aquincum
Cadiz	Gades
Cartagena	Nova Carthago
Catania	Catana
Chester	Deva
Cirencester	Corinium
Colchester	Camulodunum
Cologne	Colonia Agrippina
Constantinople (*see* Istanbul)	
Durazzo	Dyrrachium
Geneva	Genava
Gloucester	Glevum
Istanbul	Byzantium, Constantinople
Lambessa	Lambaesis
Lincoln	Lindum
Lisbon	Olisipo
London	Londinium
Lyons	Lugdunum
Mainz	Moguntiacum
Malaga	Malaca
Marsala	Lilybaeum
Marseilles	Massilia
Merida	Emerita
Messina	Messana
Milan	Mediolanum

Naples	Neapolis
Narbonne	Narbo
Nîmes	Nemausus
Nish	Naissus
Padua	Patavium
Palermo	Panormus
Rimini	Ariminum
Sagunto	Saguntum
Saragossa	Caesaraugusta
Sousse	Hadrumetum
Split	Spalato
Strasbourg	Argentoratum
Tangier	Tingis
Taormina	Tauromenium
Taranto	Tarentum
Tarragona	Tarraco
Trèves	Augusta Treverorum
Trieste	Tergeste
Vienna	Vindobona
Wroxeter	Viroconium
York	Eboracum

Glossary of Terms

Note: For words whose plural form is used in the text, both singular and plural forms are given.

Aedile—City magistrate in charge of public buildings, markets, traffic regulations, water supply, etc. Also found in the municipalities.

Ala—A cavalry squadron, numbering, after Augustus, 500 or 1,000 men recruited from the provinces.

Annona—Literally, harvest. The public grain supply of Rome. Became important at the time of Gaius Gracchus. Organized by Augustus as an imperial department.

Censor—Appointed to take the census every five years and value the estates for taxation (445 B.C.). Placed in charge of the senatorial list, and, hence, acquired great influence (312 B.C.). Later exercised a wide range of powers over morals and conduct.

Civitas (*civitates*)—Under the Empire, a local self-governing unit; often, but not always, a city.

Cohors (*cohortes*)—From the time of Marius, the tactical unit of the legion. Ten *cohortes* made up a legion of 6,000 men. Under the Empire the name was used for infantry units of provincials.

Colonate—Under the Empire, tenant farmers—especially on the imperial estates.

Colonia (*coloniae*)—Originally, a settlement of Roman or Latin citizens, founded for agriculture or defense. Later, *coloniae* were founded by the state for economic purposes, often outside Italy. Under the Empire, *coloniae* were usually for veterans.

Colonus (*coloni*)—(1) A member of a *colonia*. (2) A tenant farmer.

Consistorium—From the fourth century A.D., the Imperial Council summoned by the emperor and consisting of all the chief heads of the departments.

Consul—The supreme magistrate under the Republic; two in number, elected by the people, term of office one year. As inheritors of the powers of the king, the consuls exercised military command. Under the Empire, the consulship became largely an honorary office.

Consular—(Used as a noun.) An ex-consul.

Imperium—Supreme administrative power held by the major magistrates of the Republic within the sphere (*provincia*) of their office.

Imperium infinitum aequum—Power not limited geographically, and equal to that of any provincial governor.

Iugerum (*iugera*)—The standard Roman measure of area; equal to ⅝ths of an acre.

Legaturs (*legati*)—(1) An ambassador. (2) A deputy to a provincial governor. (3) Under the Empire, the commander of a legion, and (4) The governor of an imperial province.

Limes—Originally, a military road with fortified posts. Later, a permanent defensive front (*cf.* Hadrian's Wall).

Magistrate—In the Republic, an executive officer of the State, elected by the people and usually holding office for one year. The most important were the consuls, censors, praetors, quaestors, and aediles.

Master of Horse—An official nominated by a dictator as his deputy.

Master of the Soldiers—In the late Empire, the supreme commander of the infantry and the cavalry. Post frequently held by barbarians.

Modius (*modii*)—The standard Roman dry measure, equal to 1.1 peck.

Municipium (*municipia*)—(1) A self-governing Italian borough. (2) A self-governing community in the provinces. Less common than the *civitas* in Gaul and Britain.

Oppidum—A town or urban community, especially the Celtic towns in Gaul.

Plebs—The general body of Roman citizens, as distinct from the aristocracy (*patricii*).

Populares—From the second century B.C., the term used especially for the party which sought the support of the lower classes, but which really opposed the aristocracy in the interests of the middle class.

Praetor—Republican magistrate, chiefly concerned with the administration of justice. The *praetor peregrinus* dealt with the cases in which visitors and foreigners residing in Rome were involved.

Primipilaris—Under the Empire, the captain of the first company of a legion. After discharge, these men were frequently recruited for posts in the civil service.

Princeps—A word chosen by Augustus to describe his position as leader of the State. Later, title was assumed by Roman emperors on their accession to the throne.

Proconsul—In the late Republic, the title of the governor of a province. Under the Empire, the governor of a senatorial province.

Procurator—Under the Empire, an imperial financial officer in charge of provincial finance, mines, imperial estates, etc.

Publicanus (*publicani*)—Public contractors, especially those concerned with the collection of taxes from the provinces, who became very wealthy and powerful under the Republic, but were less important under the Empire.

Quaestor—Republican magistrate, chiefly concerned with finance.

Tribune, military—Subordinate army commander. In the late Republic, there were six tribunes in each legion.

Tribunes: *tribuni plebis*—Officers elected to preserve the interests of the people against the aristocracy, and holding wide powers of veto.

BIBLIOGRAPHY

The list is in no sense a comprehensive bibliography. It does no more than name a few books for further reading, most of which are in English. Very complete bibliographies will be found in the volumes on Rome in *The Cambridge Ancient Histories* (12 vols., ed. by J. B. Bury, *et al*, London, Cambridge University Press, 1924-39) and in *The Oxford Classical Dictionary* (ed. by M. Cary, *et al*, New York, Oxford University Press, 1949), which also contains many excellent articles. The basic work on economics is the *Economic Survey of Ancient Rome,* (ed. by T. Frank, 6 vols., Baltimore, The Johns Hopkins Press, 1933-40). There is a useful collection of original source material (selected readings in translation) compiled by N. Lewis and M. Reinhold in *Roman Civilization* (2 vols., New York, Columbia University Press, 1955). *The Loeb Classical Library* series, published by Harvard University Press, provides a text and translation of most of the major Latin authors.

General History

Boak, A. E. R., *A History of Rome to 565 A.D.*, 3rd ed., New York, The Macmillan Company, 1953.

Geer, R. M., *Classical Civilization*, 2nd ed., Vol. II, New York, Prentice-Hall, Inc., 1950.

Rostovtzeff, M. I., *A History of the Ancient World*, Vol. II, New York, Oxford University Press, 1928.

Scullard, H. H., *From the Gracchi to Nero: A History of Rome from 133 B. C. to A. D. 68*, London, Methuen & Co., Ltd., 1959.

History of the Republic and Early Empire

Carcopino, J., *Autour des Gracques*, Paris, 1928.

Ducati, P., *L'Italia antica, dalle prime civiltà alla morte di Cesare,* Milan, Arnoldo Mondadori Editore, 1936.

Ferrero, G., *The Greatness and Decline of Rome*, 5 vols., tr. by A. E. Zimmern and H. J. Chayton, New York, G. P. Putnam & Sons, 1907-09.

Whatmough, J., *Foundations of Roman Italy*, London, Methuen & Co., Ltd., 1937.

The Empire

Henderson, B. W., *Five Roman Emperors: Vespasian, Titus, Domitian, Nerva, Trajan*, New York, The Macmillan Company, 1927.

Kahrstedt, U., *Kulturgeschichte der Römischen Kaiserzeit,* Bern, A. Francke A. G., 1958.

Momigliano, A., *Claudius, the Emperor, and his Achievement*, tr. by W. D. Hogarth, London and New York, Oxford University Press, 1934.

Rostovtzeff, M. L., *The Social and Economic History of the Roman Empire*, New York. Oxford University Press, 1926. (This is the outstanding work on the Empire.)

Scramuzza, V. M., *The Emperor Claudius*, Boston, Harvard University Press, 1940.

Starr, C. G., *Civilization and the Caesars: The Intellectual Revolution in the Roman Empire*, Ithaca, Cornell University Press, 1954. (For cultural history.)

Syme, R., *The Roman Revolution*, New York, Oxford University Press, 1939. (On Augustus.)

Studi in occasione del bimillenario Augusteo, Rome, 1938.

The Late Empire

Alföldi, A., *The Conversion of Constantine and Pagan Rome*, tr. by H. Mattingly, New York, Oxford University Press, 1948.

Bury, J. B., *The Invasion of Europe by the Barbarians*, London, Macmillan & Co., Ltd., 1928.

Lot, F., *Le Fin du Monde Antique et le début du Moyen âge*, Paris, La Renaissance du Livre, 1927.

Walbank, F. W., *The Decline of the Roman Empire in the West*, Vol. III of *Past and Present: Studies in the History of Civilization*, London, Cobbett Press, Ltd., 1946.

The Provinces

Abbott, F. F., and Johnson, A. C., *Municipal Administration in the Roman Empire*, Princeton, Princeton University Press, 1926.

Bell, H. I., *Egypt from Alexander the Great to the Arab Conquest, A Study: The Diffusion and Decay of Hellenism*, New York, Oxford University Press, 1948.

Brogan, O. K., *Roman Gaul*, London, G. G. Bell & Sons, Ltd., 1953.

Broughton, T. R. S., *The Romanization of Africa Proconsularis*, Baltimore, The Johns Hopkins Press, 1929.

Chilver, G. E. F., *Cisalpine Gaul: Social and Economic History from 49 B.C. to the Death of Trajan*, New York, Oxford University Press, 1941.

Jones, A. H. M., *The Cities of the Eastern Roman Provinces*, New York, Oxford University Press, 1937.

Magie, D., *Roman Rule in Asia Minor to the End of the Third Century After Christ*, 2 vols., Princeton, Princeton University Press, 1950.

Mommsen, T., *The Provinces of the Roman Empire*, 2 vols., London 1909. (This is the classic work on the Roman provinces.)

Parvan, V., *Dacia, an Outline of the Early Civilizations*

of the Carpatho-Danubian Countries, London, Cambridge University Press, 1928.

Richmond, I. A., *Roman Britain,* Harmondsworth, Penguin Books, Ltd., 1955.

Stevenson, G. H., *Roman Provincial Administration,* 2nd. ed., New York, Oxford University Press, 1949.

Sutherland, C. H. V., *The Romans in Spain,* London, Methuen & Co., Ltd., 1939.

Literature

Bardon, H., *La littérature latine inconnue,* 2 vols., Paris, C. Klincksieck, 1952-56. (A fascinating survey of lost Latin literature.)

Grant, M., *Roman Literature,* New York, Cambridge University Press, 1954. (A good introduction.)

Hadas, M., *A History of Latin Literature,* New York, Columbia University Press, 1952.

Rand, E. K., *The Building of Eternal Rome,* Boston, Harvard University Press, 1943.

Wight-Duff, J., *A Literary History of Rome,* rev. ed., New York, Barnes & Noble, Inc., 1953.

Art

Ducati, P., *L'arte in Roma dalle origini al sec. VIII,* Bologna, L. Cappelli, 1938.

Grenier, A., *The Roman Spirit in Religion, Thought, and Art,* tr. by M. R. Dobie, New York and London, Alfred A. Knopf, Inc., 1926.

Strong, E., *Art in Ancient Rome,* 2 vols., London, William Heinemann, Ltd., 1929.

Philosophy

Arnold, E. V., *Roman Stoicism,* London, Macmillan & Co., Ltd., 1911.

Dudley, D. R., *A History of Cynicism,* London, Methuen & Co., Ltd., 1937.

Religion

Altheim, F., *A History of Roman Religion,* New York, E. P. Dutton & Co., Inc., 1938.

Cumont, F., *Oriental Religions in Roman Paganism,* Chicago, Open Court Publishing Co., 1911.

Fowler, W. W., *The Religious Experience of the Roman People From the Earliest Times to the Age of Augustus,* New York, the Macmillan Company, 1911.

Nock, A. D., *Conversion: The Old and New in Religion from Alexander the Great to Augustine of Hippo,* New York, Oxford University Press, 1933.

Christianity

Carrington, P., *The Early Christian Church,* 2 vols., London, Cambridge University Press, 1957.

Cochrane, C. N., *Christianity and Classical Culture,* New York, Oxford University Press, 1940.

Davies, J. G., *Daily Life in the Early Church,* London, Lutterworth Press, 1952.

Glover, T. R., *The Conflict of Religions in the Early Roman Empire,* 10th ed., New York and London, Charles Scribner's Sons, 1923.

Van der Meer, F., and Mohrmann, C., *Atlas of the Early Christian World,* tr. and ed. by M. F. Medlund and H. H. Rowley, London, Thomas Nelson and Sons, 1958.

Commerce

Cary, M., *The Geographic Background of Greek and Roman History,* New York and London, Oxford University Press, 1949.

Charlesworth, M., *The Trade-Routes and Commerce of the Roman Empire,* 2nd ed., New York, The Macmillan Company, 1926.

Wheeler, M., *Rome Beyond the Imperial Frontiers,* London, G. G. Bell & Sons, Ltd., 1954.

Social Life

Carcopino, J., *Daily Life in Ancient Rome: the People and the City at the Height of the Empire,* tr. by E. O. Lorimer, New Haven, Yale University Press, 1940.

Mattingly, H., *The Man in the Roman Street,* pub. by *The Numismatic Review,* New York, 1947.

Antiquities of Rome

Lugli, G., *Roma antica, il centro monumentale,* Rome, G. Bardi, 1946.

Platner and Ashby, T., *A Topographical Dictionary of Ancient Rome,* 2 vols., New York, Oxford University Press, 1929.

Scherer, M. R., *Marvels of Ancient Rome,* New York and London, The Phaidon Press, Ltd., 1955. (Well-written and splendidly illustrated.)

General

Davies, O., *Roman Mines in Europe,* New York and London, Oxford University Press, 1935.

Jolowicz, H. F., *Historical Introduction to the Study of Roman Law,* London, Cambridge University Press, 1952.

Marrou, H. I., *Histoire de l'education dans l'Antiquité,* Paris, Editions du Seuil, 1948.

Mattingly, H., *Roman Coins from the Earliest Times to the Fall of the Western Empire,* London, Methuen & Co., Ltd., 1928.

Parker, H. M. D., *The Roman Legions,* New York, Oxford University Press, 1928.

INDEX